Competition: Studies in the Recent Black Protest Movement

A Wadsworth Series:
Explorations in the Black Experience

General Editors

John H. Bracey, Jr., Northern Illinois University
August Meier, Kent State University
Elliott Rudwick, Kent State University

American Slavery: The Question of Resistance
Free Blacks in America, 1800–1860
Blacks in the Abolitionist Movement
The Rise of the Ghetto
Black Matriarchy: Myth or Reality?
Black Workers and Organized Labor
The Black Sociologists: The First Half Century
Conflict and Competition: Studies in the Recent Black Protest
Movement

The anthologies in this series present significant scholarly work on particular aspects of the black experience in the United States. The volumes are of two types. Some have a "problems" orientation, presenting varying and conflicting interpretations of a controversial subject. Others are purely "thematic," simply presenting representative examples of the best scholarship on a topic. Together they provide guidelines into significant areas of research and writing in the field of Afro-American studies. The complete contents of all books in the series are listed at the end of this volume.

Conflict and Competition: Studies in the Recent Black Protest Movement

Edited by

John H. Bracey, Jr.
Northern Illinois University

August Meier
Kent State University

Elliott Rudwick
Kent State University

Wadsworth Publishing Company, Inc.
Belmont, California

Acknowledgments

The authors wish to express their appreciation to Mrs. Barbara Hostetler, Mrs. Patricia Kufta, and Miss Eileen Petric at Kent State University for helping in the preparation of this manuscript, and to Miss Linda Burroughs and Mrs. Helen Peoples of the Kent State University Library. They are especially indebted to James G. Coke, former Director of the Kent State University Center for Urban Regionalism.

July 1970   *JHB*
AM
ER

L. C. Cat. Card No.: 73-154814
ISBN-0-534-00021-5
Printed in the United States of America

1 2 3 4 5 6 7 8 9 10—75 74 73 72 71

For
Joyce Ross

AM
ER

Contents

Introduction   1

1 Nonviolent Direct Action   5

Joseph S. Himes, "The Functions of Racial Conflict"   6

August Meier, "Negro Protest Movements and Organizations"   20

Lewis M. Killian and Charles U. Smith, "Negro Protest Leaders in a Southern Community"   34

Ralph H. Hines and James E. Pierce, "Negro Leadership after the Social Crisis: An Analysis of Leadership Changes in Montgomery, Alabama"   42

Jack L. Walker, "The Functions of Disunity: Negro Leadership in a Southern City"   54

Gerald A. McWorter and Robert L. Crain, "Subcommunity Gladiatorial Competition: Civil Rights Leadership as a Competitive Process"   65

August Meier, "On the Role of Martin Luther King"   84

2 By Any Means Necessary   93

Inge Powell Bell, "Status Discrepancy and the Radical Rejection of Nonviolence"   94

Donald von Eschen, Jerome Kirk, and Maurice Pinard, "The Disintegration of the Negro Non-Violent Movement"   113

Allen J. Matusow, "From Civil Rights to Black Power: The Case of SNCC, 1960–1966"   135

Joel D. Aberbach and Jack L. Walker, "The Meanings of Black Power: A Comparison of White and Black Interpretations of a Political Slogan"   157

David O. Sears and T. M. Tomlinson, "Riot Ideology in Los Angeles: A Study of Negro Attitudes"   192

Robert Blauner, "Internal Colonialism and Ghetto Revolt"   210

Charles V. Hamilton, "Conflict, Race, and System-Transformation in the United States"   227

Suggestions for Further Reading   238

Introduction

The black protest movement of the 1960s compelled sociologists to a reexamination of — and a renewed emphasis on — the role of social conflict in bringing about social change. The work of Lewis Coser (*The Functions of Social Conflict*, 1956) and Ralf Dahrendorf (*Class and Class Conflict in Industrial Society*, 1959) foreshadowed this interest and provided a theoretical base for much of the analysis that behavioral scientists have since made of the Negro protest.

The black protest movement is, in fact, a brilliant example of the use of various types of social conflict in an attempt to effect social change. Conflict, of course, need not be violent. At least four different types of conflict are represented in this book: (1) legal conflict, in which the attack on discrimination is made by means of litigation in the courts; (2) political conflict, involving the mobilization of the black vote to coerce governmental leaders to act upon the needs of the black community; (3) nonviolent direct action, a strategy developed by Mohandas K. Gandhi in India for the purpose of creating social change and resolving social conflict peacefully; and (4) violence, represented both by spontaneous ghetto riots and the advocacy of organized revolution.

This anthology contains scholarly articles that focus on the strategies of the black protest movement during the 1960s. As will be observed, each black protest organization adopted one or two types of social conflict as its particular strategy in the struggle for equal rights. Partly because of such differences in tactics and strategy, and partly because organizations working for the same goal tend to be rivals, the Negro protest movement of the 1960s was characterized by a great deal of interorganizational conflict and competition. Accordingly, the selections in this anthology illustrate both (1) the conflict with the larger society to overthrow discrimination and to attain racial equality and (2) the competitive struggle over strategies and tactics within the movement.

The first half of the decade — a period in which the chief thrust of the black protest movement came from the South — was an era of optimism and even millennial expectations. Such optimism was necessary if those in the movement were to have the psychological strength to engage in nonviolent direct action confrontations and to suffer the repressive measures taken against them by angry white mobs and public officials. As the preeminent mode of social conflict shifted from the legalism of the National Association for the Advancement of Colored People (NAACP) to the nonviolent direct action carried on by the Congress of Racial Equality (CORE), the Student Nonviolent Coordinating Committee (SNCC), and the Southern Christian Leadership Conference (SCLC), serious rivalies developed among the different civil rights organizations; yet they were unified in their goal of racial integration into American society and in their faith in the democratic and egalitarian values of the American system.

Optimism was evident not only among the civil rights participants but also among the social scientists who analyzed the movement. Thus, Joseph S. Himes's essay "The Functions of Racial Conflict," though written at the end of this first phase of the movement, maintains that racial conflict serves both to promote the advancement of the black race and to affirm and sustain, rather than challenge, the ultimate values of American society. Himes points to Martin Luther King's great faith in the social system and its values; and he describes how the creative confrontations brought about by King and other nonviolent direct actionists made conflict "morally justifiable" and thus legitimate.

August Meier's "Negro Protest Movements and Organizations" gives a historical background, tracing the emergence of the major black protest organizations of the 1960s, outlining their tactics and strategies, and discussing the functions of competition among them. His essay also underscores the trend toward black domination of the movement and the emerging tendencies toward nationalism.

The rest of the articles in Section One deal with the leadership struggle that developed within the black protest movement as a result of the dramatic thrust of nonviolent direct action during the late 1950s and early 1960s. Lewis Killian and Charles Smith's study of Tallahassee in the late 1950s, "Negro Protest Leaders in a Southern Community," indicates that the new militant leadership associated with the nonviolent direct action campaigns replaced the older leadership that had accommodated itself to Southern white leaders. Other studies demonstrate, however, that this was not the only possible sequence of events in the wake of the civil rights revolution. Ralph Hines and James Pierce's analysis of Montgomery, Alabama, "Negro Leadership after the Social Crisis," shows that following the successful Montgomery bus boycott, and the departure of its leader, Martin Luther King, conservative black leaders returned to influence. Jack L. Walker's study of Atlanta, "The Functions of Disunity," describes still another pattern — a situation in which both the traditional leaders and the new militants retained influence and established a complementary relationship.

Walker's article, like Meier's, advances the thesis that disunity in Negro leadership and among protest organizations has had positive effects in the battle for equal rights. Such competitive struggle was functional in two distinct ways: (1) the rivalry among the protest organizations stimulated each to more aggressive activity, thus accelerating the pace of social change; and (2) as Gunnar Myrdal suggested in *An American Dilemma* (1944), the militants' agitation served to legitimate the modes of protest of the more moderate leaders, who thus gained concessions that were impossible to secure before the rise of nonviolent direct action. Gerald McWorter and Robert Crain, in their "Subcommunity Gladiatorial Competition: Civil Rights Leadership as a Competitive Process," generally agree that competition is beneficial to civil rights activity; but they also argue that a tightly organized campaign aimed at a particular goal is most likely to succeed in the absence of competition. Their conclusion probably differs to some extent from that of Meier and Walker because rather than examining the total functioning of the protest movements in the fifteen cities under investigation, they focused primarily on campaigns aimed specifically at school desegregation.

Although the early 1960's were notable for the highly visible rivalry among civil rights organizations, one should not ignore Martin Luther King's role as a unifying force in the movement — and what this meant for its successes. Meier's essay, "On the Role of Martin Luther King," emphasizes two reasons for King's achievement: (1) his role as a symbolic leader who interpreted the black man's aspirations and the protest movement to white Americans and (2) his ability to function as a "vital center" within the black protest movement itself, bringing its divergent elements to act together at crucial moments.

But the expectations of the early 1960s far outran the achievements of the protest organizations. By the middle of 1963 Northern blacks, inspired by events in the South, were engaging in a series of massive direct action campaigns against de facto school segregation, slum housing conditions, job discrimination, and police brutality. Many of the campaigns for jobs were highly successful; but the school boycotts, the rent strikes, the demonstrations for civilian review boards to act as a check on the police, and the struggles against the exclusionary building trades unions generally ended in failure. Beginning in 1964, the disillusionment and frustration among the masses in the Northern ghettos erupted in the civil disorders that have been variously described as riots and rebellions. At the same time the continuing, often violent repression that civil rights workers suffered in the South, and the painfully slow pace of social change there, also disillusioned many of the activists. By 1966 a mood of pessimism pervaded the ranks of the most militant black protest organizations; and the movement, hitherto united on goals while divided by personalities and strategies, now became rent with ideological schisms. Nonviolent direct action faded in importance. The NAACP retained its strategy of legalism and lobbying in Congress and the legislatures, as well as its emphasis upon fighting directly for integration of blacks into American society. SNCC and CORE, in contrast, displayed a nationalist trend, becoming identified with the slogan "Black Power" in the summer of 1966. SNCC espoused a revolutionary ideology, while CORE's version of black power was essentially reformist, advocating such programs as black capitalism; but both stressed black pride, black unity, and black control of the black communities. Their ideology owed much to the former Black Muslim leader Malcolm X. SCLC was the only organization to continue in the tradition of nonviolent direct action, although to a diminished extent. The situation had become so serious that well before King was assassinated in 1968, he was no longer able to play his unifying role. CORE, and to an even greater degree SNCC, suffered a precipitous decline; but the banner of radical nationalism was taken up by other groups. Among the radical revolutionary nationalists, there was considerable talk of using organized violence as a tactic, and the urban outbreaks during the summers of the late 1960s were welcomed as ghetto rebellions.

Opening Section Two is Inge Powell Bell's "Status Discrepancy and the Radical Rejection of Nonviolence," an in-depth study of a group of black activists in

CORE which shows that the commitment to the principles of nonviolent direct action was eroding even as early as 1962 and 1963. In their article on "The Disintegration of the Negro Non-violent Movement," Donald von Eschen, Jerome Kirk, and Maurice Pinard emphasize two major factors in accounting for the erosion of this ideology. First, they point out that the movement's successes had greatly depended upon a recognition of the legitimacy of its goals by a substantial proportion of the white population. As the movement went beyond public accommodations and constitutional rights to "welfare goals" involving housing, education, and employment, it lost much of this recognition. Second, the authors observe that the movement's successes largely resulted from the ability of a small number of nonviolent activists to create social disorder — a tactic which was especially effective when it led to violence on the part of the white racists. By 1964 the movement was galvanizing into action lower-class blacks who failed to draw the distinction between disorder created by nonviolent tactics and disorder produced by outright violence on the part of blacks. In fact they simply acted on the feeling that violence works. Thus, to a considerable extent, a surge toward violent conflict replaced the previous commitment to nonviolent conflict. Finally, von Eschen, Kirk, and Pinard suggest that the involvement of more lower-class people, with their "feelings of low political efficacy," made the development of a "Black Power" rhetoric almost inevitable.

Allen J. Matusow's "From Civil Rights to Black Power" describes the transition from integrationism to nationalism and from nonviolent direct action to an espousal of violence in the case of SNCC. The SNCC ideologists who popularized this militant slogan couched their ideas in the rhetoric of conflict, and in time they came to advocate urban rioting and outright revolution. Joel D. Aberbach and Jack L. Walker's "The Meanings of Black Power: A Comparison of White and Black Interpretations" shows that many of the country's whites took the SNCC rhetoric literally and feared that "Black Power" was a thrust toward violence and black domination. But Aberbach and Walker also found that the overwhelming majority of Negroes who were favorable toward "Black Power" did not perceive it so much as a form of racial conflict as a vehicle for obtaining black unity and a fair share in American society.

David O. Sears and T. M. Tomlinson, in their "Riot Ideology in Los Angeles: A Study of Negro Attitudes," maintain that the outbreaks in major Northern urban centers in the late 1960s actually functioned as a distinct tactic of racial conflict. Robert Blauner's "Internal Colonialism and Ghetto Revolt" treats these outbreaks of violence, as well as cultural nationalism and the movement for black control of the black ghettos, as types of racial conflict, analagous to the techniques used by colonial peoples to drive out white imperialist powers. The concluding essay, by Charles V. Hamilton, "Conflict, Race, and System-Transformation in the United States," though written in the context of the late 1960s returns to the theme of the functions of racial conflict in removing racial inequities and fulfilling the democratic values of American society.

Nonviolent Direct Action

1

The Functions of Racial Conflict

Joseph S. Himes

When one contemplates the contemporary American scene, he may be appalled by the picture of internal conflict portrayed in the daily news. The nation is pictured as torn by dissension over Vietnam policy. The people are reported being split by racial strife that periodically erupts into open violence. Organized labor and management are locked in a perennial struggle that occasionally threatens the well-being of the society. The reapportionment issue has forced the ancient rural-urban conflict into public view. Religious denominations and faiths strive against ancient conflicts of theology and doctrine toward unification and ecumenism. Big government is joined in a continuing struggle against big industry, big business, big finance, and big labor on behalf of the "public interest."

The image created by such reports is that of a society "rocked," "split" or "torn" by its internal conflicts. The repetition of such phrases and the spotlighting of conflict suggest that the integration, if not the very existence of the society is threatened. It thus implied, and indeed often stated that the elimination of internal conflict is the central problem for policy and action in the society.

These preliminary remarks tend to indicate that there is widespread popular disapproval of social conflict. In some quarters the absence of conflict is thought to signify the existence of social harmony and stability. According to the human relations theme, conflict, aggression, hostility, antagonism and such devisive motives and behaviors are regarded as social heresies and therefore to be avoided. Often the word conflict is associated with images of violence and destruction.

At the same time, in contemporary sociology the problem of social conflict has been largely neglected. As Coser, Dahrendorf and others have pointed out, this tendency issues from preoccupation with models of social structure and theories of equilibrium.[1] Conflicts are treated as strains, tensions or stresses of social structures and regarded as pathological. Little attention is devoted to the investigation of conflict as a funtional social process.

However, some of the earlier sociologists employed social conflict as one central

Joseph S. Himes, "The Functions of Racial Conflict," *Social Forces* Vol. 45, September, 1966, pp. 1–10. Reprinted by permission of The University of North Carolina Press.

Presidential address delivered at the annual meeting of the Southern Sociological Society, New Orleans, April 8, 1966. I am indebted to Professors Ernst Borinski, Lewis A. Coser, Hylan G. Lewis, and Robin M. Williams, Jr., for their critical reading of this manuscript.

element of their conceptual systems. Theory and analysis were cast in terms of a process model. Conflict was viewed as natural and as functioning as an integrative force in society.

To Ludwig Gumplowicz and Gustav Ratzenhofer conflict was the basic social process, while for Lester F. Ward and Albion W. Small it was one of the basic processes. Sumner, Ross, and Cooley envisaged conflict as one of the major forces operating to lace human society together.[2] Park and Burgess employed social conflict as one of the processual pillars of their sociological system.[3]

At bottom, however, the two analytic models of social organization are really not inconsistent. Dahrendorf argues that consensus-structure and conflict-process are "the two faces of society."[4] That is, social integration results simultaneousuly from both consensus of values and coercion to compliance. Indeed, in the present study it is observed that the two sources of social integration are complementary and mutually supporting.

Coser has led the revival of sociological attention to the study of social conflict. In this task he has injected the very considerable contributions of the German sociologist Georg Simmel into the stream of American sociological thought. Ralf Dahrendorf, among others, has made futher substantial contributions to the sociology of social conflict. One latent consequence of this development has been to sensitize some sociologists to conflict as a perspective from which to investigate race relations. Thus race relations have been called "power relations" and it has been proposed that research should be cast in terms of a "conflict model."[5] This approach is consistent with Blumer's thesis that race prejudice is "a sense of group position" and that empirical study involves "a concern with the relationship of racial groups."[6]

In the present discussion the term racial conflict is used in a restricted and specific sense.[7] By racial conflict is meant rational organized overaction by Negroes, initiating demands for specific social goals, and utilizing collective sanctions to enforce these demands. By definition, the following alternative forms of conflict behavior are excluded from the field of analysis.

1. The aggressive or exploitative actions of dominant groups and individuals toward minority groups or individuals.
2. Covert individual antagonisms or affective compensatory or reflexive aggressions, and
3. Spontaneous outbursts or nonrationalized violent behavior.

As here treated, racial conflict involves some rational assessment of both means and ends, and therefore is an instance of what Lewis Coser has called "realistic conflict."[8] Because of the calculating of means and ends, racial conflict is initiating action. It is a deliberate collective enterprise to achieve predetermined social goals. Of necessity, conflict includes a conscious attack upon an overtly defined social abuse.

Merton has pointed out that groups sometimes resort to culturally tabooed means to achieve culturally prescribed ends.[9] Under such circumstances one might assume that if legitimate means were available, they would be employed. But, Vander Zanden has observed, "Non-violent resistance is a tactic well suited to struggles in which a minority lacks access to major sources of power within a society and to the instruments of violent coercion."[10] He goes on to add that, "within the larger American society the Negro's tactic of non-violent resistance has gained a considerable degree of legitimacy."[11] Three principal manifestations of Negro behavior fit this definition of racial conflict.

1. Legal redress, or the calculated use of court action to achieve and sanction specific group goals. Legal redress has been used most often and successfully in the achievement of voting rights, educational opportunities and public accommodations.
2. Political action, or the use of voting, bloc voting and lobby techniques to achieve legislative and administrative changes and law enforcement.
3. Non-violent mass action, or organized collective participation in overt activity involving pressure and public relations techniques to enforce specific demands.

This paper examines some of the social functions of conflict as here defined. It is asked: Does realistic conflict by Negroes have any system-maintaining and system-enchancing consequences for the larger American society? To this question at least four affirmative answers can be given. Realistic racial conflict (1) alters the social structure, (2) enhances social communication, (3) extends social solidarity and (4) facilitates personal identity. Because of space and time limitations, considerations of societal dysfunctions and goal achievements are omitted.

Structural Functions

H. M. Blalock has noted that within the American social structure race relations are power relations.[12] Thus, realistic social conflict is an enterprise in the calculated mobilization and application of social power to sanction collective demands for specific structural changes. Yet, because of minority status, Negroes have only limited access to the sources of social power. Robert Bierstedt has identified numbers, resources and organization as leading sources of power.[13] Of these categories, resources which Bierstedt specifies as including money, prestige, property and natural and supernatural phenomena, are least accessible to Negroes.

Perforce then, realistic racial conflict specializes in the mobilization of numbers and organization as accessible sources of power. Thus a boycott mobilizes and organizes numbers of individuals to withhold purchasing power. A demonstration organizes and mobilizes numbers of individuals to tap residual moral sentiments and to generate public opinion. Voter registration and bloc voting mobilize and organize numbers of citizens to influence legislative and administrative processes. Legal redress and lobby techniques mobilize organization to activate legal sanctions or the legislative process.

The application of mobilized social power in realistic racial conflict tends to reduce the power differential between actors, to restrict existing status differences, and to alter the directionality of social interaction. First, in conflict situations, race relations are defined unequivocally in power terms. Sentimentality and circumlocution are brushed aside. The power dimension is brought into central position in the structure of interaction. The differential between conflict partners along this dimension is thus reduced. The power advantage of the dominant group is significantly limited. In this connection and perhaps only in this connection, it may be correct to liken embattled Negroes and resisting whites to "armed camps."

Second, alteration of the power dimension of interracial structure tends to modify status arrangements. In the traditional racial structure, discrimination and segregation cast whites and Negroes in rigid and separate orders of superiority and inferiority. The limited and stylized intergroup contacts are confined to a rigid and sterile etiquette. However, in realistic conflict initiating actors assume, for they must, a status coordinate with that of the opposition.[14]

Status coordination is one evident consequence of power equalization. Moreover, it is patently impossible to make demands and to sanction them while acting from the position of a suppliant. That is, the very process of realistic conflict functions to define adversaries in terms of self-conception as status equals. Martin Luther King perceives this function of realistic conflict in the following comment on the use of non-violent action and deliberately induced tension.[15]

Non-violent direct action seeks to create such a crisis and foster such a tension that a community which has constantly refused to negotiate is forced to confront the issue. It seeks so to dramatize the issue that it can no longer be ignored.

That is, social power is used to bring interactors into status relations where issues can be discussed, examined and compromised. There are no suppliants or petitioners and no condescending controllers in a negotiation relationship. By the very nature of the case, interactors occupy equal or approximately equal positions of both status and strength.

Third, power equalization and status coordination affect the interactional dimension of social structure. The up and down flow of interaction between super- and subordinates tends to level out in relations between positional equals. That is, rational demands enforced by calculated sanctions cannot be forced into the molds of supplication and condescension.

The leveling out of social interaction is inherent in such realistic conflict mechanisms as sit-ins, freedom rides, bloc voting, voter registration campaigns and boycotts. Thus, for example, the interruption of social interaction in a boycott implies an assumption of status equality and the leveling of interaction. The relationship that is interrupted is the up and down pattern inherent in the status structure of inequality. No relationship is revealed as preferable to the pattern of supplication and condescension. Whether such structural functions of realistic conflict become institutionalized in the larger social system will depend on the extent of goal achievement of the total Negro revolution. That is, structural consequences of conflict may be institutionalized through the desegregation and nondiscrimination of education, employment, housing, recreation and the like. Changes in these directions will provide system-relevant roles under terms of relatively coordinate status and power not only for the conflict participants, but also for many other individuals. Developments in these directions will also be influenced by many factors and trends apart from the process of realistic racial conflict.

We may now summarize the argument regarding the structural functions of realistic racial conflict in a series of propositions. Realistic conflict postulates race relations as power relations and undertakes to mobilize and apply the social power that is accessible to Negroes as a minority group.

In conflict, the traditional interracial structure is modified along three dimensions. The power differential between interactors is reduced; status differentials are restricted; and social interaction tends to level out in directionality. Whether these structural consequences of realistic conflict become institutionalized in the general social system will depend on the extent and duration of goal achievement in the larger social structure.

Communicational Functions

It is widely claimed that Negro aggression interrupts or reduces interracial communication. Whites and Negroes are thought to withdraw in suspicion and hostility from established practices of communication. The so-called "normal" agencies and bridges of intergroup contact and communication are believed to become inoperative. Such a view of conflict envisages Negroes and whites as hostile camps eyeing each other across a "no man's land" of antagonism and separation.

It is true that racial conflict tends to interrupt and reduce traditional communication between whites and Negroes. But traditional interracial communication assumes that communicators occupy fixed positions of superiority and inferiority, precludes the consideration of certain significant issues, and confines permitted interchanges to a rigid and sterile etiquette. "The Negro," write Killian and Grigg, "has always been able to stay in communication with the white man and gain many favors from him, so long as he approached him as a suppliant and as an inferior, and not as a conflict partner."[16]

It will be evident that intergroup communication under such structural conditions is both restricted in content and asymmetrical in form. However, our analysis indicates that realistic conflict functions to correct these distortions of content and form and to extend the communication process at the secondary mass media level.

First, realistic racial conflict heightens the individual level and extends the social range of attention to racial matters. Individuals who have by long custom learned to see Negroes only incidentally as part of the standard social landscape, are brought up sharply and forced to look at them in a new light. Persons who have been oblivious to Negroes are abruptly and insistently confronted by people and issues which they can neither avoid nor brush aside. Many individuals for the first time perceive Negroes as having problems, characteristics and aspirations that were never before recognized, nor at least so clearly recognized. Racial conflict thus rudely destroys what Gunnar Myrdal aptly called the "convenience of ignorance."[17]

In *Freedom Summer,* Sally Belfrage gives a graphical personal illustration of the attention-arresting function of realistic racial conflict.[18] In the most crowded and hottest part of an afternoon the daughter of one of Greenwood's (Mississippi) leading families walked into the civil rights headquarters. In a lilting southern voice she asked to everybody in general: "I jus' wanted to know what y'all are up to over here."

At the same time the "race problem" is brought into the focus of collective attention by realistic conflict. Negroes as well as their problems and claims insist upon having both intensive and extensive consideration. To support this contention one has only to consider the volume of scientific, quasi-scientific and popular literature, the heavy racial loading of the mass media, and the vast number of organizations and meetings that are devoted to the racial issue.

Further, realistic racial conflict tends to modify both the cognitive and affective content of interracial communication. Under terms of conflict whites and Negroes can no longer engage in the exchange of standardized social amenities regarding safe topics within the protection of the status structure and the social etiquette. Communication is made to flow around substantive issues and the calculated demands of Negroes. Communication is about something that has real meaning for the communicators. It makes a difference that they communicate. In fact, under terms of realistic conflict it is no longer possible to avoid communicating. Thus Martin Luther King argued that nonviolent mass action is employed to create such crisis and tension that a community which has refused to negotiate is forced to confront the issue.[19]

In conflict the affective character of communication becomes realistic. The communicators infuse their exchanges of cognitive meanings with the feelings that, within the traditional structure, were required to be suppressed and avoided. That Negroes are permitted, indeed often expected to reveal the hurt and humiliation and anger that they formerly were required to bottle up inside. Many white people thus were shocked to discover that the "happy" Negroes whom they "knew" so well were in fact discontented and angry people.

Thus the cognitive-affective distortion of traditional interracial communication is in some measure at least corrected. The flow of understanding and affection that was permitted and encouraged is balanced by normal loading of dissension and hostility. The relationship thus reveals a more symmetrical character of content and form.

Finally, attrition of primary contacts between unequals within the traditional structure and etiquette is succeeded, in part at least, by an inclusive dialogue at the secondary communication level. The drama of conflict and the challenges of leaders tend to elevate the racial issue in the public opinion arena. The mass media respond by reporting and commenting on racial events in great detail. Thus millions of otherwise uninformed or indifferent individuals are drawn into the public opinion process which Ralph H. Turner and Lewis M. Killian have analyzed as defining and redefining the issue and specifying and solving the problem.[20]

Much obvious evidence reveals the secondary communication dialogue. Since 1954 a voluminous scientific, quasi-scientific and popular literature on the race issue has appeared. Further evidence is found in the heavy racial loading of newspapers, magazines, television and radio broadcasting and the motion pictures. The race problem has been the theme of numerous organizations and meetings at all levels of power and status. From such evidence it would seem reasonable to conclude that few if any Americans have escaped some degree of involvement in the dialogue over the race issue.

We may now summarize the argument briefly. Realistic racial conflict tends to reduce customary interracial communication between status unequals regarding trivial matters within the established communication etiquette. On the other hand, conflict tends to extend communication regarding significant issues with genuine feelings and within noncustomary structures and situations. At the secondary level both the volume of communication and the number of communicators are greatly increased by realistic conflict. These observations would seem to warrant the conclusion that communication within the general social system is extended by realistic racial conflict.

Solidarity Functions

A corollary of the claim that racial conflict interrupts communication is the assertion that conflict also is seriously, perhaps even radically disunifying. Struggles between Negroes and whites are thought to split the society and destroy social solidarity. It is at once evident that such a claim implies the prior existence of a unified or relatively unified biracial system. Notwithstanding difference of status and condition, the racial sectors are envisaged as joined in the consensus and structure of the society.

A judicious examination of the facts suggests that the claim that racial conflict is seriously, perhaps even radically, disunifying is not altogether correct. On the one hand, the image of biracial solidarity tends to be exaggerated. On the other, realistic racial conflict serves some important unifying functions within the social system.

As Logan Wilson and William Kolb have observed, the consensus of the society is organized around a core of "ultimate values."[21] "In our society," they assert, "we have developed such ultimate values as the dignity of the individual, equality of opportunity, the right to life, liberty, and the pursuit of happiness, and the growth of the free personality."

Far from rejecting or challenging these ultimate values, the ideological thrust of realistic racial conflict affirms them.[22] That is, the ultimate values of the society constitute starting points of ideology and action in racial conflict. As Wilson Record and others have observed, Negro protest and improvement movements are thoroughly American in assumption and objectives.[23]

This fact creates an interesting strategic delemma for the White Citizens Councils, the resurgent Ku Klux Klan and similar manifestations of the so-called "white backlash." The ideology of racial conflict has preempted the traditional high ground of the core values and ultimate morality. The reactionary groups are thus left no defensible position within the national ethos from which to mount their attacks.

One consequence of realistic racial conflict, then, is to bring the core values of the society into sharp focus and national attention. People are exhorted, even forced to think about the basic societal tenets and to consider their meaning and applications. A dynamic force is thus joined to latent dedication in support of the unifying values of the society. Thus, as Coser has observed, far from being altogether disunifying, realistic conflict functions to reaffirm the core and unifying values of the society.[24] In other words the "two faces of society" are seen to be complementary and mutually supporting.

The primacy of core values in realistic racial conflict is revealed in many ways. Martin Luther King places the ultimate values of the society at the center of his theoretic system of non-violent mass action.[25] In his "Letter from Birmingham Jail" he refers to "justice," "freedom," "understanding," "brotherhood," "constitutional rights," "promise of democracy" and "truth." See how he identifies the goal of racial freedom with the basic societal value of freedom. "We will reach the goal of freedom in Birmingham and all over the nation, because the goal of America is freedom."[26]

One impact of realistic racial conflict is upon interpretation of core values and the means of their achievement. Thus, the issue is not whether or not men shall be free and equal, but whether these values are reserved to white men or are applicable to Negroes as well. Or again, the phrases "gradualism" and "direct action" depict an important point of disagreement over means to universally affirmed ends. But, it may be observed that when men agree on the ends of life, their quarrels are not in themselves disunifying.

Further, the very process of realistic racial conflict is intrinsically functional. Participants in the conflict are united by the process of struggle itself. The controversy is a unique and shared social possession. It fills an interactional vacuum maintained in the traditional structure by limited social contacts and alienation.

At the same time, as Coser has argued, a relationship established by conflict may lead in time to other forms of interaction.[27] It is conceivable that Negroes and whites who today struggle over freedom and justice and equality may tomorrow be joined in cooperation in the quest of these values.

Conflict is also unifying because the object of struggle is some social value that both parties to the conflict wish to possess or enjoy. The struggle tends to enhance the value and to reveal its importance to both actors. A new area of consensus is thus defined or a prior area of agreement is enlarged. For example, that Negroes and whites struggle through realistic conflict for justice or freedom or equality tends to clarify these values for both and join them in the consensus regarding their importance.

"Simultaneously," as Vander Zanden observes, "within the larger American society the Negro's tactic of non-violent resistance has gained a considerable degree of legitimacy."[28] That is, conflict itself has been defined as coming within the arena of morally justifiable social action. The means as well as the ends, then, are enveloped within the national ethos and serve to enhance societal solidarity. In this respect, realistic racial conflict, like labor-management conflict, tends to enter the "American way of life" and constitutes another point of social integration.

Many years ago Edward Alsworth Ross pointed out that nonradical conflicts may function to "sew" the society together.[29]

Every species of conflicts interferes with every other species in society . . . save only when lines of cleavage coincide; in which case they reinforce one another. . . . A society, therefore, which is ridden by a dozen oppositions along lines running in every direction may actually be in less danger of being torn with violence or falling to pieces than one split just along one line. For each new cleavage contributes to narrow the cross-clefts, so that one might say that society is sewn together by its inner conflicts.

In this sewing function, realistic racial conflict is interwoven with political, religious, regional, rural-urban, labor-management, class and the other persistent threads of struggle that characterize the American social fabric. What is decisive is the fact that variously struggling factions are united in the consensus of the ultimate societal values. The conflicts are therefore nonradical, crisscrossing and tend to mitigate each other.

The proposition on the solidarity function of realistic racial conflict can now be formulated briefly. The claims that racial conflict is disruptive of social solidarity, though partially true, tends to obscure other important consequences. Conflict not only projects the combatants into the social consensus; it also acts to reaffirm the ultimate values around which the consensus is organized. Moreover, conflict joins opposing actors in meaningful interaction for ends whose importance is a matter of further agreement. From this perspective and within a context of multifarious crisscrossing threads of opposition, realistic racial conflict is revealed as helping to "sew" the society together around its underlying societal consensus. We now turn to a consideration of certain social-psychological consequences of realistic racial conflict.

Identity Functions

The fact is often overlooked that realistic racial conflict permits many Negroes to achieve a substantial measure of identity within the American social system. This function of racial conflict is implied in the foregoing analyses of communication and solidarity. However, the analysis of the identity function of racial conflict begins with a consideration of the alienation of the American Negro people. Huddled into urban and rural slums and concentrated in menial and marginal positions in the work force, Negroes are relegated to inferior and collateral statuses in the social structure. Within this structural situation discrimination prevents their sharing in the valued possessions of the society. Legal and customary norms of segregation exclude them from many meaningful contacts and interactions with members of the dominant group.

Isolated and inferior, Negro people searched for the keys to identity and belonging. The social forces that exclude them from significant participation in the general society also keep them disorganized. Thus identity, the feeling of belonging and the sense of social purpose, could be found neither in membership in the larger society nor in participation in a cohesive racial group. Generation after generation of Negroes live out their lives in fruitless detachment and personal emptiness. In another place the alienation of Negro teenagers has been described as follows.[30]

The quality of Negro teenage culture is conditioned by four decisive factors: race, inferiority, deprivation and youthfulness. Virtually every experience of the Negro teenager is filtered through this complex qualifying medium; every act is a response to a distorted perception of the world. His world is a kind of nightmare, the creation of a carnival reflection chamber. The Negro teenager's culture, his customary modes of behavior, constitute his response to the distorted, frightening, and cruel world that he perceives with the guileless realism of youth.

Yet the search for identity goes on. It takes many forms. In the Negro press and voluntary organizations it is reflected in campaigns for race pride and race loyalty. One sector of the Negro intelligentsia invented the "Negro history movement" as a device to create a significant past for a "historyless" people. For the unlettered and unwashed masses the church is the prime agent of group cohesion and identity. The National Association for the Advancement of Colored People and other militant organizations provide an ego-enhancing rallying point for the emancipated and the aggressive. The cult of Negro business, escapist movements like Father Divine's Heaven, and nationalist movements like Marcus Garvey's Universal Negro Improvement Association, and the Black Muslims provide still other arenas for the Negro's search for identity.

Despite this variegated panorama of effort and search, the overriding experience of Negroes remains isolation, inferiority and the ineluctable sense of alienation. Whether involved in the search or not, or perhaps just because of such involvement, individuals see themselves as existing outside the basic American social system. Vander Zanden puts it this way: "By virtue of his membership in the Negro group, the Negro suffers considerably in terms of self-esteem and has every incentive for self-hatred.[31] Thus self-conception reflects and in turn supports social experience in a repetition of the familiar self-fulfilling prophecy.

In this situation, collective conflict had an almost magical although unanticipated effect upon group cohesion and sense of identity among Negroes. Group struggle, as Coser and others have pointed out, functions to enhance group solidarity and to clarify group boundaries.[32] The separations among collective units are sharpened and the identity of groups within a social system is established. In the course of conflict collective aims are specified, defined and communicated. Cadres of leaders emerge in a division of labor that grows clearer and more definite. Individuals tend to find niches and become polarized around the collective enterprise. All participants are drawn closer together, both for prosecution of the struggle and for common defense.

As the racial conflict groups become more cohesive and organized, the boundaries with other groups within the American social system become clearer. The distinction between member and nonmember is sharpened. Individuals who stood indecisively between groups or outside the fray are induced or forced to take sides. The zones of intergroup ambiguity diminish. Internally, the conflict groups become more tightly unified and the positions of members are clarified and defined more precisely.

Further, conflict facilitates linkage between the individual and his local reference group as the agent of conflict. The individual thus achieves both a "commitment"[33] and a "role" as a quasi-official group representative in the collective struggle. Pettigrew writes:[34]

Consider the Student Non-Violent Coordinating Committee (SNICK), . . . The group is cohesive, highly regarded by Negro youth, and dedicated entirely to achieving both personal and societal racial change. Recruits willingly and eagerly devote themselves to the group's goals. And they find themselves systematically rewarded by SNICK for violating the 'Negro' role in every particular. They are expected to evince strong racial pride, to assert their full rights as citizens, to face jail and police brutality unhesitatingly for the cause. . . . Note, . . . that these expected and rewarded actions all publicly commit the member to the group and its aims.

In the general racial conflict system individuals may act as leaders, organizers and specialists. Some others function as sit-inners, picketers, boycotters, demonstrators, voter registration solicitors, etc. Many others, removed from the areas of overt conflict, participate secondarily or vicariously as financial contributors, audience members, mass media respondents, verbal applauders, etc.

In the interactive process of organized group conflict self-involvement is the opposite side of the coin of overt action. Actors become absorbed by ego and emotion into the group and the group is projected through their actions. This linkage of individual and group in ego and action is the substance of identity.

Paradoxically, the personal rewards of participation in conflict groups tend to support and facilitate the larger conflict organization and process. Edward Shils and Morris Janowitz have noted this fact in the functions of primary groups in the German Army in World War II.[35] That is, for the individual actor the sense of identity is grounded and sustained by gratification of important personal needs.

In the case of realistic racial conflict, group-based identity functions to facilitate sociopsychic linkage between the individual and the inclusive social system. It was shown above that racial conflict is socially unifying in at least two ways. First, the conflict ideology identifies parties to the conflict with the core values of the social heritage. Thus sit-inners, and demonstrators and boycotters and all the others in the drama of racial conflict conceive of themselves as the latter-day warriors for the freedom, justice and equality and the other moral values that are historically and essentially American. For many Negroes the sense of alienation is dispelled by a new sense of significance and purpose. The self-image of these embattled Negroes is consequentially significantly enhanced.

Second, the conflict process draws organized Negroes into significant social interaction within the inclusive social system. Some of the crucial issues and part of the principal business of the society engage Negroes of all localities and stations in life. Though often only vicariously and by projection, life acquires a new meaning and quality for even the poorest ghetto dweller and meanest sharecropper. The sense of alienation is diminished and the feeling of membership in the inclusive society is enhanced.

We may now formulate the argument as follows. Intense alienation kept alive the Negro's quest for identity and meaning. Miraculously almost, realistic racial conflict with its ideological apparatus and action system functions to alleviate alienation and to facilitate identity. Conflict enhances group solidarity, clarifies group boundaries strengthens the individual-group linkage through ego-emotion commitment and overt action. In-group identity is extended to the larger social system through the extension of communication, the enlargement of the network of social interactions and ideological devotion to national core values. It may be said, then, that through realistic racial conflict America gains some new Americans.

Notes

[1] Lewis A. Coser, *The Functions of Social Conflict* (Glencoe, Illinois: The Free Press, 1956), p. 20; Ralf Dahrendorf, *Class and Class Conflict in Industrial Society* (Stanford: Stanford University Press, 1959), chap.5.

[2] William Graham Sumner, *Folkways* (Boston: Ginn, 1906); Edward Alsworth Ross, *The Principles of Sociology* (New York: Century, 1920); Charles Horton Cooley, *Social Process* (New York: Charles Scribner's Sons, 1918), and *Social Organization* (New York; Charles Scribner's Sons, 1909).

[3] Robert E. Park and Ernest W. Burgess, *Introduction to the Science of Sociology* (Chicago: University of Chicago Press, 1924).

[4] Dahrendorf, *op. cit.,* pp. 157–165. Arthur I. Wastow makes the same point in his concepts of "church," "state," and "government" as models of social integration. See *From Race Riot to Sit-in, 1919 and the 1960s: A Study in the Connections Between Conflict and Violence* (New York: Doubleday & Co., 1966).

[5] Lewis M. Killian and Charles M. Grigg, *Racial Crisis in America* (Englewood Cliffs, New Jersey: Prentice-Hall, 1964), p. 18 ff.; H. M. Blalock, Jr., "A Power Analysis of Racial Discrimination," *Social Forces,* 39 (October 1960), pp. 53–59; Ernest Borinski, "The Sociology of Coexistence — Conflict in Social and Political Power Systems," unpublished, pp. 6–7; Wilson Record, *Race and Radicalism* (Ithaca: Cornell University Press, 1964); Ernst Borinski, "The Litigation Curve and the Litigation Filibuster in Civil Rights Cases," *Social Forces* 37 (December 1958), pp. 142–147.

[6] Herbert Blumer, "Race Prejudice as a Sense of Group Position," in J. Masuoka and Preston Valien (eds.), *Race Relations* (Chapel Hill: The University of North Carolina Press, 1961), p. 217.

[7] In much authoritative literature the concept conflict in racial relations is used in various other ways. See for example, George Simpson and J. Milton Yinger, *Racial and Cultural Minorities* (New York; Harper & Row, 1965), chap. 4; Killian and Grigg, *op. cit.;* Leonard Broom and Norval D. Glenn, *Transformation of the Negro American* (New York: Harper & Row, 1965), esp. chaps. 3 and 4.

[8] Coser, *op. cit.,* pp. 48–55.

[9] Robert K. Merton, *Social Theory and Social Structure* (Glencoe, Illinois: The Free Press, 1957), pp. 123–149.

[10] James W. Vander Zanden, "The Non-Violent Resistance Movement Against Segregation," *American Journal of Sociology,* 68 (March 1963), p. 544.

[11] *Ibid.,* p. 544.

[12] Blalock, *op. cit.,* pp. 53–59.

[13] Robert Bierstedt, "An Analysis of Social Power," *American Sociological Review,* 15 (December 1950), pp. 730–738. Bierstedt argues that numbers and organization as sources of social power are ineffectual without access to resources.

[14] Thomas F. Pettigrew, *A Profile of the Negro American* (Princeton: D. Van Nostrand Co., 1964), p. 167.

[15] Martin Luther King, *Why We Can't Wait* (New York; Harper & Row, 1963), p. 81.

[16] Killian and Grigg, *op. cit.,* p. 7.

[17] Gunnar Myrdal, *An American Dilemma* (New York: Harper & Bros., 1944), pp. 40–42.

[18] Sally Belfrage, *Freedom Summer* (New York: The Viking Press, 1965), p. 48.

[19] King, *op. cit.,* p. 81.

[20] Ralph H. Turner and Lewis M. Killian, *Collective Behavior* (Englewood Cliffs, New Jersey: Prentice-Hall, 1957), chaps. 11 and 12.

[21] Logan Wilson and William L. Kolb, *Sociological Analysis* (New York: Harcourt, Brace & Co., 1949), p. 513.

[22] Pettigrew, *op. cit.,* p. 193.

[23] Record, *op. cit.;* Pettigrew, *op. cit.;* Broom and Glenn, *op. cit.*

[24] Coser, *op, cit.,* pp. 127–128.

[25] King, *op. cit.,* pp. 77–100.

[26] *Ibid.,* p. 97.

[27] Coser, *op. cit.,* pp. 121–122.

[28] Vander Zanden, *op. cit.,* p. 544.

[29] Ross, *op. cit.,* pp. 164–165. Dahrendorf, *op. cit.,* pp. 213–215, argues that conflicts tend to become "superimposed," thus threatening intensification. "Empirical evidence shows," he writes, "that different conflicts may be, and often are, superimposed in given historical societies, so that the multitude of possible conflict fronts is reduced to a few dominant conflicts. . . . If this is the case, (class) conflicts of different associations appear superimposed; i.e., the opponents of one association meet again — with different titles, perhaps, but in identical relations — in another association." (Pp. 213–214.) Such an argument, however, fails to recognize that conflicts may superimpose along religious, regional, ethnic or other fronts and thus mitigate the strength of the class superimposition.

[30] Joseph S. Himes, "Negro Teen Age Culture," *Annals,* 338 (November 1961), pp. 92–93.

[31] Vander Zanden, *op. cit.,* p. 546.

[32] Coser, *op. cit.,* p. 34.

[33] Amitai Etzioni employs the concept "commitment" to designate one dimension of cohesiveness and operational effectiveness in complex organizations. See his *Complex Organizations: A Sociological Reader* (New York: Henry Holt Co., 1961), p. 187; and *A Comparative Study of Complex Organization* (Glencoe, Illinois: The Free Press, 1961), pp. 8–22.

[34] Pettigrew, *op. cit.,* pp. 165–166.

[35] Edward A. Shils and Morris Janowitz, "Cohesion and Disintegration in the Wehrmacht in World War II," *Public Opinion Quarterly,* 12 (Summer 1948), p. 281.

Negro Protest Movements and Organizations

August Meier

After the Second World War, the general drift of American public opinion toward a more liberal racial attitude that had begun during the New Deal became accentuated as a result of the revolution against Western Imperialism in Asia and Africa that engendered a new respect for the nonwhite peoples of the world, and as a result of the subsequent competition for the support of the uncommitted nations connected with the Cold War. In this context of changing international trends and shifting American public opinion, the campaign for Negro rights has, since mid-century, broadened rapidly and has, in fact, in certain fundamental respects changed its character. Thus there has been a shift in emphasis from legalism to direct action. At the same time the scope of the attack has widened. Meanwhile the civil rights movement has become both more and more a Negro movement, and more and more a mass movement. Finally the movement has become infused with a new militance, a new sense of urgency, a new psychology of immediatism as, despite increasing Southern resistance, the racial barriers have begun to crumble in an accelerating fashion.

Pre-eminent among the civil right organizations in 1950 was the NAACP. Often interlocked with NAACP leadership, though in a number of places operating independently, were the voters leagues that had arisen in the South after the Supreme Court outlawed the white primary (1944); together with the NAACP they had raised the number of Negro registered voters in twelve southeastern states from about 233,000 in 1940 to about 1,110,000 by 1952. Playing second fiddle to the NAACP, but holding the key to future strategy, was the tiny Congress of Racial

August Meier, "Negro Protest Movements and Organizations," *Journal of Negro Education,* XXXII, Fall 1963, pp. 437–450. Reprinted by permission of the *Journal of Negro Education.* Annotation is sparse for this article because the printed sources available are only of limited usefulness. Pre-eminent among them are the annual reports of the NAACP, various CORE publications (most notably, James Peck, *Cracking the Color Line* [1962]), SCLC's irregularly issued *Newsletter* and brochures, SNCC's sporadically published *Student Voice,* James Peck, *Freedom Ride,* (New York, 1962), Martin Luther King, *Stride Toward Freedom,* (New York, 1958), and publications of The Southern Regional Council.

Consquently this article is based very largely on two types of sources: interviews and conversations with a substantial number of leaders and activists in the civil rights field — notably in the NAACP, CORE and SNCC — and observations growing out of my close connection with SNCC's Baltimore affiliate, the Baltimore Civic Interest Group.

Equality. The nationalist movements were only a speck on the horizon, for since Garvey the alienated lowest class of urban Negroes tended to find hope and dignity in the pentecostal churches and in such chiliastic sects as those of Daddy Grace, Elder Macheaux and Father Divine.

At mid-century the NAACP could look back upon a forty-year history of deliberate but definite advance. Often regarded as conservative today, its program of agitation, and political and legal action, and its insistence upon attacking segregation and other forms of discrimination, was originally considered radical in contrast to the accommodating ideology of Booker T. Washington, then in the ascendancy. Leaving the task of enlarging employment opportunities to the conciliatory methods of the more conservative Urban League, the NAACP had tried to attain the Negro's full constitutional rights through political pressure and the courts. By 1950, in fact, the NAACP could pride itself upon an imposing series of Supreme Court victories, particularly in the fields of due process and equal protection in criminal cases, residential segregation, and voting. Taken together, *Smith v. Allwright,* (1944), invalidating the white primary, and *Shelly v. Kraemer,* (1948), declaring restrictive covenants unenforceable, seemed to open a new era. As early as 1946 the NAACP had made its first dent in the system of transportation segregation, and the McLaurin and Sweatt decisions in 1950, though applicable only to graduate and professional schooling, suggested that the separate-but-equal principle itself would soon be completely overturned. During the early 1950s the NAACP's Legal Defense and Educational Fund concentrated on both interstate and intrastate transportation, discrimination in publicly owned recreational facilities, and segregation in the public schools. By the middle of the decade the Supreme Court had made clearcut decisions in support of the NAACP's position in each of these areas, thus firmly establishing the basic legal principles supporting desegregation.

Due to a rise in membership fees, the NAACP had lost nearly half its members in 1948; in 1950 the total was just under 200,000. Since then there has been a gradual rise, the number doubling to nearly 400,000 in 1962. Income for the Association rose more rapidly: between 1954 and 1958 its revenues increased from $465,000 to $1,000,000. Today the NAACP spends at the rate of well over a million dollars annually, while the National Legal Defense Fund (founded in 1939 and since 1955 a completely separate institution legally and administratively) spends almost as much. Significantly the major increase in membership in the late 1940s and early 1950s was in the South, so that by 1955 fully half of the NAACP members lived there. The legislative attack on the NAACP in the South after the 1954 Supreme Court decision (the Association is still under injunction not to operate in Alabama), the economic reprisals taken against NAACP leaders and parents who tried to register their children in previously all-white schools, and the harrassment and violence to which the Association's leaders were subjected in the white South's campaign against the organization, did not lead to a decline in membership — in fact Negroes rallied to it just because it was under such bitter attack.

During the late 1940s and early 1950s branch activity in the North concentrated largely on obtaining passage of fair employment and fair housing acts; in the border states and upper South the principal emphasis was on litigation to secure the use of public recreational facilities; and in the South generally this period witnessed considerable voter registration activity. During the second half of the decade Southern branches were engaged in extensive litigation against the South's massive resistance to school desegregation and subsequently against the more subtly drawn pupil-placement laws. Throughout the country during the late fifties there was a heavy accent on voter registration: it was felt that in the ballot lay the key to obtaining civil rights legislation and a sympathetic policy on the part of public officials. Increased income for the association made it possible to employ staff specialists first in labor, since 1958 in housing and voter registration, and quite recently in education. Both these, by advising branches on how to work in their fields, and the burgeoning field staff (which grew from less than half a dozen in 1950 to twenty-seven in 1963), vastly stimulated NAACP activity on all fronts. The effort to eliminate discriminatory practices by trade unions had become a major concern by the middle of the decade; political and legal pressures were employed to see that publicly financed housing would be open to all; and recently the attack on de facto school desegregation in the North has become a major concern. Prior to 1960 nonviolent direct action was a more peripheral matter for NAACP branches — but in 1958 and 1959 NAACP college and youth chapters in Oklahoma City and St. Louis engaged in successful sit-ins, and elsewhere, as in Louisville and Baltimore, adult branches sponsored direct action. Nevertheless, looking back over the decade of the 1950s it is clear that the NAACP's chief concerns had been to increase the number of voters and to attack segregation in all its manifestations with both legal and political pressures.

Established in 1942, CORE was much younger than the NAACP, and in 1950 was still a small, chiefly white organization, confined to the North and a few border communities, and lacking even a single paid staff member. Contrary to popular impression, the use of nonviolent direct action was not a product of the postwar era, but of the depression, for CORE's origins lay in the activities of the Fellowship of Reconciliation, a pacifist social-action organization. This group of religious pacifists combined Gandhi's technique of *satyagraha* with the sit-*down* tactics of the Detroit automobile strikers, to produce the sit-*in.* F.O.R.'s synthesis of union tactics (including picketing) with Gandhian nonviolence was tested on a limited scale beginning around 1940. Then, in order to attract people whose interests lay in reace relations rather than in philosophical pacifism, some of the F.O.R. leaders founded CORE.

CORE's membership[1] and activity had been in the North during the 1940s and in the border states at the turn of the decade and early 1950s. In 1956 CORE employed a paid field worker for the first time, and began its work in the Deep South, both by nibbling at the edges and, more daringly, engaging in activity in South Carolina.[2] Like the NAACP, CORE always aimed at the attainment of full citizenship in all areas. But at first it was chiefly concerned with public accommodations.

Though back in the early 1950s St. Louis CORE pioneered in the technique — later so effectively employed and popularized by the Philadelphia ministers — to obtain employment through selective buying campaigns, this did not become a major emphasis until fairly recently, and not until 1959–1960 did CORE use direct action to secure desegregation of privately owned apartment houses. Today in the North CORE concentrates on unemployment and housing, with some work in school desegregation; in the South it concentrates on places of public accommodation and to a lesser extent on voter registration.

CORE pioneered in the use of *satyagraha* in this country, but it was the Montgomery bus boycott of 1955–1956 that dramatically brought it to the attention of the nation, and the Negro community in particular. And it has been Martin Luther King, whom the bus boycott catapulted into prominence, who has now become the leading symbol of this strategy. Even before a court decision (obtained by NAACP lawyers) had spelled success for the Montgomery Improvement Association, a similar movement had started in Tallahassee,[3] and afterwards one was undertaken in Birmingham where, following the state's injunction against the NAACP, a group of ministers headed by Fred Shuttlesworth had established the Alabama Christian Movement for Human Rights. About the same time there appeared the Tuskegee Civic Association, which undertook a three-year long boycott of local merchants in response to the state legislature's gerrymander that placed practically all Negro voters outside of the town's limits — a campaign crowned with success when the Supreme Court ruled the gerrymander illegal in 1960.

The happenings in Montgomery, Tallahassee, Birmingham and Tuskegee were widely heralded as indicating the emergence of a "New Negro" in the South — militant, no longer fearful of white hoodlums, police and jails, and willing to use his collective economic weight to attain his ends. Seizing upon the new mood, King in 1957 established the Southern Christian Leadership Conference — an organization of affiliates rather than a membership organization like NAACP. Ideologically committed to a thoroughgoing philosophical pacifism of the Gandhian persuasion, SCLC's program includes not only the now-familiar demonstrations but also citizenship training schools which prepare leaders to go out into local communities and push voter-registration. SCLC's budget comes chiefly from contributions — its income for the year ending August 31, 1961, was nearly $200,000; its budget this year is almost two and a half times as much — approximately $375,000.

The NAACP thought it saw the beginning of the end in the 1954 Supreme Court decision. And truly, it was only the *beginning* of the end. Impressive as it was to cite the advances — especially legal advances — made in the post-war years, in spite of state laws and supreme court decisions something was clearly wrong. Negroes were still disfranchised in most of the Deep South; Supreme Court decisions in regard to transportation facilites were still largely ignored there; discrimination in employment and housing was the rule, even in states with model civil rights laws; and after 1954 the Negro unemployment rate grew constantly due to recessions and automation. And then, as we have noted, there was the rise of Southern white militance in response to the 1954 decision, best represented by the White Citizens Councils.

At the very time that legalism was thus proving itself a limited instrument, Negroes were gaining a new self-image of themselves as a result of the rise of the new African nations; King and others were demonstrating that nonviolent direct action could be effective in the South; and the new laws and court decisions, the gradually increasing interest of the federal government, the international situation, and the evident drift of white public opinion, had developed in American Negroes a new confidence in the future. In short there had occurred what has appropriately been described as a revolution in expectations. Negroes no longer felt that they had to accept the humiliations of second-class citizenship, and consequently these humiliations — somewhat fewer though they now were — appeared to be more intolerable than ever. This increasing impatience — and disillusionment — of Negroes accounted for the rising tempo of nonviolent direct action in the later 1950s which culminated in the student sit-ins and the Freedom Ride of 1960–1961.

Symptomatic of this impatience and disillusionment was the stepped-up campaign against trade-union discrimination. During the 1930s the CIO unions had made a new departure in establishing nondiscriminatory policies. However, the Civil Rights Committee of the merged AFL-CIO made little, if any, significant progress. While the chief charges of discrimination were still directed at the old AFL unions, notably in the building trades, there was also increasing dissatisfaction with the policies of the industrial unions. For example, even the United Automobile Workers — known for its liberalism — until 1962 had no Negroes among its chief executives and policy makers. Beginning in 1958 the NAACP openly attacked its allies in the labor movement for abdicating their responsibility in regard to erasing the color line within the trade unions. In the Spring of 1960, A. Philip Randolph established the Negro American Labor Council, to fight against discrimination from within the AFL-CIO. With a board consisting chiefly of staff people from the AFL-CIO unions, the NALC is made up of affiliates in a number of cities; a year after its formation it claimed between seven and ten thousand members. It lacks a paid staff, but it has been a valuable platform for agitation and a mighty symbol of the Negro worker's discontent.

Many date the new departure in the tactics of the civil rights movement from the Montgomery bus boycott in 1955 — and the impact of this event is not to be minimized. But it seems to me that the really decisive break with the past came with the college student sit-ins that started spontaneously at Greensboro in 1960. This was so for several reasons. For one thing these sit-ins involved the use of nonviolent direct action on a massive, South-wide scale, never before attempted. Secondly, they involved tens of thousands of students, thousands of whom were arrested — an involvement of numbers of people heretofore inconceivable. Thirdly, it began a period — in which we are still living — in which the spearhead of the civil rights struggle has come from the youth. Of course the adults in the Negro community rallied to the aid of the students and supplied essential legal and financial assistance. But it has been the youth who have been the chief dynamic force in revamping the strategy of the established civil rights organization — who in turn felt it necessary to do something in order to retain leadership in the movement.

The NAACP almost immediately swung into action, and the national office deliberately speeded up the formation of youth councils and college chapters with the specific purpose of engaging in demonstrations, while national staff members went to regional NAACP conferences that spring and knocked heads together in a strong effort to obtain local NAACP participation and support for this type of mass action. In fact, much of the sit-in activity during 1960 was carried on by NAACP youth councils and college chapters. Like the NAACP, SCLC sought to get on the student bandwagon, and it sponsored the Raleigh Conference at which the Student Nonviolent Coordinating Committee was established — though SNCC and SCLC later drifted apart. SNCC is theoretically a coordinating committee of affiliated youth groups in the Southern and border states; actually, for the most part a small group in Atlanta engages in action of its own choosing, and enlists the aid of people in the local communities where it decides to work. SNCC has been extraordinarily effective. Though it has the most modest budget of any of the civil rights organizations (it operated last year on $120,000), and its field secretaries work on a subsistence basis, and although it has been less publicized than the other organizations, it has probably supplied the major drive for the civil rights movement in the South. CORE in 1960 seemed to be in the doldrums, its techniques appropriated by more vigorous and lusty successors. But in 1961, following the Freedom Ride to Alabama and Mississippi, CORE re-emerged as in many ways the most imaginative and resourceful of the civil rights organizations in the application of the tactics in which it had pioneered.

The events of 1960 and 1961 ushered in a period of intense competitive rivalry for prestige and power in the civil rights field. It has been a four-way struggle — between SCLC, NAACP, SNCC and CORE (though even the Urban League has set forth upon more aggressive policies). Of the four it may be said that SNCC has probably been the most dynamic force, closely seconded by CORE. While various SCLC affiliates have taken the lead in nonviolent direct action in their communities, especially where local NAACP branches are dominated by conservative leadership, King, functioning chiefly as a symbolic or "spiritual" leader, has ordinarily moved into situations which others have begun, to lend the magic of his image to the support of the local movement. Moreover, in many communities there have sprung up local organizations, established very often by ministers of working-class churches, taking various names, and unattached to any national body. Sometimes these are "umbrella" organizations, including within them local units of national organizations; at times they are entirely independent of, though not necessarily inimical to, the NAACP or other established groups. As the oldest and therefore the most bureaucratic of the civil rights organizations, in many localities dominated by older, conservative leaders, the NAACP has quite naturally been on the defensive in a number of places. But it is impossible to generalize about the NAACP. While some branches have resisted the direct action techniques, others have embraced them wholeheartedly. There are cases of militant cliques ousting conservative leadership within NAACP branches; in Philadelphia for example the older leaders found their homes picketed with signs calling them "Uncle Toms." While the NAACP can scarcely take credit for initiating the direct action techniques, it is clearly invalid to stereotype it as run by a conservative Black Bourgeoisie wedded to legalism. Pushed and shoved by the exclusively action-oriented groups, the NAACP has pretty effectively met the challenge posed by them. In fact at the 1963 annual convention, militants among the rank and file and the "radicals" on the paid staff triumphed against the more conservative elements. The convention enthusiastically endorsed direct action as the major NAACP tactic for the future, granted greater autonomy to the youth, and called upon the National Board to adopt procedures for removing do-nothing conservative leadership from the branches.

However, the NAACP's predominance in the civil rights field, not seriously contested as late as 1960, has been broken. Often in fact one gets the impression that the rivalry among the different groups is not due so much to differences in philosophy, tactics or degree of militancy as much as to a power struggle for hegemony in the civil rights movement. Painful as these conflicts have been, the rivalry of civil rights groups has actually proven to be an essential ingredient of the dynamics of the civil rights movement over the past three and a half years; for in their attempt to outdo each other, each organization puts forth stronger effort than it otherwise would, and is constantly searching for new avenues along which to develop a program.[4] And despite all rivalries, when the chips are down, the different organizations usually do manage to cooperate. Especially significant has been the growing cooperation this past spring between CORE and SNCC. The best example of this cooperation amidst rivalry is the fact that all of these organizations, along with others, worked together in sponsoring the August 28th March on Washington.

Two of the most significant aspects of the civil rights movement since 1960 are that it has become increasingly a Negro movement and at the same time increasingly a mass movement. The two developments are not unrelated; and both of them, of course, had their origins well before 1950. The NAACP membership and branch leadership has always been almost entirely Negro; but at the start most of the staff and executive board were liberal whites. In 1921 the NAACP employed its first Negro executive secretary, James Weldon Johnson; in 1933 its legal staff came under Negro direction when Charles Houston took over; and today only two NAACP staff members are white (though the NAACP Legal Defense Fund's chief counsel has been a white man, Jack Greenberg, since Thurgood Marshall was elevated to the bench). Constitutional changes made in 1947 and 1962 have permitted greater membership participation in the election of the national board; one result of this has been a decline in the number of whites on it — today only a dozen whites remain out of a membership that in the coming months will reach a maximum of sixty. CORE started off as a predominantly white liberal middle-class organization; as late as 1960 perhaps only one third of its membership was Negro, and at that time its four chief executive officers, as well as its national chairman, were white. With the selection of James Farmer as national director in 1961, CORE's image changed markedly in the Negro community, and it was thereby able to attract far more Negro support. Today, of CORE's four chief executive officers two are white and two are Negro. While the majority of Northern CORE members are still white there has been growing Negro participation in that section, and in the South CORE's membership is almost entirely Negro. The climax to these developments came at CORE's 1963 convention, the first one at which a majority of the delegates were Negroes. The Southern Negro delegates really set the tone for the convention, and moved into positions of leadership. And for the first time in CORE's history a Negro was selected as national chairman. Randolph's March on Washington Movement during the Second World War adumbrated current tendencies in its insistence upon an all-Negro membership and leadership; Negroes, he said, must fight their own battle for citizenship rights. More recently, organizations like SCLC, the Alabama Christian Movement for Human Rights, the Tuskegee Civic Association, the Negro American Labor Council, and the newer local groups have been Negro organizations from the start. SNCC has avoided any form of organic union with the predominantly white Northern Student Movement for Civil Rights — though it and Northern white students generally have been a prime source of SNCC's financial support; and while SNCC has a number of white field secretaries, it consciously projects itself as a Negro led organization. There has been in fact a growing insistence that Negroes must take the initiative and leadership in achieving their freedom; that white liberals tend to be compromisers who cannot be fully trusted, though their financial support and participation in direct action is welcomed.

CORE's experience has shown clearly that in order to attract large numbers of Negroes to the civil rights movement Negro leadership is essential. And white liberals — and radicals — in the movement have accepted this fact. The NAACP had originally appealed to the elite Negroes, and during the 1930s some of the younger intellectuals like Ralph Bunche attacked it for doing nothing about the problems of the masses. The Association modified its program somewhat, and during the 1940s and 1950s made an increasing appeal to working-class people, as its growing membership testifies. Actually it would be impossible to make any generalizations about the sources of NAACP branch membership and leadership today, because the variations from branch to branch are so considerable. At the risk of a great deal of oversimplification, and on the basis of general impression rather than careful investigation, one might say that in the South leadership tends to come from ministers, in the West from professional people, and in the Northeast from lower-middle class people such as postal workers. Leadership thus generally tends to be more middle class rather than either lower class or upper class. The nature of the membership of a branch, like leadership, depends to a great extent upon specific local conditions and personalities. In some branches the more elite people in the community set the tone; in others the professional and business people show no interest and blue-collar workers predominate. CORE, originally composed of white-collar middle-class people, since 1960 has found more blue-collar skilled and even semi-skilled workers joining its ranks, both in the North where it has moved into the area of obtaining employment for working class Negroes, and in the South. The youthful sit-inners of 1960–1961 were chiefly people of working-class origins — that is they tended to be upward mobile members of the Negro lower-middle and upper-lower classes — though their leadership was more likely to be drawn from people of middle-class origins. From the beginning the bus boycotts in the South were mass movements, and the same is true of newer movements like the Albany Movement and the selective buying campaigns being undertaken in a number of cities, though it should be pointed out that all classes of the community are involved in these efforts and that the middle and even upper classes are dispro-portionately represented in the leadership.

A striking development of the past few months has been the involvement of lower-lower class people, many of whom are unemployed or chronically so. It is this group that apparently was responsible for the brick and bottle-throwing in Birmingham and Jackson. Even more significantly some individuals of this class, heretofore avoiding participation in demonstrations sponsored by the direct-action groups, have begun to join in with the nonviolent direct actionists, but unlike them have not remained nonviolent in the face of attacks from white hoodlums, but have become involved in fracases with them in places like Cambridge, Maryland, and Nashville. In the North this group is chiefly concerned with obtaining jobs; in the South, despite a high rate of unemployed it is becoming involved in the struggle for public accommodations, though this is very possibly a result of the growing tendency to package demands for desegregation of lunch counters and other facili-ties with demands for jobs.

There are those who believe that overt violence on the part of Negro demonstra-tors is on the rise and that in hard-core areas of the South, Gandhian techniques will not work and that disillusionment with nonviolent tactics will set in. This line of thinking and the recent outbreaks are reminiscent of the events at Monroe, North Carolina, in 1959, and recall Robert Williams' assertion that federal intervention would not occur until Negroes struck back at their attackers.[5] Moreover, there is the possibility that the dire predictions in the daily press about possible racial violence may act in the nature of a self-fulfilling prophecy. Whether or not extensive violence occurs, astute leadership in the civil rights organizations will undoubtedly employ its possibility as a means of forcing quicker action from the white commu-nity.

In any event one must conclude that there has emerged a real thrust for achieving "Freedom Now" from the working class people — that is from the lower and lower-middle class people. SNCC, highly critical of the Black Bourgeoisie and white liberals alike, regards itself as the vanguard of the Negro masses — and to a remarkable extent that is exactly what the youthful demonstrators of the years since 1960 have proven to be. And this thrust from the working class — especially from the working class youth — has been largely responsible for the recent dynamics behind the civil rights movement. In fact the competiton for prestige and power among the major civil rights organizations is in large part a competition for control over the masses of working class Negroes. It is likely that a large part of the increasing militancy of middle and upper class Negroes is derived from the new militancy of the working classes. As Bayard Rustin has said of Birmingham, here was a "black community [that] was welded into a classless revolt. A. G. Gaston, the Negro millionaire who with some ministers and other upper-class elements had publicly stated that the time was not ripe for such a broad protest, finally accommodated himself, as did the others, to the mass pressure from below and joined the struggle."[6]

Now until recently it seemed quite possible that the unskilled, lowest-class urban Negroes might turn to the escapist nationalist ideology of the Black Muslims, for this sect offered a sense of dignity and a future to those whom the civil rights movement seemed to neglect. More than anything else the increasing unemployment with the revolution in expectations created a climate in which the Black Muslims thrived. The Black Muslims are simply one of several nationalist movements — but the only one of any size: estimates of their number vary, but it is almost certainly below 100,000, though there are many sympathizers and admirers. Historically nationalism of the extreme variety typified by the Black Muslims has been usually found among the most dispossessed of the Negro masses (the principal exception being the large scale interest in colonization exhibited by the Negro elite during the 1850s), though there are certain tiny groups of nationalist intellectuals, like the avowedly black Marxist Monro Defense Committee, and the Liberation Committee for Africa.

Just as the Garvey Movement was the lower-lower class counterpart of the New Negro of the 1920s, so the Black Muslims are the counterpart of the new "New Negro" of the 1960s. The literature about this movement is so extensive that it would be superfluous to discuss its program here.[7] However, despite the stark contrast between the integrationist aims of the civil rights organizations, and the separatist ideology of the Black Muslims, it is important to recognize that the two have much in common. Both are manifestations of a militant rejection of white doctrines of Negro inferiority and white policies of discrimination; both are essentially a quest for recognition of the Negroes' human dignity. Both reflect the new self-image of American Negroes arising out of the rise of the new African state. Both exhibit dissatisfaction with the traditional, accommodating, otherwordly Christianity of the Negro masses, which offered rewards in heaven rather than on earth. And both are indications of Negro rejection of the philosophy of gradualism, and both exhibit a rejection of liberal white paternalism. In part perhaps because they have sensed the increasing attraction of the direct-action activities of the civil rights organizations which have been moving more vigorously into the area of employment discrimination; in part perhaps because they thought the moment opportune to make a bid for leadership of the entire Negro community, since March

1963 the Black Muslims seem to have made a turn to the right. There is now less emphasis upon separatism, more emphasis on the generalized abstractions of justice and freedom, and support is even urged for the programs of other groups which are working for freedom and justice for the race.

The influence of the Black Muslims on the civil rights movement is somewhat speculative. Negroes of all classes approve of their dramatic indictment of the American race system, and of their ability to place white men on the defensive. Their renown may have contributed to some extent to the tendency to assert pride in being black, or even of being black nationalists, that has enjoyed some vogue among Negro activists in recent years. Their activity may also have contributed not a little to the intensified activity of the more traditional organizations like the NAACP and Urban League, and may have helped alert the civil rights organizations generally to the importance of doing something vigorous about employment discrimination. Certainly fear of the Black Muslims has accelerated the efforts of influential whites to satisfy the demands of the civil rights organizations.

The new thrust from the Negro masses, the complex patterns of rivalry and cooperation among the various civil rights organizations, the increasing power of the Negro vote in the urban centers, the growing relization of the Negro's economic power that has derived from the successful boycotts, the obvious sensitivity of the government to foreign criticism of our racial system, have together resulted in a broadening and intensification of the Negro protest movement. Year by year and month by month the Negroes of the United States have been growing more militant, more immediatist. Civil rights organizations now make several demands together in a package, rather than fighting on single issues, as before, and are no longer satisfied with tokenism. The result is that the rate of change is being accelerated, and the Kennedy administration has been brought to seriously commit itself to sponsor major legislative remedies. But the dynamics of the situation are such that whatever Kennedy does will not be enough — both because Negro demands increase with every advance, and because the President is subject to counter-pressures from interest groups inimical to civil rights. Large-scale violence may or may not come about as a result of large-scale unemployment, Southern white intransigeance, and increased Negro militance. But two things are certain — Negro militancy is bound to increase, and an accelerated tempo of advancement in civil rights appears inevitable.

Postscript

The preceding pages were completed early in July. Over the past two months the Negro protest movement has been characterized by varied, and in a sense, contradictory tendencies. There appears to be a waxing nationalist spirit, and yet also evidence of increasing white support and participation; a growing belief that unity with white labor and greater socialization of the economy will be necessary to assure freedom and equality, and at the same time increasing evidence that white moderates — most notably churchmen and businessmen — are becoming involved.

The rising spirit of nationalism would appear to be the product of two forces. One is the growing sense of confidence and self-respect as advances are made. Evidence of this is to be found, for example, in a burgeoning interest among Negroes in Negro history. The other source of this nationalist spirit is the disillusionment with the pace of change, the continuing tendency of the Kennedy administration to compromise with Southern racists, the shock of increasing police brutality and white violence in the Deep South. All these combine to give Negroes a greater sense of isolation and alienation at the very time that white support for the cause of civil rights is increasing. One manifestation of this trend is the sentiment for an all-Negro "Freedom Now" political party. Oddly enough it would appear that this idea has been projected chiefly by the Socialist Workers Party (the Trotskyites), who are deliberately attempting to capitalize upon this nationalist sentiment in order to destroy the Democratic Party and thereby create, they hope, a truly revolutionary situation.[8]

Universal among civil rights leaders is the belief, growing over the past year, that there can be no really meaningful solution to the civil rights question without a solution to the nation's economic problems. Mass unemployment lends urgency to the Negro protest at the same time that it makes the attainment of desegregation and equal rights a largely empty gain for the masses. Some civil rights leaders foresee an "inevitable" shift toward the left and toward increasing socialization in the American economic system; and they suggest that potentially the Negro protest movement can play an important role in eliminating poverty for whites as well as for Negroes.[9] Moreover, as a result of the March on Washington there has been something of a rapproachement between the civil rights organizations and the more "progressive" elements among the former CIO unions, and if this proves fruitful there will certainly be sharply increased pressure on the national administration to take more radical steps to eliminate unemployment.

On the other hand the March on Washington also actively involved in civil rights, for the first time, a number of white moderates — a few even from the South — who had heretofore displayed no interest. In addition to the March itself, the shock of the outrages in Birmingham both in the spring and in recent weeks, has served to arouse moderate elements hitherto unconcerned. An even more re-markable manifestation of this trend is the $1.5 million raised among businessmen this past summer by Stephen Currier of the Taconic Foundation for the recently-established Council for United Civil Rights Leadership and its allied Committee for Welfare, Education and Legal Defense.[10]

Thus the future direction of the civil rights movement is uncertain. It seems likely that the Urban League and NAACP will probably continue to be — relatively speaking — conservative forces, while SNCC obviously will continue to be the most radical. (It is undoubtedly sound strategy that there continue to be diverse approaches among Negro protest organizations.[11]) It is predictable that the white moderates are also likely to act as something of a relatively conservative influence. The joining of disparate elements in the two major current civil rights coalitions will inevitably mean a degree of instability within them. For the Council for United Civil Rights Leadership ranges from the "moneybags" represented by Stephen Currier to the parsimonious SNCC people, while the March on Washington Movement ranges from churchmen who dread the idea of "revolution" to the SNCC activists who revel in the idea that they are "revolutionists." Strictly speaking the civil rights movement (including SNCC) is not properly labelled revolutionary, for the vast majority of Negro activists do not desire to overturn the social structure — however much they say they want to do this[12] — but rather they want to be included in it on a basis of equality. The Negro protest movement therefore is more properly described as a reform movement. Of course the differences between the radical and conservative elements in the civil rights movement are not by any means a matter of mere semantics. There is a marked difference between eminent clergymen getting themselves arrested for trespassing — and getting bailed right out — at the Gwynn Oak Amusement Park in Maryland, last July 4, and the type of radical civil disobedience that would create a breakdown in the government of Alabama which SNCC is now recommending.

Negro protest organizations are therefore posed with knotty problems of strategy. It is apparent that, unlike Africa, the Negro protest movement in this country must depend upon substantial numbers of white allies for its success. Should, then, the major effort be made to hold and increase the support from the white moderates, as the abolitionists and other successful reform movements in this country's history were eventually able to do? Or should the stress be laid upon forging an alliance with the working-class whites and upon striving toward a more socialized economy? Indubitably the threat of an all-Negro party will push the Kennedy administration further along the road of civil rights; but would a successful party of this type, if it resulted in the victory of a reactionary Republican in 1964, serve to advance or retard the cause of civil rights? Should radical civil disobedience as proposed by SNCC be undertaken, at the risk of alienating considerable white support, but generating considerable international publicity and pressure? It is likely that all of these approaches will be attempted, and that like the competing civil rights organizations each of the competing strategies will play a part in the achieving of racial democracy in the United States.[13]

Notes

---

[1] There is no accurate record of CORE's membership, since the national office lists only contributors to the national body and chapter officers. Its growth, however, is reflected in the

fact that these numbered less than 2,000 in 1950, 26,000 on the eve of the 1961 Freedom Ride, and 61,000 as of May 1963.

[2] Actually CORE's first foray into the South was its Freedom Ride in the Upper South in 1947.

[3] A superb illustration of the subtleties and complexities involved in any analysis of the competitive rivalry among the various civil rights organizations, which will be discussed below, is the fact that this movement was led by Rev. Mr. C. K. Steele, president of the Tallahassee branch of the NAACP, and subsequently (while still NAACP president) a vice-president of King's SCLC and chairman of its Tallahassee affiliate. Similar situations existed for a while in Atlanta and in Nashville.

[4] For a fuller discussion of this thesis see August Meier, "The 'Revolution' Against the NAACP: A Critical Appraisal of Louis Lomax's *The Negro Revolt,*" *Journal of Negro Education,* 32:148–152, Spring 1963.

[5] Perhaps the best treatment of the Monroe, N.C., situation (from the point of view, however, of a Marxist), is Julian Mayfield, "Challenge to Negro Leadership: The Case of Robert Williams," *Commentary,* 21:297–305, April 1961.

[6] Bayard Rustin, "The Meaning of Birmingham," *Liberation* (organ of the War Registers' League), June, 1963.

[7] C. Eric Lincoln, *The Black Muslims in America* (Boston, 1961), and E. U. Essien-Udom, *Black Nationalism: The Search for an Identity in America,* (Chicago, 1962).

[8] For statement of the Trotskyite position see statement adopted by the 1963 convention of the Socialist Workers Party, in *International Socialist Review,* 24:103–113, Fall, 1963.

[9] See statement by Bayard Rustin given at the Socialist Party Conference held in Washington, August 29–31, and published in *New America,* September 24, 1963; see also Loren Miller, "Freedom Now — But What Then?," *Nation,* 196:539–542, June 29, 1963.

[10] The best discussion of this money-raising effort and its significance is probably Reese Cleghorn, "The Angels Are White — Who Pays the Bills for Civil Rights?," *New Republic,* 149:12–14, August 17, 1963.

[11] For suggestive case study see Jack L. Walker, "The Functions of Disunity: Negro Leadership in a Southern City," *Journal of Negro Education,* 32:227–236, Summer, 1963.

[12] Thus the use of revolutionary-sounding language in John Lewis's censored speech at the March on Washington was actually metaphorical, rather than representing a genuine revolutionary ideology.

[13] For perceptive comments on new directions in the Negro protest movement following the March on Washington, see article by Tom Kahn and remarks of Bayard Rustin and Norman Hill in the Socialist Party newspaper, *New America,* Sept. 24, 1963. For further discussion of the role of the radical revolutionary left-wing groups in the Negro protest movement see August Meier, "New Currents in the Civil Rights Movement," *New Politics,* 3:27–29, Summer, 1963.

Negro Protest Leaders in a Southern Community

Lewis M. Killian
Charles U. Smith

One of the significant features of race relations in the past five years has been the emergence of new patterns of Negro leadership in southern communities. Prior to the various court decisions which withdrew legal support from the traditional framework of segregation, Negro leadership gave the appearance of conforming to the pattern of "accommodating" or "compromise" leadership. Analyses of leadership in southern Negro communities, such as the treatment found in Myrdal's *American Dilemma*,[1] suggest that the compromise leaders held their positions primarily because they were acceptable to white leaders. They were also accepted by Negroes because accommodation was regarded as the most practical and effective mode of adjustment in the existing power situation.

The desegregation decisions of the U.S. Supreme Court, even without extensive implementation, redefined this power situation. In the years following 1954, militant leaders, reflecting the protest motive instead of the theme of patience and accommodation, have moved into the focus of attention of both whites and Negroes. Whereas the accommodating leaders had not been widely known to the white public, largely because they operated in a noncontroversial and often clandestine manner, the new leaders quickly rocketed to fame or notoriety, depending upon the observer's point of view. Martin Luther King, defying the white power structure of his community and being featured on the cover of *Time* magazine, symbolizes this new leadership. Many white leaders have reacted by bewailing the "breakdown of communication" between the races, denouncing the militant Negro leaders as reckless, radical parvenues, and attempting to isolate them by parleys with hand-picked, "responsible" leaders. Both practical and theoretical considerations dictate the need for a new appraisal of Negro leadership in the South.

Lewis M. Killian and Charles U. Smith, "Negro Protest Leaders in a Southern Community," *Social Forces*, XXXVIII March 1960, pp. 253–257. Reprinted by permission of the University of North Carolina Press.

The authors are indebted to the Society for the Psychological Study of Social Issues for a grant-in-aid which helped make this study possible. This is a revised version of a paper read at the twenty-second annual meeting of the Southern Sociological Society, Gatlinburg, Tennessee, April 17, 1959.

The north Florida community of Tallahassee is one of the southern communities in which a change in the pattern of Negro leadership seemed to accompany a crisis in race relations. The critical situation arose from a challenge to segregation on city busses, culminating in a boycott. Here, too, news media featured daily the names of militant Negroes who previously had been anonymous ciphers in the Negro community as far as most whites were concerned. There were allegations to the effect that "newcomers" had come into the community and stirred up the erstwhile contented population, and that the Negro leadership had "split" with the result that white leaders did not know with whom to deal. Hence this community was well suited for a case study of Negro leadership in crisis.

The situation proved an opportunity to get the answers, for this community, to certain questions. Was the leadership in this Protest Movement actually new to the Negro community, or were the new leaders merely people who had suddenly become known to the white community because of a change or strategy? If they were new to the higher levels of the power structure in the Negro community, had they actually displaced the old group of leaders or was the community split between two competing sets of leaders? A corollary is the question whether these "new leaders" drew their strength from popular support or simply from a tightly organized, activist minority.

Method of Study

The study, executed shortly after the end of the bus boycott, consisted of two related parts. The first was an assessment of the structure of Negro leadership through interviews with a panel of 21 Negroes tentatively designated as "leaders" by social scientists familiar with the community. This list subsequently proved to include what came to be defined as "old" and "new" leaders in almost equal proportions.

A panel of 21 white leaders was also selected. This panel included all of the white leaders who had dealt with the Negro community in connection with the bus protest, in either an official or unofficial capacity. It also included white functionaries who were known to have worked directly with the Negro community in connection with other matters, such as fund drives, civic projects, and communtiy problems, both before and after the boycott. They are white leaders who most often speak to the Negro community in behalf of the white community. Some of them are high in the power structure. That this group represents fairly the position of the white leadership in Tallahassee is indicated by the absence of opposition to their representations to the Negro community.

The names of the 21 Negroes tentatively listed as "leaders" were placed on a card which was handed to the subject during the interview. Then he was asked a series of questions about Negro leadership *before* and *after* the bus boycott, and told to respond by giving names from the list. The questions which are of interest here were:

1. As best you can recall, which would you have identified as "leaders" among Tallahassee Negroes 2 years ago?
2. At that time, which do you feel were able to influence large numbers of Negroes on important public issues?
3. Which ones were able to express most accurately the feelings of most Negroes in Tallahassee on important public issues?
4. Which ones were able to deal most effectively with white leaders as representatives of the Negro group?
5. Now, at the present time, which do you feel are most able to influence large numbers of Negroes on important public issues?
6. Which are able to express most accurately the feelings of most Negroes, etc.
7. Which are able to deal most effectively with white leaders, etc.

Subjects were allowed to give as few or as many responses to each question as they wished, and Negro subjects were encouraged to include their own names if they felt they should.

After the data had been collected, the answers of white and Negro informants were tabulated separately. Each of the 21 potential Negro leaders was given a score and a rank on each question, according to the number of times his name was mentioned in response to the question. Hence each Negro had, for each question, a rank assigned him by the Negro informants and a rank assigned by the white leaders.

The second portion of the study was an attitude survey of a sample of the adult Negro population of Tallahassee. Every fifth address was taken from a list of all the households in blocks occupied only by Negroes. Any adult available at the address was interviewed. A total of 196 usable interviews were obtained. A Likert-type scale of questions concerning attitudes toward segregation in general, the bus boycott, and the leadership of the Bus Protest Movement was used. Key questions for purposes of this study were:

1. The Negro should not boycott to achieve his goals. (Agreement with this statement would represent a repudiation of the militant leaders.)
2. The old, established leaders in Tallahassee were more effective than the ones leading the bus protest.
3. The leadership in the Tallahassee Bus Protest is very good.

Subjects were grouped in three categories on the basis of whether their answers to these three questions reflected approval or disapproval of the leaders who had called for the bus boycott. Those who answered all three of the questions favorably were classified as "Highly favorable," those who answered two favorably were classified as "Favorable," and those who answered only one or none in this manner were placed in the "Unfavorable" category.

Findings

The interviews with the panel of potential Negro leaders revealed that a real change in leadership had indeed taken place between the "Pre-Boycott" and "Post-Boycott" periods. On the basis of high rankings on the answers to the questions "Who were the leaders?" "Who were influential?" and "Who were representative?" two years previously, six individuals were classified as "Pre-Boycott Leaders." Of these six, not one was found in the first five ranked on "influence" and "representativeness" in the Post-Boycott period. None of them were ranked even in the first ten on "influence," although two did remain in the first ten on "representativeness." An indication of how complete the turnover of leadership personnel was in the fact that of the first five ranked as both "influential" and "representative" in the Post-Boycott period, not one was among the first ten named as "leaders" in the Pre-Boycott period.

This change of leadership was also found to involve, as had been postulated, a replacement of Accommodating Leaders by Protest Leaders. Of the six Pre-Boycott leaders, five were ranked by Negroes as being most able to deal effectively with white leaders during this period. Five of the six were also ranked by whites as most able to deal effectively with white leaders. Four, including the three ranked highest by Negroes as "leaders," were ranked in the first five as "emissaries" by both Negroes and whites. This finding bears out the theory that, in the era of accommodation in race relations, leadership in the Negro community was based primarily on acceptability to white leaders and ability to gain concessions from them.

In contrast, none of the five New Leaders were ranked by either Negroes or whites as among the five Negroes able to deal most effectively with white leaders in the Post-Boycott period. In fact, none of them ranked in the first ten on acceptability to white leaders as it was perceived by Negroes. Clearly these New Leaders were not seen by other prominent Negroes as "Compromise Leaders."

The panel of Negroes interviewed included both the Old Leaders and the New Leaders, plus some individuals who did not receive high rankings for either period. The Negro panel was divided, for purposes of further analysis, into an "old group" of subjects who had ranked in the first ten on the question concerning Pre-Boycott leadership, and a new group. The new group identified as the five most influential leaders in the Post-Boycott period the same five men who had been ranked as New Leaders by the entire panel. The "old group" ranked four of these five men as the five most influential leaders in this same period, indicating that their perception of the change in leadership was almost the same as that of the "new group." Moreover, none of the "old group," including the Old Leaders, gave their own names in response to the question of ability to influence large numbers of Negroes. Although during the course of the boycott some of the Old Leaders had openly challenged the influence of the New Leaders, by the time of this study they seemed to have accepted the fact that they had been displaced. It is accurate, therefore, to say that a change, not a split, in leadership had occurred.

Although no intensive study of the individual characteristics of the Old and New Leaders was made, certain ones were evident. Even though at the time of the study, the boycott had ended and had obviously failed of its purpose to force desegregation of city buses, all of the New Leaders were strongly identified with it. All were officers of the organization which had led the boycott and all had been arrested and fined for "operating an illegal transportation system" (a car pool). In contrast, not one of the Old Leaders had been active in promoting the boycott, and at least two of them had opposed it as a tactic. Of the six Old Leaders, three were employed in the state-supported school system; none of the five New Leaders were state employees. There were three ministers among the New Leaders, none among the old. Although the Old Leaders had, as a group, indeed lived in the community a longer time than their successors, the shortest time that any of the New Leaders had lived in Tallahassee was three years. One of them had lived there over thirty years. It was only in a limited and relative sense that they could be described as "new-comers."

Since the New Leaders had been identified as synonomous with the leaders of the Bus Boycott, the questions asked in the opinion poll were suited to serve as a measure of their popular support. Were they leaders not only in the eyes of the small panel of prominent Negroes but also in the eyes of the Negro community? The results of the survey indicate that they were. When asked if the leadership in the Bus Protest was very good, 84 percent of the sample agreed that it was. Some inconsistency was found between the answers to this question and the question, "The old established leaders in Tallahassee were more effective than the ones leading the Bus Protest," since only 62 percent of the sample disagreed with this statement. But, to the extent that this sample can be taken as representative, it appears that the New Leaders did have majority support in the Negro community. Subjects were also asked to agree or disagree with the statement, "Should the Negro population of Tallahassee need to develop united action to obtain rights or services not connected with the Bus Protest, the people leading the Protest would probably be selected to lead such action." Again, strong majority support of the New Leaders was indicated, 82 percent of the sample agreeing with this statement.

Using the categories "Highly Favorable," "Favorable," and "Unfavorable," established earlier, an analysis was made of certain differences between Negroes showing greater or lesser support for the boycott and its leaders. The chi-square test of independence was used. Differences significant beyond the .01 level were found in age and education, the more favorably disposed subjects being younger and better educated. Those who were favorably disposed toward the boycott were more likely to own automobiles than those who were not, this difference also being significant beyond the .01 level. This difference may have reflected the fact that the boycott caused less personal inconvenience for car owners than it did for others, or it may have been that car ownership was an indirect measure of socio-economic status. No significant difference in ownership of real property was found between supporters and non-supporters, however, so the former explanation seems the more likely. This is also suggested by the fact that differences in occupation were not significant at the .05 level.

Summary and Conclusions

In the community studied, the impression that there has been a change in the quality of race relations is borne out. The clearest indication of this change is the replacement of the Old Leaders by New Leaders who clearly reflect the protest motive rather than any spirit of accommodation. These New Leaders have widespread popular support, and the extent of their influence is conceded by the Old Leaders whom they displaced.

Additional findings lend added significance to this shift in Negro leadership. The panel of white leaders were found to perceive Negro leadership in the Post-Boycott period in almost the same way that the Negro leaders did. Of the six men ranked highest by whites as "most influential" in the Post-Boycott period, four were among the Negroes' New Leaders. At the same time, most of these white leaders indicated that they were unwilling to deal with these New Leaders because the militant spokesmen were uncompromising in their opposition to segregation. It is only in this sense that communication has broken down between the races. The New Leaders are unwilling to communicate and negotiate with whites in the circumscribed, accommodating fashion of yesterday. The Old Leaders can no longer claim the support of the Negro population, no matter how acceptable they might be to the whites. As long as this situation prevails, the structure of the situation seems to permit only one kind of communication between the Negro community and the white power structure: formal, peremptory demands, backed by the threat of legal action, political reprisal, or economic boycott. So long as the New Leaders are not accepted as bona fide, albeit antagonistic, emissaries of the Negro community in the same way that the Old Leaders were, this would seem to be the only way in which they can get the attention of the white leaders.

While the present study was principally concerned with a description of the changes in Negro leadership in Tallahassee during the Bus Protest, there is evidence which indicates that the New Leaders and new leadership are permanent in this community. Although they may have been "issue leaders" at first, they have continued to maintain their position of leadership as the sample of the Negro population predicted they would.

In the first place some of the Old Leaders were called upon by the Tallahassee City Commission to get the Negroes to agree to a compromise settlement in the early days of the Bus Protest. The efforts of the Old Leaders to do this failed completely and ever since they have made no overt efforts to regain the following they had prior to the protest. This is apparently due to their belief that neither the ·Negro population nor the city officials have confidence in them. The Negroes do not trust them because of what they regard as underhanded dealing with the City Commission. The city officials apparently feel that these erstwhile leaders cannot be trusted to gauge Negro sentiment accurately or to deliver results when called upon, because they lack following.

Secondly, the New Leaders have continued to enjoy reasonable support for their undertakings. Some of them have moved into other areas of leadership, such as the NAACP, the Southern Christian Leadership Conference, and the Florida Council of Human Relations. One of them is president of the Tallahassee Chapter of the NAACP. Another is on the State NAACP Board and on the Board of Directors of the Southern Christian Leadership Conference.

Finally these New Leaders have sought to keep the Negro community of Tallahassee militant and dynamic by continuing weekly meetings of the ICC, the organization formed to promote the bus protest, conducting institutes on nonviolence, taking preliminary steps toward school integration, working to get more Negroes registered and voting, and making many local and nonlocal public appearances in connection with the uplift of of Negroes. Furthermore, the press has done much to contribute to their status as permanent leaders by seeking their opinions and comments on various matters affecting the Negro community in Tallahassee (e.g. the recent rape case).

The writers feel that the New Leaders are becoming permanent leaders not because of the attractiveness of their personalities or their skill at organizing, but rather because they adhere rigorously to the *form* of militant leadership which is becoming the trend for Negroes throughout the United States. This new leadership is not of the accommodating type. It seeks gains for the Negro community through formal demands and requests, boycotts, lawsuits, and voting. The protest leaders are not concerned with whether or not the whites high in the power structure know, like, or want to deal with them. Until the Old Leaders are willing or able to translate their mode of leadership into a form similar to this, it appears that they will not again rise to prominence as leaders in Tallahassee.

Notes

---

[1] Gunnar Myrdal, *An American Dilemma* (New York: Harper and Bros., 1944) pp. 768–780.

Negro Leadership after the Social Crisis: An Analysis of Leadership Changes in Montgomery, Alabama

Ralph H. Hines
James E. Pierce

Contemporary interest in the problem of leadership and the social crisis is closely related to inquiries into the nature of social solidarity, group identification, social roles and the general problem of intergroup and interpersonal relations. In a sense, all these problems are practical as well as theoretical considerations of the basic preoccupation of our age. We live in a world in which the individual finds it increasingly difficult to adjust to or cope with the growing complexities of his social, economic and political environment.

Within recent years an emerging and evolving Negro leadership has been one of the significant factors effecting new forms of social interaction in the field of human relations. The cause of the emergence of a wholly new type of leadership in the Negro community, unknown a decade or so ago, has been the focus of attention of numerous social scientists.[1] This new Negro leadership, a "protesting" rather than an "accommodating" type, has emerged as the champion of Negro rights.

In the era following the Supreme Court school desegregation decision of May, 1954, an unprecedented vitalization of Negro leadership has surged in various parts of the country. By and large, the mercurial rise of a militant and protesting type Negro leadership is a product of the South. Discrimination is real, overt and recurrent in the South. Unlike their Northern compatriots who experience more subtle and less definitive expressions of discrimination, Negroes in the South know the limitations of their freedom and feel, therefore, that they have little about which to be complacent.

Ralph H. Hines and James E. Pierce, "Negro Leadership after the Social Crisis: An Analysis of Leadership Changes in Mcntgomery, Alabama," *Phylon,* XXVI, 2nd Quarter, 1965, pp. 162–172. Reprinted by permission of the publisher.

A protest movement as a means of correcting group-defined wrongs is not a novel approach to the problem of race relations in America nor to American history generally.[2] Oliver Cox, in his analysis of Negro leadership, points out that protest has been the most prolonged and significant line of action of Negro rights fighters since the days of slavery. Further, protest was the instrument of the abolitionists and "since the Civil War almost all the Negro newspapers and magazines have been protest organs."[3]

This paper analyzes the continuities and discontinuities of leadership surrounding the social crisis. The bus boycott in Montgomery, Alabama, from December, 1955, to February, 1957, serves as a model of the social crisis where a decided racial cleavage developed. Both symbolic and actual conflict existed in Montgomery between the superordinate and subordinate groups. This analysis considers some of the factors, latent and manifest, which created the crisis as well as those which fostered varying types of leadership responses.

The concept "leader" is used here to delineate that individual identified as sufficiently influential to direct or control collective behavior and having a number of followers who, implicitly or explicitly, legitimatize his leadership function.[4]

In order to determine the leadership structure of the Negro community during three periods studied, the pre-protest, the protest and post-protest, a panel of thirteen Negro social science teachers were asked to identify leaders in terms of degrees of prominence.[5] Three categories of prominence were outlined, including most prominent leaders, prominent leaders, and not prominent but leaders. An analysis will be given of leadership for each period as well as changes in leadership types.

The Pre-Protest Community

Montgomery, Alabama, a city of approximately 125,000 population, is located in the middle expanse of the Alabama midlands in an area commonly referred to as the "Black Belt."[6] The capital city of Alabama, Montgomery, is the governmental, administrative and political center of the state. A few small industries supply goods, services and employment for the population. These are, however, relatively insignificant forces in the over-all economic structure of the community.

The Negro community, of about 50,000 population, is divided into two major sectors. An intervening white residential and shopping area separates them.[7] The ideological and practical world of Montgomerians is that of racial separatism. Few social, commercial or public facilities are available to the Negro members of the community. Six night clubs, four movie houses, one community center, eleven schools, and forty churches constituted the major means of social, educational and recreational services for Negroes during the pre-protest period. The Negro college, located in the smaller of the two major sectors of town, afforded limited opportunities for use of its facilities by citizens of the town.[8]

An analysis of the leadership structure of pre-protest Montgomery reveals several interesting configurations. The panel was able to identify twenty-two individuals who could, with justification, be called community leaders. Of this group, only six received a sufficient number of choices by the panel to warrant inclusion in the prominence construct. Table 1 shows the occupational categories of these leaders and the frequency of their choice by the panel.

Table 1: Identified Leaders in the Pre-protest Negro Community by Occupation and Frequency of Choices

Category	Occupation	Frequency of Choices*
Most prominent	Ralroad employee	13
	College teacher	11
Prominent	College teacher or official	11
	Businessman	11
Not prominent but a leader	Minister	11
	Public school teacher	10

* Frequency of choices refers to the number of choices made by the panel of "experts" in delineating community leaders. If a presumed leader did not receive 50 percent of the panel's choices, he was not considered eligible for inclusion in any category. Leadership in this study relates to those individuals having some community-wide appeal and recognition.

A breakdown of all identified leaders, regardless of the degree of prominence in the Negro community, is given in Table 2. Two occupation categories stand out as significant sources of leadership in this period: the ministry and the teaching profession. Jointly, these professions represented 54 percent of the total known and identified leaders of Montgomery's Negro community. As was expected, the minister assumed an important role in the life of the community. He was a natural leader to a people who had access to a minimum of social, political and economic opportunities.

The pre-protest community appeared to have had little sense of "we-ness" or group solidarity. Community-wide leadership was essentially latent and certainly impotent in the areas of racial and social change. Few public articulations of discontent and unrest originated from the leadership. No issue or event with unifying effects upon the total community had come.

The manifest role of Negro leaders in pre-protest Montgomery was accommodative. Negro leadership was what Myrdal called "typical" of Southern American towns. Leaders not only tended to be accommodative and compromising but their positions were held principally because of their acceptability to whites.[9]

While the spiritual and civic leaders of the Negro population were believed to be in the community, the intellectual leadership was to be found, presumably, at

Table 2: All Identified Negro Leaders by Occupation
(Pre-Protest Period)

Occupation	Number	Percentage of Total
College teacher or official	5	22.8
Minister	4	18.2
School teacher	3	13.6
Doctor, Dentist	2	9.1
Insurance agent	2	9.1
Businessman	2	9.1
Domestic worker	2	9.1
Railway employee	1	4.5
Lawyer	1	4.5
	22	100.0

the local college. The college, however, provided little overt and demonstrative support to the undercurrent of social unrest permeating the Negro population. The inability of the college to function in both the pre-protest, and, as we shall see, in the protest period, grew out of a rather delicate balance between its obligations to the Negro community and the accommodative forces inherently attached to its own operation. Oliver Cox makes this point patently clear in his assessment of the leadership ability of Negroes connected with educational institutions in the Deep South. He shows that Negro intellectuals can seldom rise to be real or great leaders because they can never take an unequivocal position. The ruling class, says Cox, does not have complete confidence in them and the people do not know exactly in what social situation it will become convenient for them to champion their cause. Therefore, the accommodative leader "does not inspire courage and faith in himself among the people, though he may claim their respect and sympathy."[10]

In summary, to the extent that Negro leadership existed in Montgomery prior to the protest, it must be recognized as an accommodative type. It tended to be slight, parochial, interest-group centered, and fundamentally powerless in the over-all structure of the wider community. The leadership of the pre-protest period mirrored more or less the self-conception and social expectations of Southern Negroes. As social types, Negroes tended to be acquiescent, accommodative and obedient to the rules of interracial etiquette.[11] Pre-protest leadership was composed of neither power wielders nor decision makers in the sense these terms are used by Floyd Hunter,[12] nor participants in the power structure of the wider community as power is described and analyzed by Bierstedt.[13]

The Protest: An Emergence of New Leadership

Initially, the Montgomery bus protest was intended as a short-range method to correct one and only one humiliating and socially distasteful pattern of Negro-white interaction. At the start, there were no broad and comprehensive demands for total redress of the "wrongs" inflicted for generations upon the Negro population of the area. This was a specific issue. In fact, the general approach of the first group of Negro leaders who interceded on behalf of Mrs. Rosa Parks,[14] and the Negro population generally, was ameliorative rather than punitive. Three concessions were sought: (1) that Negro bus riders be given courteous treatment; (2) that all bus riders be seated on a first-come-first-served basis — Negroes from back to front, whites from front to rear; and, (3) that Negro drivers be hired on routes which served predominantly Negro Neighborhoods.[15]

White reaction to the unaccustomed demands of an otherwise silent, accommodative and complacent minority was bitter. The arrest of ninety-five Negroes swiftly resulted as an answer to Negro "insurrection." Bus officials were intransigent in their refusal to negotiate even though 70 percent of their revenue was derived from Negroes. The refusal by white officials to move on otherwise "mild" demands inadvertently altered the course of events from a protest to a full scale boycott. When the base was broadened to include the larger issues of segregation and racial discrimination, the National Association for the Advancement of Colored People offered legal and financial assistance. At the inception of the boycott, pre-protest leaders attempted to "work things out." Dissatisfaction was expressed on all sides. It was clear that "new blood" was needed. The boycott was now a mature social crisis with determination on both sides to oppose to the end the aims of each. A new style Negro leadership came forward to take the reins.

Identification of the new leadership by the panel revealed that thirty-five individuals were involved, one way or another, in leadership capacities during the protest period. Not all of these persons were, however, of equal importance to the leadership structure of the Negro community or stood out in prominence among the rank and file. Table 3 indicates all leaders by occupation.

An examination of Table 4 demonstrates what we believe to be a more realistic view of the effective leadership structure in Montgomery during the boycott. It is

Table 4: Identified Leaders in Protest Negro Community by Occupation and Frequency of Choice

Category	Occupation	Frequency of Choices*
Most prominent	Minister	13
	Minister	8
	College teacher	7
Prominent	Businessman	13
	Minister	13
	Lawyer	10
	Railroad employee	7
Not prominent but a leader	School teacher	13
	Minister	10
	Housewife	11
	Minister	10
	Minister	8

* See explanation for frequency of choices under Table 1.

of interest to note that the ministry and other "independent" occupations provided the bulk of potential leaders for the Negro protest. This seems to have been the establishment of a pattern for other communitites where interracial conflict developed.

In Montgomery, a minister, Martin Luther King, Jr., stood at the apex of a new leadership pyramid unprecedented in the history of the Negro community. Using the Gandhian technique of non-violence, he brought to the protest that symbolic representation needed to transform frustrations into demands. In his person and program, King achieved what Leslie W. Dunbar described as the symbolic impressions necessary to all social movements.[16] Through King's leadership, the transition was made from accommodation and compromise to assertativeness and protest.

The non-violent protest and assertative Negro leadership were unexpected events for the white community. The leading daily newspaper called upon "whites" to awaken to the problems now facing them in view of the "new Negro" they had to meet.[17]

The Montgomery bus boycott lasted for three hundred and eighty-one days. The degree of total community involvement and a new sense of social solidarity, engendered by the organized efforts of a dynamic and forceful leadership, undeniably accounted for its ultimate success. The masses stood behind their leaders, pushing and being pushed.[18]

Martin Luther King was catapulted to national and international fame and became the undisputed leader of the Negro mass movement. He is by far the most popular Negro leader in America today and speaks with the voice of charismatically endowed authority.[19] The charisma of King's leadership first became apparent during the Montgomery bus boycott.[20] His willingness to undergo severe personal privations in the interest of social justice for the Negro population enhanced his "calling." His departure from Montgomery, however, left a vacuum in the leadership pyramid which, as we shall see, has never been filled. He left unresolved the more basic factors which gave rise to the original crises.

Post-Protest Leadership: The Aftermath of the Crisis

The boycott was over, but the spirit of protest, however, was not dead. For several months following the departure of King, the upper-and-middle-echelon Negro leaders who had carried the bulk of the organizational responsibilities felt compelled to continue a program toward complete desegregation. The leadership structure, however, unquestionably was altered. It lacked both depth and the broad base from which it had operated so efficiently during the protest period. Table 5 and Table 6 show identified leaders and preferred leaders respectively.

More striking than the reduction of leaders immediately following the protest period is that which followed from 1959 to the present. Table 7 is a combined representation of all identified leaders and preferred leaders in the Negro community. The sharp decline in leadership coincides with the decline of Negro participa-

Table 5: All Identified Negro Leaders by Occupation
(Post-Protest Period—1957–1960)

Occupation	Number	Percentage of Total
Minister	8	42.1
Lawyer	4	21.1
School teacher	1	5.2
College teacher or official	1	5.2
Insurance agent	1	5.2
Railroad employee	2	10.5
Businessman	2	10.5
Total	19	100.0

Table 6: Identified Leaders in Post-Protest Period by Occupation
and Frequency of Choices

Category	Occupation	Frequency of Choices
Most prominent	Minister	13
	Businessman	13
Prominent	Minister	13
	Lawyer	12
	College teacher or official	7
Not prominent but a leader	Businessman	12
	Railroad employee	7

Table 7: All Identified Negro Leaders by Occupation,
Frequency of Choices and Category
(Period: 1960–1964)

Category	Occupation	Number	Frequency of Choices
Most prominent	—	—	—
Prominent	Lawyer	1	13
	Minister	1	13
Not prominent but a leader	College teacher	1	13

tion and group action since the closing phase of the post-protest period. This becomes more significant when it is remembered that parks, schools, playgrounds and other public facilities in Montgomery remained segregated until 1965.

Conclusion

Any analysis of a social crisis must take into account the social milieu in which the crisis occurs. Montgomery, Alabama, is a Deep South community in tradition, temperament and experience. It is the "Home of the Confederacy," the "Heart of Dixie" and the gateway to plantation culture. There has been little visible alteration in the "Southern Credo" or the "Southern way of life" since the bus boycott. Fundamentally, the white community is resistant to change. Those social forces which have produced changes represent superficialities scarcely penetrating the important layers of resistance.

Negroes recognize the extreme degree of race consciousness which permeates almost every facet of social interaction between themselves and whites. Some insist that accommodation is the only means whereby the social and economic goals of Negroes can be achieved.

Fishman and Solomon point out that aggression toward whites under circumstances of accommodation has to be expressed in greatly disguised form. In previous periods of race relations in the South, "demonstration of laziness, stupidity and passivity gave expression to Negro resentment against an oppressive social system (almost as a slackdown in a factory), but it came in sufficiently disguised form so as to hide the meaning from the white community and minimize provocation and physical retaliation."[21]

In this same context, it should be remembered that the protest of Montgomery used the technique of non-violence as a means to achieve resolution of that city's interracial problems. A non-violent type of social protest is, according to Fishman and Solomon, "both practical in the southern context and, at the same time, quite syntonic with the psycho-social background of the participants."[22]

In view of the above, it would seem that the culmination of the protest and the diminution of Negro leadership in Montgomery were consequences of an almost indestructible social situation. It would further seem that the bus boycott was successful because it had an attainable goal.

Regardless of the validity of these positions, it is clearly indicated that the leadership structure of the community was transformed radically after the protest period because it followed a course in which accommodation rather than protest was the line of social action.

Both the white and the Negro communities advanced two arguments which forced the decision in favor of reversion to accommodation. (1) Since the boycott had been conducted over an extended period of time, it was viewed as desirable that a *modus vivendi* be found. The length of the boycott spent the energies and enthusiasm of many for renewed civil rights struggles. Those who presented this argument pointed with pride to the manner in which a community, otherwise loosely bound together, had found solidarity and common interest through the protest. Pride was also noted in the fact that Negroes had withstood threats, physical intimidation, harassment and terrorization in the posture of a group committed to non-violence because of the justness of their cause. (2) When the life of the community as a whole is considered, few if any other areas of interracial contact carried the same level of emotional and universal appeal as the everyday necessity of riding a bus. Those who used this line of reasoning suggested that other inconveniences were occasional rather than daily frustrations and could be resolved through more "normal" means, *i.e.*, accommodation.

The final step favoring a return to accommodation came with the resolution of the bus boycott. The white community was given notice of the dissatisfaction of Negroes with the status quo but was also advised of their willingness to discuss, arbitrate and work toward reconciliation.

The reversion to accommodation as the leadership form for Montgomery's Negro population was an accomplished fact within eighteen months after the boycott. Since that time, Negro leadership has remained in the hands of those who tacitly or explicitly subscribe to the theory of accommodation. A recent bi-racial committee[23] drawn by the white community includes approximately forty Negroes who serve as consulting members. The characteristics of this group show remarkable differences from those of Negro leaders who spearheaded the protest. One striking difference is found in occupation and dependence upon the white community. While the protest leaders tended, by and large, to be in "independent" occupations, the recent leadership list contains persons largely connected with semi-public and salaried positions.

Killiam and Smith in their study of the Tallahassee bus protest suggested that the emergence of a new and protesting-type leadership in their community seemingly has had a permanency attached to it.[24] This has not been the case in Montgomery. On the contrary, the leadership has returned, if not to its old perspective of pre-protest days, to something closely resembling it.

Our analysis suggests therefore the following conclusions: (1) Protest movements do not necessarily make for permanent alterations of the Negro leadership structure from an accommodative to a protest type. (2) Where the protest leader replaces the accommodative type as a response to public demand for social action, the symbolic representation needed often requires charismatic leadership. The realization of a limited goal may, in time, however, diminish the importance of the charismatic leader. The protest leader, having served as a unifying force, is no longer needed and the accommodative leader can resume routine and perhaps more realistic goal achievement.[25]

Finally, our study would suggest that leadership in the social crisis may indeed be a correlate of the changing conditions of the community as well as a factor in the process of change itself. Gouldner and Gouldner suggest that great social upheavals frequently find persons, rather than events or objects, as the most potent symbols of change. In this connection, when Negro protest for social change reaches cataclysmic proportions, leadership form usually takes on a dynamic, protesting and forceful mantle. When, however, the social situation approaches reconciliation, protest leadership seems no longer desirable or necessary.

Notes

[1] See Tilman C. Cothran and William Phillips, Jr., "Negro Leadership in a Crisis Situation," *Phylon,* XXII (Second Quarter, 1961); Thomas P. Monahan and Elizabeth H. Monahan, "Some Characteristics of American Negro Leaders," *American Sociological Review,* XXI (October, 1950); Oliver C. Cox, "Leadership among Negroes in the United States," in Alvin W. Gouldner (ed.), *Studies in Leadership* (New York, 1950); Louis E. Lomax, *The Negro Revolt* (New York, 1962); Frederick Solomon and Jacob R. Fishman, "Non-violence in the South: A Psychosocial Study" (mimeographed), Presentation of the Annual Convention of the American Psychiatric Association (St. Louis, May, 1963); Lewis M. Killiam and Charles V. Smith, "Negro Protest Leaders in a Southern Community," *Social Forces,* XXXVIII (March, 1960).

[2] Protest is indeed as basic to American tradition and development as trial by jury, writ of habeas corpus and representative government. Note, for example, the role of protest in the creation of the American Republic. The Boston Tea Party, Shay's Rebellion, the woman's suffrage protest, the Veteran Marchers, the prohibition protests are all illustrations of the manner in which protest movements have influenced social action.

[3] Oliver C. Cox, *op. cit.,* p. 242.

[4] See George Homans, *The Human Group* (New York, 1950); Alvin W. Gouldner (ed.) *Studies in Leadership* (New York, 1950); Mapheus Smith, "Leadership: The Management of Social Differentials," *Journal of Abnormal and Social Psychology,* XXXIV (March, 1939), 348; Cecil A. Gibb, "The Principles and Tracts of Leadership," *Journal of Abnormal and Social Psychology,* XLII (April, 1947), 267–84; E. C. Devereux, Jr., "Community Participation and Leadership," *Journal of Social Issues,* XVI, No. 4 (March, 1960), 29–45.

[5] The use of social science teachers in this study rests upon several assumptions which necessitate caution in interpretation and understanding. In the first place, we assume a degree of expertness which may or may not be present. Secondly, because of their professional

training, we assume a degree of social awareness which may or may not be obvious. Finally, we assume an objectivity which may be fettered by the interpersonal relationships between the rater and those rated. No attempt was made to neutralize the variable of personal involvement or non-involvement. In spite of these limitations, the reconstruction of conditions of concern to this study meant some interplay of contingent interpersonal and subjective elements. Awareness of these factors should serve, however, as caution against unnecessary generalization.

[6] The term "black belt" refers specifically to the soil typography of the region rather than a characterization of the racial or ethnic resident groups. It is coincidental, however, that the bulk of Alabama's Negro population lives in this region.

[7] For a complete description of the socio-economic and political setting of Montgomery and environs, see Lawrence D. Reddick, *Crusader Without Violence: A Biography of Martin Luther King, Jr.* (New York, 1959); Martin L. King, Jr., *Strive Toward Freedom* (New York, 1958); and Norman W. Walter, "The Walking City, A History of the Montgomery Boycott," *Negro History Bulletin,* XX (October, 1956), (November, 1956), (February, 1957) and (April, 1957).

[8] Alabama State College is situated on the east side of Montgomery.

[9] Gunnar Myrdal, *et. al., An American Dilemma* (New York, 1944), pp. 768–80. In this same connection it is interesting to note that accommodation was acceptable to both factions of the community to the extent that the employment of three Negro policemen and three policewomen was considered consonant with harmonious race relations. With the boycott, all Negro police personnel were displaced and have not, to date, been reinstated on the police rolls.

[10] Cox, *op. cit.,* p. 259.

[11] For a detailed elaboration of this point see Ralph H. Hines, "Social Expectations and Cultural Deprivation," *Journal of Negro Education,* XXXIII, No. 2 (Spring, 1964).

[12] Floyd Hunter, *Community Power Structure: A Study of Decision Makers* (Chapel Hill, 1954).

[13] Robert Bierstedt, "An Analysis of Social Power," *American Sociological Review* (October, 1957), 493–507.

[14] Mrs. Rosa Parks was the Negro bus rider who refused to move when ordered by a white bus driver having constabulary powers. Her arrest sparked the subsequent bus boycott which lasted from December 1, 1955, to February, 1957.

[15] Cited in King, *op. cit.,* p. 63.

[16] Leslie W. Dunbar, "Reflections on the Latest Reform of the South," *Phylon,* XX (Third Quarter, 1961), 249–57.

[17] *Montgomery Advertiser,* December 17, 1955.

[18] In this connection Walter observes, *op. cit.,* (October, 1956), p. 33, "The Negro leaders finally caught up with the masses. The lower elements, the proletariat, were ready and waiting for the leadership of the educated and intelligent groups."

[19] While it is not our aim to present a personality analysis of Martin Luther King, Jr., it is unavoidable that mention should be made of the qualitative aspects of his leadership which enabled diverse forces and interests to be welded into one. In this connection King displayed all the qualities of true charisma. These attributes of leadership have been described in detail by Max Weber, *The Theory of Social and Economic Organization,* A. M. Henderson and Talcott Parson (trans.) (New York, 1947), pp. 329–30; and, Harold D. Lasswell, *Psychopathology and Politics* (Chicago, 1930), ch. VIII: see also Max Weber, "The Sociology of Charismatic Authority," in Hans H. Gerth and C. Wright Mills (trans. and eds.), *From Max Weber: Essays in Sociology* (New York, 1946), pp. 245–52; and Dorothy Emmett, *Function, Purpose and Powers* (London, 1958), p. 233.

[20] In his book King refers to a vision which marked the turning point in the line of action he felt compelled to follow. See *Strive Toward Freedom, op. cit.,* pp. 134–35.

[21] Fishman and Solomon, *op. cit.,* p. 8.

[22] *Ibid.,* p. 8.

[23] The *Montgomery Advertiser,* February 16, 1964, gives the full list.

[24] Killiam and Smith, *op. cit.,* p. 257.

[25] The dichotomy between the charismatic and bureacratic leader is the closest parallel we have found which relates to the leadership reversion noted in the Montgomery crisis. The accommodative or bureaucratic leader works toward compromise, adjustment and routine. Organizing and the minutiae of details attached to organizations are usually scorned by the charismatic leader. On this point see Earl H. Bell, *Social Foundations of Human Behavior* (New York, 1961), p. 469.

The Functions of Disunity: Negro Leadership in a Southern City

Jack L. Walker

Introduction[1]

During the last five years waves of Negro protest demonstrations have swept across the Southern states. Incidents like the Montgomery bus boycott, the freedom rides and the sit-ins have spread with amazing speed, provoking racial crises in numerous towns and cities, even in the Deep South, and often taking the white leaders by surprise. From these crises a new type of Negro leadership seems to be arising: one dedicated to protest rather than accommodation and determined to press its demands for equality with a wide range of weapons including economic boycotts, civil disobedience, and political reprisals, tactics that Southern Negroes have never used in the past.

As the new, more militant leaders have arisen in Negro communities, the established leadership has usually offered resistance, and as a result many Southern Negro communities have been torn by disunity and internal conflict. Lewis M. Killian and Charles U. Smith in investigating Tallahassee, Florida, following a sharp dispute over bus segregation in the city found that the more militant, "protest" leaders had completely displaced the established Negro leadership. They found that after the crisis had passed, not one of the six persons named by a panel of both whites and Negroes as the top Negro leaders before the dispute were included as top leaders after the dispute. Also not one of the five persons that the panel named as top Negro leaders after the dispute had been ranked among the first ten before the dispute took place. Even the old, established leaders seemed to be aware that they had been displaced, and the study also indicated that a majority of the Negro community had shifted their allegiances to the protest leaders. Killian and Smith argue that:

Jack L. Walker, "The Functions of Disunity: Negro Leadership in a Southern City," *Journal of Negro Education,* XXXII, Summer 1963, pp. 227–236. Reprinted by permission of the *Journal of Negro Education* and the author.

. . . the new leaders are becoming permanent leaders not because of the attractiveness of their personalities or their skill at organizing, but rather because they adhere rigorously to the *form* of militant leadership which is becoming the trend for Negroes throughout the United States.[2]

The situation in Tallahassee, however, does not seem to have been duplicated in all other Southern cities, or even in all those that have experienced a racial crisis within the last five years. Leslie Dunbar in commenting on the findings of Killian and Smith has argued that:

There is some evidence in the stories of how a number of Southern cities have desegregated lunch counters to suggest that the older Negro leadership and the protest leaders can and do fruitfully complement each other, though coordination and mutual trust have sometimes been hard come by. My guess would be that this is the true interpretation. Negro leadership in the South is being broadened by an infusion of new elites.[3]

The subject of this essay is the relations between the established Negro leadership and the new protest leaders in a Southern city, the issue raised by Dunbar, Killian and Smith. The analysis is based on a case study of the sit-in controversy in Atlanta, Georgia, and is concerned particularly with the social and economic factors associated with the leaders differing attitudes towards goals and techniques of social action. It will be argued that both the conservative and the protest leaders can play an important part in such racial disputes, and unless the conservatives are completely displaced by the protest leaders, disputes among the leadership tend to increase, not decrease, the effectiveness of the Negro community's battle against the institutions of segregation.

Sit-ins in Atlanta: A Case Study[4]

On February 1, 1960, several Negro students sat down at a lunch counter in Greensboro, North Carolina, and refused to leave when told that the store did not serve Negroes. The manager is reported to have said: "They can just sit there. It's nothing to me." But within a week similar groups were sitting down in protest all over the South, and a major social movement was underway. The sit-ins spread even into the Deep South, and in response to fears and rumors that sit-ins were being planned the Georgia legislature passed a special trespass law on February 17, 1960.

Their fears were well founded, for as early as February 4 students at Atlanta University were planning demonstrations, but they were persuaded by faculty members and an apprehensive administration to postpone their action until they had drawn up a statement of their grievances. This statement was quickly completed and printed in the form of a full page advertisement in all local newspapers on March 9, 1960, under the title: "An Appeal for Human Rights." The advertisement caused a sensation in the state and it was commented on by politicians and public figures all over the country. This was followed on March 15 by the first wide-spread sit-in demonstrations in Atlanta in which 77 students were arrested under the new Georgia trespass law.

While their cases were pending in court the students began to work on several other projects. They mounted picket lines against food stores which had large Negro clienteles yet did not hire Negroes above the menial level, they held a series of meetings in Negro churches explaining the student movement and asking for support, they began publishing a weekly news sheet that eventually became a full fledged weekly newspaper, and on May 17, 1960, they gathered 1400 students together to march on the State Capitol in downtown Atlanta to celebrate the Supreme Court's 1954 anti-segregation decision. This march was diverted by Atlanta's Chief of Police to prevent the students from meeting a large, ugly crowd that had gathered at the capitol. When the students left for summer vacation tension was running high in the city.

During the Spring of 1960 there was considerable dispute among adult Negroes about the student movement. Although there were few who spoke out directly against the students, there were those who expressed their disapproval by keeping silent or withholding praise. The conservative adults, many of whom were businessmen, were opposed on principle to the student's use of picket lines and boycotts against businesses which practiced discrimination in hiring. They were also apprehensive when they understood that the students were not satisfied with their first sit-ins and their march on the State Capitol, but were planning repeated demonstrations in an effort to force the issue. The adult community began to divide on their support for the students and rumors that all the Negro adults did not approve of the students' efforts passed through the white community.

Regardless of the criticism, the leaders of the student movement continued organizational and propaganda work during the summer. On June 27 they met privately with the president of the city's leading department store who tried to convince them to give up their demonstrations promising that he would consider their grievances later on after the schools had been safely desegregated. This meeting broke down into a heated argument in which the student leaders are reported to have threatened the merchant with a boycott and the merchant shouted: "I don't need Negro trade!"

Following this incident conservative Negroes came into the open with criticisms of the students, and a few even made public speeches attacking their methods. But even so, after the students had returned for the fall term, on October 19, 1960, widespread sit-ins were mounted once again, and once again large numbers of demonstrators were arrested.[5] The students refused to leave the jail on bail at this time. Once again tension built up in the city. At this point the mayor asked for, and was granted, a 30-day truce period in which he promised to try to reach a settlement of the dispute.

The mayor's efforts were completely unsuccessful. The leading merchants were in no mood to compromise with the demonstrators and were suspicious of the mayor who was quite anxious to get a settlement and whose political power rested firmly on Negro support. When the mayor called a meeting of the downtown merchants in his office, only the small ones attended who depended heavily on Negro trade and feared a boycott.

On their own the leading merchants decided to try informal methods to bring an end to the disturbances. The conservative leaders of the Negro community, those who had criticized the students during the summer and who had been considered the "spokesmen" of the Negro community in the past, were asked to attend a private meeting with the merchants. The meeting was secret but it seems that the Negroes were being asked to use their influence to persuade the demonstrators to cease their efforts and to wait until after the schools were desegregated to discuss the issue of lunch counter desegregation. After meeting twice they decided to invite one adult Negro leader who had been a close advisor of the students, and the most influential student leader to a secret meeting in the Negro section of town so that the white merchants could offer their proposals. When these two men were contacted, however, they immediately became suspicious of the proceedings and decided to expose them. They made a public announcement that they were not a party to these secret negotiations, and when the conservative Negroes and the whites arrived at the meeting place television cameras were already set up and reporters were everywhere clamoring for statements.

After this incident, on November 25, 1960, the students resumed their sit-ins and also organized a full scale boycott of the downtown shopping area. A stalemate continued through the months of December and January, during which most of the lunch counters remained closed and the boycott of the downtown stores remained in effect.

Throughout this three month period of stalemate the students, equipped with short wave radios, had been sitting-in at lunch counters all over the city without incident. Either they had been ignored, or the counters had been closed, but on February 7, 1961, one restaurant manager in a federal office building invoked the trespass law and had the demonstrators arrested. During the next three days arrests continued daily with the students refusing once again to come out on bail. A protest march and rally was planned to take place in front of the jail on February 19, and it was feared that such a demonstration might result in a riot.

At this tense moment the student leaders themselves turned to one of the oldest, most respected Negro leaders and asked him to try to get negotiations started again. This man had made public statements backing the students at the beginning of the movement, but he was also widely considered to be a conservative and had attended the secret meetings with the white merchants in November, 1960. At this juncture, however, by utilizing friendships he had with influential white leaders, he was able to get negotiations started which eventually led to a settlement of the controversy. The agreement was announced on March 7, 1961. It called for desegregation of the lunch counters after the school desegregation had been completed during the fall of 1961, and, except for the firm agreement that the counters would be desegregated, it was essentially what the merchants had pressed for from the beginning. The actual desegregation took place on September 27, 1961.

The Functions of Disunity

The sit-in controversy in Atlanta took place in a community which is still basically segregated. Although a few of the barriers have been broken down during the past five years there are still almost no social contacts between the leadership of the two racial groups and residential segregation places their homes far apart. This isolation of the leadership of the two communities from each other is a potentially disruptive element in the social structure of the city. If a crisis arises involving the crucial issue of race, communication between the leaders of the two racial groups, which is normally tenuous and rather formal, becomes very hard to maintain, and it is even more difficult to establish the circumstances in which negotiation of the difficulties that caused the crisis can take place.

During the controversy over the sit-in demonstrations in Atlanta such a breakdown in communications between whites and Negroes occurred, and at the same time relations among the Negro leaders were strained because of their disagreements over tactics. The conservative Negro leaders are primarily older businessmen, although there are also social workers, college administrators and ministers in this group. The more liberal group is made up of students, members of the staffs of various Negro improvement groups, college teachers, younger businessmen and ministers.[6]

The dispute within the Negro community revolves around the use of protest demonstrations and economic boycotts to press the attack on segregation. The conservatives never questioned, throughout the sit-in controversy in Atlanta, the goals of the students, and even when they agreed to attend secret meetings with the merchants they never failed to inform the whites that they thought the students' demands were justified, even if they did not approve of their methods.[7] The conservatives oppose boycotts and protest demonstrations primarily because they feel these public displays of discontent cause bitterness and rancor and tend to destroy the cordial, settled atmosphere which they feel is a necessary precondition to effective negotiations. They also fear economic retaliation more than the protest leaders, not only because of their own businesses, but also because they have worked hard to build institutions such as the Y.M.C.A., the Urban League, and many churches which depend heavily on contributions from influential whites. During the boycott that accompanied the sit-in affair in Atlanta some of these organizations began to lose white contributors as tension mounted. To some extent the conservative leaders have each made adjustments to the traditional position of the Negro in Southern society. Although none seems completely satisfied, in varying measures they have given up efforts to penetrate the dominant white society and consequently they have a greater commitment to the institutions within the Negro community.

The businessmen among the conservatives have frequent dealings with influential whites in the city; both the bank and savings and loan association operated by Negroes in Atlanta have very sizeable deposits from white customers. In fact, to a large extent, the power of the conservatives depends on their influence with the white community. They are spokesmen for the Negro community primarily because they have gained white recognition and favor, although their own achievements placed them in a position to be chosen for this role. Because of this process of selection, the protest leaders regard the conservatives with almost the same hostility they have for the whites, if not more so. They complain that the conservatives' power is based essentially on the Negro's fear of the power of the white man. They think that the established leaders have profited from the injustices of segregation by trading their human dignity for the opportunity to represent the whites within the Negro community.

The protest leaders are not so directly engaged in activities and institutions that serve the whole community as are the conservatives, and they deal more exclusively with the Negro community than the conservatives. Yet even so they do not feel as much committed to its maintenance; in fact they hate all that it stands for. Their work brings them into closer contact with the social, economic and political deprivations suffered by the Negro, and they tend to concentrate on these injustices and have fewer reasons to try to protect institutions, both charitable and commercial, that presently exist in the Negro community. They are under less compulsion than the conservatives to act with restraint or to compromise their demands in order to make limited material gains or to promote the fortunes of Negro businessmen. In this sense they stand outside the economic and social life of the established community and they try to keep the dominant leaders, both white and colored, at arm's length, guarding against being too friendly with politicians and certainly never asking them for favors or help of any kind. They try to conduct their affairs strictly on the basis of their moral principles, and for these reasons conservatives frequently regard them as "irresponsible" and find their attitudes toward politics and community leaders "unrealistic" or "hateful." One conservative leader in Atlanta, who has a reputation as a good tactician and organizer, acknowledged the importance of the student protests in bringing "more integration in less than two years than we gained in ten," but he also argued that "they will never get anything done on their own because they are cut off; they work in a righteous vacuum over there."

The protest leaders and the conservatives manifest considerable suspicion for each other, and in Atlanta a complete breakdown in relations between them is prevented primarily by the existence of several influential men who stand between these two groups and are not so deeply committed to either political style, or who are caught in ambiguous circumstances that prompt them to maintain contact with both protest and conservative leaders. These men tend to bind the Negro community together by providing lines of communication between leaders of all persuasions.

Even though the conservative and protest leaders distrust each other, during the Atlanta sit-in controversy at least, their efforts were complementary. In fact, if the Negro community is conceived of as a system designed to fight the institutions of segregation, each of these groups performed a function in this situation. The students and the adult protest leaders, by organizing demonstrations and economic boycotts, created a crisis which had to be resolved, even if in doing so they raised the level of tension between the two racial groups in the city and caused a rather dangerous breakdown of communications. But the leaders of the protests did not have the power to resolve the crisis they had created because they had no basis for contact with the dominant white leaders. As James Q. Wilson suggests, one of the inherent difficulties of protest action is "that the discretion of the protest leader to bargain after he has acquired the resources with which to bargain is severely limited by the means he was forced to employ in order to create those resources."[8] From the beginning of the dispute the leading merchants refused to negotiate directly with the demonstrators whom they considered to be irresponsible troublemakers. In fact, the tactics pursued by the protest leaders were almost certain to antagonize the dominant whites. As Killian and Smith point out in describing the political style of the protest leaders:

This new leadership is not of the accommodating type. It seeks gains for the Negro community through formal demands and requests, boycotts, lawsuits and voting. The protest leaders are not concerned with whether or not the whites high in the power structure know, like or want to deal with them.[9]

The more conservatively inclined leaders, utilizing their reputations and the connections they had built up with the white community through the years, had the function of resolving the crisis situation created by the protest leaders. In this case even the antagonism between the two groups was functional because it made the conservatives seem more reliable and responsible in the eyes of the whites, and so they were still able to act as negotiators when both sides were ready to compromise.

Those leaders in the middle, who did not identify completely with either the conservative or the protest leaders, had the function of moderating this conflict over tactics. Some individuals find themselves in this situation because they are subject to cross-pressures which restrain them from becoming attached to either side in the controversy. Others are not committed because they have a flexible attitude toward social action which prompts them to regard all tactical weapons as potentially useful. Regardless of the influences that put them in this position, however, these leaders in the middle provide both formal and informal links between the conservative and protest leaders.

The situation in Atlanta does not seem to have been unique. Something of this same kind of unanticipated cooperation and sharing of functions between protest and conservative Negro leaders seems to have taken place during the sit-in controversy in Knoxville, Tennessee. Negotiation began initially there without any demonstrations, but broke down after four tedious months of talks. Sit-ins began on June 9, 1960, and a boycott was started five days later on June 14. Merrill Proudfoot describes a meeting of the executive committee of the protest movement which took place on July 2, 1960, after about three weeks of demonstrations. The meeting was attended by the president of Knoxville College, who had not been involved in planning or staging the demonstrations, and he revealed that he had been contacted by an official of the Knoxville Chamber of Commerce who informed him that there was a movement underway to reopen negotiations. Proudfoot rather indignantly comments:

The circuitous means of communicating with one another has lent a comic-opera aspect to the way this major community problem has been handled. It would seem sensible for one of the merchants to have called Crutcher or James [the leaders of the demonstrations] and said, "Come on down and let's talk!" Instead the merchants hint to the Chamber of Commerce official that they might be willing; he contacts not Crutcher or James, but Colston — the one person in the Negro community who has the greatest status . . . and he in turn makes the contact within the Negro community.[10]

Also when a negotiating team was formed to formulate the final agreement to desegregate, Colston was included once again, but this time he was accompanied by Crutcher. Although the description is not so complete it seems that a similar process operated at Winston-Salem, North Carolina, where the agreement to desegregate the lunch counters was not formulated by the protest leaders. Clarence H. Patrick reports that:

The demonstrators several times sought unsuccessfully for someone to organize and mediate a meeting between them and the store managers in an attempt to resolve the antisegregation movement on the basis of some mutual agreement. The leaders of the protest never met, as a group, with the managers of the stores where the protests occurred.[11]

Conclusion

The evidence presented here suggests that not all Southern Negro communities have experienced the same changes in leadership that Killian and Smith detected in Tallahassee. In some cases it seems that a kind of tactical balance exists with both conservative and protest leaders playing a part in the fight for equality. However, there is no evidence that the period of change and transition in Negro leadership in Atlanta has ended. In fact, a major unsettling force seems to be developing beneath the level of leadership. Almost all the leaders interviewed, including the conservatives, felt that expectations are rising perceptibly throughout the Negro community as a result of recent successful attacks on the institutions of segregation. The Negro masses, who have traditionally been apathetic toward politics and efforts to fight segregation, seem to be gaining hope that change is possible and are shaking off the mood of cynical resignation that has paralyzed them in the past.

Looking forward, these circumstances suggest a prediction that the drive to break down racial barriers will not stall once a few victories are won, but will continue and intensify in the foreseeable future. However, there are some uncertain features of this development. First of all, it is unclear whether the conservatives, who were once the dominant leaders within the Negro community, are being completely supplanted by the protest leaders, or whether in the future there will continue to be a mixture of conservative and protest elements in Atlanta's Negro leadership. It is uncertain, because of increasing demands for equality from the masses, whether the aging conservative group will be replaced with leaders of similar stature and influence within the Negro community. If this does not occur, the present tactical balance within the Negro community will be altered in favor of the militants.

The full impact of such a change in Negro leadership on race relations in the city would depend in large measure on the reactions of the whites. Several local observers, when asked to comment on this prospect, emphasized that a new, younger and more liberal group of white leaders is emerging in the city to replace the older, more conservative whites. There is also a widely held impression in Atlanta that the majority of the white population has accepted, or at least is resigned to, the end of segregation. These observers saw a prospect of diminishing resistance from the whites, faster integration, and improving race relations as the younger leaders of both races take control.

The accuracy of this prediction depends, to a large extent, upon the nature of the issues that face the community in the future, and upon the pliability of the whites as the Negroes begin aggressively attacking segregation in such potentially explosive areas as housing and employment. It also seems likely that in the future the Negro community may become more united behind the protest leaders, but this may not automatically result in an increased effectiveness in gaining their ends. This study brings into question the assumption commonly made that a weak minority within the society must maintain unity and solidarity if it is to be effective in gaining its objectives.

It seems clear that the Atlanta Negro community became more effective in breaking down the barriers of segregation after the militant, protest leaders came on the scene; even their arrival caused considerable bickering and disunity among Negro leaders in the city. However, the protest leaders' outspoken desire to destroy the institutions of segregation, their habit of treating all issues in moral terms, and their willingness to employ force in the form of economic boycotts to gain their objectives alienated them from the dominant white leadership. The conservative leaders were much more acceptable to the whites because they tended to concentrate primarily on improving the economic welfare of the Negro without demanding an immediate end to segregation. The conservative Negro leaders' primary interest in maintaining the institutions within the Negro community along with their antipathy for the protest leaders and their obvious disapproval of boycotts and demonstrations made them seem "responsible" in the eyes of the whites, and thus acceptable as bargaining agents. Therefore, it would seem that a Negro community in a Southern city is likely to be more effective in eliminating the institutions of segregation if it has both conservative and protest elements within its leadership. Without the protest leaders it will lack the capacity to precipitate tension through the use of boycotts, demonstrations and other "direct action" techniques. And without the conservative leaders it is in danger of losing contact with the dominant white leaders and being unable to negotiate a peaceful, compromise solution to a racial crisis. Seen in this light, there seems to be a part to play in the Negro's fight for equality for both the more accommodating, conservative leaders and the liberal, protest leaders. As long as a broad agreement exists on the ultimate goals of equality and an end to racial discrimination, some disunity over the proper methods of social action may be positively desirable.

Notes

[1] The research on which this essay is based was financed by a grant from the Iowa Citizenship Clearing House and the National Center for Education in Politics. Neither of them, of course, is responsible for any errors of fact or interpretation in this study.

[2] Lewis M. Killian and Charles U. Smith, "Negro Protest Leaders in a Southern City," *Social Forces* (March, 1960), p. 257.

[3] Leslie Dunbar, "Reflections on the Latest Reform of the South," *Phylon,* 22:253, Fall, 1961.

[4] This case study is based on the record of the controversy found in the files of *The Atlanta Constitution, The Atlanta Journal, The Atlanta Daily World,* and *The Atlanta Inquirer,* and on a series of interviews with the principal actors conducted during April and May of 1962.

[5] These demonstrations received nationwide attention, especially because of the arrest of Martin Luther King, Jr. and the series of events that led to the famous phone call to the King family from John F. Kennedy.

[6] The principal actors in the sit-in controversy were interviewed at length, and frequently they voluntarily described themselves with such terms as "conservative" or "liberal." These self-identifications were used, along with an analysis of each participant's actions and statements during the dispute to decide which were conservatives and which were protest leaders.

[7] It should not be surprising that the older leaders would be in sympathy with the goals of the students because the students' protests did not grow out of alienation from any of the society's basic orienting values except those, such as white supremacy, that underpin segregation. Searles and Williams found that the student protests "were precipitated by Negro students' reference to the white middle class as a standard of comparison . . ." They also discovered that: "Far from being alienated, the students appear to be committed to the society

and its middle-class leaders." Ruth Searles and J. Allen Williams, "Negro College Students' Participation in Sit-ins," *Social Forces,* 40: 219, March, 1962.

⁸ James Q. Wilson, "The Strategy of Protest," *Journal of Conflict Resolution* (September, 1961), p. 293.

⁹ Killian and Smith, p. 257.

¹⁰ Merrill Proudfoot, *Diary of a Sit-in,* Chapel Hill: University of North Carolina Press, 1962, pp. 111–112.

¹¹ Clarence H. Patrick, *Lunch Counter Desegregation in Winston-Salem, North Carolina* (Pamphlet Distributed by the Southern Regional Council, 1960), p. 7.

Subcommunity Gladiatorial Competition: Civil Rights Leadership as a Competitive Process

Gerald A. McWorter
Robert L. Crain

As is often the case, the folklore of American politics contains two conflicting statements about the value of competition for political leadership. On the one hand, competition for political office is assumed to be the measure of a thriving democracy. On the other hand, we tend to think of intensely competitive politics as the breeding ground for the spectacular demagogue. In particular, the American Negro civil rights movement is seen as an example of a situation in which high levels of competition have promoted "irresponsible" leadership.[1] In this paper we will examine the civil rights movement in 14 cities, and present an analysis of the factors which cause variations in the degree and character of leadership competition and the way in which this competition has affected these movements.

The Problem

Much of the literature on the social bases of competition for leadership centers around the word "pluralism." One position is that stated by Kornhauser:

A plurality of independent and limited-function groups supports liberal democracy by providing social bases of free and open competition for leadership, widespread participation in the selection of leaders, restraint in the application of pressures on leaders, and self-government in widespread areas of social life. Therefore, where

Gerald A. McWorter and Robert L. Crain, "Subcommunity Gladitorial Competition: Civil Rights Leadership as a Competitive Process," *Social Forces*, Vol. 46, September, 1967, pp. 8–21. Reprinted by permission of The University of North Carolina Press.

social pluralism is strong, liberty and democracy tend to be strong; conversely, forces which weaken social pluralism also weaken liberty and democracy.[2]

Here, the competiton referred to is clearly functional to a democracy. While the mass society theorists claim that severe social conflict is prevented by these same forces which produce moderate competition, Gusfield has described ways in which pluralism can encourage such conflict.[3] This is clarified by James S. Coleman, who distinguishes between participation in voluntary organizations which tend to integrate a community by weaving community-wide patterns of communication and influence, and attachments to ethnic and other subcommunity organizations which encourage a division of the community.[4] William A. Gamson's study of 16 middle-sized and small New England cities presented evidence to support this distinction, showing that rancorous conflict was more likely to occur in communities which had isolated subcommunities within their boundaries.[5] By either argument, we might expect the pluralistic community, with a more elaborate network of voluntary organizations, and a larger supply of potential leaders, to provide the greatest degree of leadership competition, although whether such competition sustains or weakens democratic values is left an open question.

However, one apparent difficulty with the pluralism argument is that it would lead us to expect a fairly low level of leadership competition. There is no reason to expect a more elaborate structure of voluntary associations within the generally low socioeconomic-status Negro community than in a white community of similar status.[6] And there is little basis for severe ideological cleavage on civil rights as major civil rights leaders command the overwhelming endorsement of the Negro community.[7]

There is another approach to the question which provides a somewhat different set of hypotheses; Ralf Dahrendorf has noted that one can contrast an "integration" theory of society — stressing equilibrium and continuity — with a coercion theory which emphasizes strains and change.[8] He accepts these as compatible viewpoints reflecting the "two faces" of society, but focuses on the coercion theory and writes:

I shall try to show how, on the assumption of the coercive nature of social structure, relations of authority became productive of clashes of role interest which under certain conditions lead to the formulation of organized antagonistic groups within limited social organizations as well as within total societies.[9]

This suggests that in analyzing groups such as those of the civil rights movement, we should keep in mind the possibility that a seemingly stable status hierarchy within the Negro community can itself create competition and conflict. Dahrendorf's remarks lead us back to a traditional viewpoint which says that conflict in politics is to be expected as long as there are bases of power available to competitors.

Much of the existing discussion of the consequences of competition is irrelevant to our concern because it assumes a competition between stable two-party systems. Local studies of competition in nonpartisan or one-party political systems would be more relevant, but there is little material. V. O. Key and others have pointed out the way in which "every man for himself" politics in southern states rewards ideological extremists,[10] and several writers have noted that in Louisiana, where stable party factions have persisted for several decades, racism did not play a major role in electoral contests.[11] James Q. Wilson has noted that the structured politics of Chicago has produced Congressman William Dawson, while the unstructured (and probably more competitive) politics of New York City has recruited Adam Clayton Powell.[12] Following this line of reasoning, Wilson has hypothesized that the growth of amateur political clubs in both major political parties has caused ideology to become more important in electoral campaigns and has tended to restrict the freedom of elected officials by binding them to more detailed party platforms.[13] Whether introducing ideology and platform loyalty are good or bad depends not only on one's point of view, but also on the particular community studied. Hunter, for example, suggests that the limiting of competition by the influentials of Atlanta has tended to discourage innovation and prevent the masses from winning new programs.[14]

There does seem to be one consistent finding: (political party competition results in increased political participation) Milbrath found a high correlation between party competition and general turnout for senatorial and gubernatorial elections,[15] and Agger et al., in a comparative study of four cities, demonstrate how elite competition stimulates mass participation in politics.[16] This is especially true if the basis of the competition is ideological. Lane,[17] and Matthews and Prothro[18] have presented similar findings about contested primary elections and rates of voter turnout.

Similar themes have emerged from studies of leadership in the Negro subcommunity. Hunter found the Negro subcommunity of Atlanta had managed to sustain a monolithic leadership structure despite considerable competition for leadership.[19] Studies of Providence, Rhode Island[20] and "Pacific City"[21] suggest the same pattern. More recently, Ladd has found similar monolithic patterns in Greenville, South Carolina, and Winston-Salem, North Carolina.[22] However, Ladd notes that Winston-Salem does have considerable competition for leadership, and suggests that this is the pattern for the Negro communities of the "new South."

One study found that during periods of intense racial controversy new leaders appeared;[23] another study noted that during a similar controversial period, the opposing factions within the Negro subcommunity merged during the crisis.[24]

Both Glick[25] and Walker[26] hypothesize that competition within the civil rights movement has unanticipated consequences which benefit the Negro subcommunity. Walker concludes that "disputes among the leadership tend to increase, not decrease, the effectiveness of the Negro community's battle against the institution of segregation."[27]

In general, our analysis follows the essential questions being raised in this literature. After clarifying the concept of leadership competition in the civil rights movement, we will investigate: (1) What are the social bases which generate and sustain competition? and (2) What are the social consequences of competition?

The Data

The research reported here is part of a larger study conducted by the National Opinion Research Center on decision-making with regard to school integration.[28] Fifteen cities were studied by teams of graduate student interviewers who spent from ten to 15 man-days in each city during the winter of 1964–65. Techniques employed included (a) formal questionnaire interviews with decision-makers, (b) unstructured interviews (up to eight hours in length) with decision-makers and informants, and (c) collecting documentary materials. An average of 20 respondents were interviewed in each city, including an average of four civil rights leaders. In general, there was no difficulty in obtaining interviews with the leading civil rights leaders. The civil rights leaders interviewed included those with important formal positions (e.g., the NAACP president) and those identified as important actors in the school segregation issue. The sample is thus biased (partly, but not completely) toward those persons concerned with education.

The 15 cities included eight in the North, drawn from a sampling frame including all cities between 250,000 and 1,000,000 which were at least ten percent Negro in population. The cities were selected randomly, with substitutions then made for cities which had not faced demands for school integration. The seven southern cities were selected to maximize the range of behavior on school integration, and include three cities which are the largest in their state, three smaller cities from the same states for comparison, and a fourth small city; the smallest city contained 158,623 people. One small southern city is deleted from this analysis because of insufficient direct interviews.

Variations in Levels of Competition

As the word is used here, competition for leadership includes competition for formal offices in the government and in voluntary organizations such as the NAACP; but also (and more importantly) competition for status, influence, and power, for the loyalty of masses of civil rights activists, and for control over the policy and the program of the civil rights movement. A civil rights leader may be one who has the reputation for leadership, has the loyalty of a following, holds a formal office, or who is able to use other sources of prestige and status to influence the white subcommunity regarding civil rights. A civil rights leader, by our definition, may be either white or Negro. While it follows that competition can occur in several different ways, the most important distinction is between organized and individual competition. By organized competition we refer to competition between competing organizations or groups, each committed more or less permanently to a program or ideological stance. By individual competition, we refer to the competition between individuals for leadership in such a way that a majority of the civil rights leaders are not permanently committed to one side of a conflict. While in principle it would be useful to distinguish competition for leadership from conflict over ideology, in practice the two go hand in hand.

The variables were constructed primarily from the interviews with civil rights leaders. Our judgment of the leader and types of competition is based largely upon three factors — the response to sociometric questions about other leaders; the attitudes expressed by leaders about different civil rights organizations; and a detailed history of the relationships between the groups during the course of the school desegregation issue, which in the North was usually the most important civil rights issue. While the result is a largely impressionistic judgment, we are more confident about its reliability than we might otherwise be because of the great variance among the cities. The differences among cities is quite large, as will be shown when some of the cases are described.

In all 14 cities there is some degree of competition and conflict among civil rights leaders. However, in five of the cities the level of competition is so low that for present purposes we describe them as having minimal competition. These five cities are Baltimore and Miami, where most civil rights activity is handled by the NAACP and competition within the NAACP is light; Columbus, Georgia, where a "ruling elite" of five men work as a close-knit unit; and Pittsburgh and Buffalo, where various groups work in reasonable harmony, again with only a small number of highly active leaders. In all five of these cities, there are no civil rights leaders who were willing to criticize other leaders, and no case when a civil rights group opposed or criticized publicly a program advanced by another.

Four cities — St. Louis, Newark, Atlanta, and Jacksonville — fit our model of having intense organized competition. In all four cases, the conflict can be briefly described as between the establishment and the outsiders. The conflict tends to polarize the entire movement; even the leaders who try to think of themselves as nonaligned can only be understood by their relationships to one of the opposing factions. In each case, most leaders interviewed were critical, not merely of other leaders, but other particular civil rights groups as well.

The remaining five cities have individual competition for leadership. In two, San Francisco and Montgomery, the competition can be described as intense and persisting over long periods of time without clear factional alignments. In the other three — Oakland, Boston, and New Orleans — competition and conflict tend to come and go, and are often pushed into the background. Because, as we shall see, the cities without competition are in some ways intermediate between those which have organized competition and those which have individual competition, it is useful to present them graphically in the center of the typology. The civil rights leaders in these cities often qualified their criticism of other leaders in terms of how much support was offered or available for their own program. Since each actor appeared to be a free agent, everyone was considered a possible ally, as well as a potential enemy.

Table 1: Level and Intensity of Civil Rights Leadership
Competition in 14 Cities, by Region

Level of Competition	Region of Cities	
	North	South
Individual competition:		
Intense	San Francisco	Montgomery
Moderate	Oakland	New Orleans
	Boston	
Minimal competition	Baltimore	Miami
	Pittsburgh	Columbus
	Buffalo	
Organized competition	St. Louis	Jacksonville
	Newark	Atlanta

The five cities with individual competition have in common a volatile style of civil rights activity. In all five, since the temporary withdrawal of one or another leader can alter the picture considerably, it is difficult to predict the level and style of civil rights activity. This is especially true of Montgomery, whose leaders have been consistently drafted into the national civil rights movement. As new leaders appear, the pattern of competition changes, and civil rights programs change with them.

The Social Bases of Organized Competition

Let us first consider the roots of organized competition; later we will consider the causes of individual competition. In all four cities in this category, it is possible to locate sources of structural competition in the different bases of power available to competing factions. In the two northern cities the conflict is between the political "establishment" and militant neighborhood-based groups. In St. Louis, the demands for school integration were first made by the West End Community Council with the support of CORE. At first, the NAACP lent its support to the campaign, but later they began to withdraw. After some important victories, an open split between the militant grass-roots groups and the NAACP brought about the collapse of the school integration drive. The militants generally accused the NAACP of being conservative and tied to the Democratic party organization in the Negro wards, though one of the militants used his civil rights activity to win control of one ward.[29]

In Newark the pattern was nearly identical. The most militant leader in the NAACP was also a leader of the community organization in a middle-income integrated neighborhood. Under the stress of the school integration campaign, he left the NAACP and the community group continued to battle the school system without the NAACP branch's support. Again, the militants accused the NAACP of being too close to the ruling faction of the Democratic party.

The only other city in the sample with a strong patronage-based Negro political machine is Jacksonville, and here again the result has been organized competition for leadership. However, the cast is a bit different, since the NAACP is militant and anti-machine, and the machine leadership does not have a civil rights organization. In part, this is the effect of Jacksonville being a southern city; the NAACP is not legitimate enough to be accepted by white politicians, and Negro political leaders without autonomous bases of power cannot afford to be active in it. In addition, there is less distinction in the South between generalized community leadership and civil rights leadership, so that the Negro political leader does not need to be a representative of a civil rights group in order to claim status as a civil rights leader.[30]

The fourth city with organized competition is Atlanta. The competition here is between the generations, older and less militant leaders being attacked by young upwardly-mobile militants.[31]

A general but simple proposition fitting all four cities is that organized competition will occur if and only if one faction has access to status independent of an appeal to mass support, and the other faction can successfully appeal to the masses for its power. In the first three cities the political machine can supply patronage and other material incentives maintaining Negro political leaders without requiring that they make a mass appeal on ideological grounds. The competing group is a neighborhood-based mass organization in St. Louis and Newark, and a traditional civil rights group in Jacksonville. Since their claim to leadership is based upon the loyalty of a visible group of followers, all three cities have engaged in considerable direct action. Neighborhood-based groups are more successful competitors to the NAACP than city-wide groups such as CORE, probably because they have a more committed following. Thus in all four cities the contest is between militant direct-action groups and moderates.

In Atlanta the same proposition seems to hold. One faction draws its power from its association with the elites of Atlanta's Negro business and academic communities. Of all the cities, Atlanta has the greatest amount of resources for such an elite; the second largest Negro-owned life insurance company and the second largest Negro-owned bank are in Atlanta,[32] in addition to seven Negro colleges and universities. These same resources (especially the colleges) have produced the following for the mass-oriented activists.[33]

To put it another way, the machine city makes it possible for the white leadership to offer resources to particular Negro leaders in exchange for conservative behavior on civil rights. It was probably once true that most cities were able to maintain a conservative group of leaders in this way by offering money or various symbols of honor and prestige. Indeed, the threat of physical violence in some cases might have made such an offering unnecessary. But in the eleven nonmachine cities in our sample, we found little evidence of this today. One reason is that the civil rights revolution has placed these Negro leaders under attack, and the white community has usually been unwilling or unable to counter by inflating their payments to them.

The white leadership also has a negative sanction; it can withhold recognition from civil rights leaders by simply refusing to deal with them. While we have no example of a city which was able to suppress an issue in this fashion, it seems probable that this tactic has increased the turnover of leadership as unrecognized leaders drop into the background. Actually, this is not an "effective" device; as we shall see, an increase in competition tends to increase militancy, so that the whites may find the new leadership more difficult to deal with.

At first it would seem that almost any city could provide a basis for power independent of a mass following, and hence have organized competition, but this is apparently not the case. In Boston there is only one Negro elected official and very few in appointed posts. In the other northern cities the absence of a machine vote requires that ambitious political leaders take militant positions, or at least give public support to the militant leaders. Of the northern cities, none has the elaborate Negro economy of Atlanta; furthermore, the Negro economic leaders are sometimes either politically active or are newspaper publishers and therefore still dependent upon a mass following. Similarly, in the South, Jacksonville is represented as a home office of one of the large Negro-owned insurance firms but is otherwise not an important Negro economic center, and the other cities have even less Negro-owned business.[34] Outside of Atlanta, there are so few Negroes holding political positions that they can hardly constitute a faction. One might expect competition on general ideological grounds between militants and conservatives, but there has been a constantly accelerating rise of militancy in the Negro community since World War II. Conservative ideologies no longer offer a competitive alternative to this increased militancy. Unless the "Uncle Tom" is propped up with a considerable number of favors from white sources, it seems he is fast becoming a mere anachronism.[35]

The general hypothesis predicts that one other type of city will not have organized competition; this is the city where there is no basis for a grass-roots movement. A city with a low-status population, without (for example) the resources of a Negro college, might fall into this class. But even here this is unlikely because of a strong general endorsement of civil rights activity by the Negro masses. If any city in our sample can be described this way it is Columbus, Georgia, where the "ruling elite" has up to now been able to handle civil rights activity with little competition from direct-action groups. Columbus has the lowest status Negro population of the cities in our sample; with a higher status population, there might be a conflict between the generations here as in Atlanta (but it is also possible that the elite might become more militant).

It would also be possible for a city to be led by a group of elites who have enough prestige to be "above criticism." This may have been the case in Montgomery during the early days of the Montgomery Improvement Association, when the MIA leadership combined their prestige as nationally recognized civil rights leaders with their local prestige as ministers of the church.[36] And of course this would have been more often the case before the current thrust of civil rights activities. But in most cities, the holders of traditional status can be attacked (with or without justification) as being conservative. Even when the traditional prestige hierarchy retains its importance, an increase in civil rights activity may encourage competition among elites for the leadership of the movement.

The Bases for Individual Competition

If by individual competition we refer to competition between individuals without permanent factional coalitions or stable ideological differences, we can choose between two seemingly contradictory hypotheses. First, competition will be most present in the "mass society" since there will be few loyalties or agreements binding people into "follower" roles; anyone who wants to be a leader is free to do so. This is a special case of Coleman's hypothesis that a person without an elaborate network of social attachments is free to take controversial positions.[37] However, the more commonly accepted opposing hypothesis is that the pluralistic society, with its complex network of associations, is the training ground for potential leaders. The arguments are not really contradictory, and taken together suggest that we should find greatest competition in (a) the community with many leadership roles and many people in high-status positions, but with little in the way of interdependent relations and a weak internal prestige structure, and less competition in either, (b) the community with a large number of roles for training potential leaders, but with a stable prestige hierarchy and interdependence, or (c) the community with few leadership roles, which will not have competition even if it has an inadequate prestige hierarchy.[38]

We would expect a city of type (a) to have a fast growing middle-class Negro community which is partially assimilated. In such a situation, many persons with leadership skills will be holding "white" jobs, some of the civil rights leaders will be white, and there will not be a traditional prestige structure. All three of the northern cities with individual competition seem to fit this description. In Boston,

San Francisco, and Oakland, a large number of civil rights leaders are either white, hold "white" jobs, or live in predominantly white areas. Thus they are autonomous vis-à-vis the Negro economic structure, and have ambiguous status in the Negro prestige hierarchy. Table 2a suggests the lack of autonomy of the Negro community in these cities compared to the less competitive Pittsburgh and Baltimore. In all three individual competition cities, Negroes are less segregated, and the lack of autonomy of the Negro community is reflected in the unimportance of the Negro press. The table also suggests that if it were not for the political organization of St. Louis and Newark, these two cities would have little competition — St. Louis because it has a Negro elite which would maintain considerable power, Newark because it has almost no basis for a grass-roots movement. In general, Table 2a indicates that in the nonmachine cities of the North, the higher the status of the Negro community, the greater the individual competition. This pattern does not hold in the four southern cities which do not have organized competition.

In the South, Negro subcommunities are somewhat more self-sufficient, have more visible prestige structures, and have lower status populations. There is little variation in the degree of autonomy of these highly segregated subcommunities. Hence, we would expect them to have less individual competition. Two cities, New Orleans and Montgomery, do have a limited amount of individual competition, but this may be the result of unique historical factors in each case. A pioneering thrust of civil rights activity in 1955 established the MIA as the model for a mass-based organization in the South. However, several key leaders moved to regional and national levels of leadership, notably Dr. Martin Luther King and Rev. Ralph Abernathy (successive presidents of the MIA). At the time of our interviews, several leaders in the MIA were struggling to organize activity, and thus were competing for power. But our proposition holds that if a direct-action program was organized successfully, the level of competition would decline considerably. Similarly, this appears to be the case for New Orleans which has always had a relatively weak civil rights movement.[39] The cities without competition do have in common a lower supply of "troops" for mass demonstrations; neither has a Negro college whose student body could be used for demonstrations.

Social Sources of Competition: A Summary

There seems to be some evidence in these data to support several propositions about the causes of competition.

1. A necessary condition for competition is an adequate supply of social resources.

2. A necessary condition for competition to be organized or factional is that there be distinctly different ways to mobilize resources. In our case, this means a

Table 2a: Selected Social Factors Influencing Competition (North)

Level of Competition	Socioeconomic Status		Size	Level of Segregation	
	Percent White Collar	Percent High School Graduates	Percent Population Negro	Index of Residential Segregation*	Importance of Negro Newspapers†
Individual competition:					
Intense:					
San Francisco	27	40	9.0	69.3	Low
Moderate:					
Boston	17	37	9.8	83.9	Low
Oakland	18	32	26.4	73.1	Low
Minimal competition:					
Baltimore	15	19	35.0	89.6	High
Pittsburgh	14	25	16.7	84.6	High
Buffalo	11	22	13.8	86.5	Low
Organized competition:					
St. Louis	15	24	28.8	90.6	Medium
Newark	11	22	34.4	71.6	Medium

* Data compiled from Karl E. Taeuber and Alma F. Taeuber, *Negroes in Cities* (Chicago: Aldine Publishing Co. 1965).
† Data compiled from *Negro Newspapers in the United States* (Jefferson City, Missouri: Lincoln University, Dept. of Journalism, 1964). The Baltimore *Afro-American* and the Pittsburgh *Courier* are well known: the St. Louis *Argus* and the Newark *Afro-American* are weeklies with circulations of 9,000 and 7,000 respectively.

Table 2b: Factors Influencing Competition (South)*

Level of Competition	Socioeconomic Status		Percent Population Negro	Number of Negro Colleges†
	Percent White Collar	Percent High School		
Individual competition:				
Intense:				
Montgomery	14.3	17.8	38.1	1
Moderate:				
New Orleans	11.6	14.5	30.8	2
Minimal competition:				
Miami	8.5	18.1	14.7	0
Columbus	11.9	12.7	29.0	0
Organized competition:				
Atlanta	12.7	21.1	38.2	6
Jacksonville	10.7	18.2	23.2	1

* Importance of Negro Newspapers and the Index of Residential Segregation are not relevant to the study of southern Negro leadership: see text.
† Data compiled from Earl J. McGrath, *The Predominantly Negro Colleges and Universities in Transition* (New York: Columbia University, Teachers College, 1965).

choice between appealing for mass support and obtaining resources in other ways; in another context it would include appealing to different sectors of the population for support.

3. Individual competition is facilitated by a weak or ambiguous prestige structure. Social control over potential leaders and loyalty to factions can exist only to the extent that the Negro subcommunity is in fact a subcommunity with binding integrative attachment mechanisms.

Social Consequences of Leadership Competition

In a competitive environment, prospective leaders must make appeals for support. It is commonly assumed that this produces a more militant movement, and our data support this assumption. Without competition, leadership remains in traditional hands, which suggests that the leadership in noncompetitive cities will be older and have higher status. Our data indicate that this is also the case, at least partially. Table 3 gives the age, educational attainment, and income of the civil rights leaders interviewed in each class of city; the data suggest that the noncompetitive cities have older leaders who have high incomes, but without especially high educational attainment. However, the South presents a reverse pattern with the noncompetitive cities having younger leaders who are better educated with lower incomes. In both of the noncompetitive southern cities, the leadership was occupied by upwardly-mobile professionals. The Negro professional holds an indisputable status in the Negro subcommunity functionally similar to that of a member of a traditional elite.[40]

Table 3: Social Characteristics of Civil Rights Leaders, by Type of Leadership Competition and Region

	Competition	Median Age		Percent with Professional Education		Percent Income over $10,000	
North	Individual	33	(8)	67	(9)	50	(8)
	Minimal	41	(12)	42	(12)	67	(9)
	Organized	34	(6)	58	(12)	20	(5)
South	Individual	53	(7)	43	(7)	50	(4)
	Minimal	46	(7)	50	(8)	0	(6)
	Organized	49	(9)	44	(9)	67	(9)

Militancy is measured by a four-item scale from a longer agree-disagree questionnaire.[41] The meaning of this militancy scale is perhaps best captured by one of these items which asks the respondent to agree or disagree that "Too many times Negroes have compromised when they could have made more progress if they had held out a little longer." But another component of militancy is the willingness to disagree that "The average white man really wants the Negro to have his rights." Apparently the militant feels there is little to be gained from appealing to the better nature of whites, and therefore the only hope is to make discrimination so unpleasant or costly that whites will give in out of self-interest. In Table 4, we see that the cities with competition, both organized and individual, have more militant leaders. It is understandable that the southern leaders would generally be more militant than those in the North.

Table 4: Militancy of Civil Rights Leaders, by
Competition Level of City and Region*

Level of Competition	Region of Cities					
	North		**South**		**Total†**	
Individual competition	2.14	(7)	2.74	(9)	1.78	(16)
Minimal competition	1.30	(10)	2.00	(7)	1.07	(17)
Organized competition	2.00	(9)	2.50	(10)	1.72	(19)
Mean	1.77	(26)	2.42	(26)	1.77	(52)

* Each civil rights leader interviewed was given a militancy score, the average number of militant responses to four statements. The possible range of scores is from very militant (score = 4) to not militant at all (score = 0).
† The total column is derived after reducing the southern militancy scores by .65 so that the North-South differences will not influence the result. In the total column the level of militancy in the two competitive cases are each significantly higher than the militancy in the minimal competition case (at the .05 level, one-tailed test).

Thus far, we have observed that leadership in competitive cities differs in means-orientations. Let us now consider two other factors, differences in goal orientation, and differences in the actual amount of civil rights activity. Here we will draw upon the 15 case studies without attempting to present the data in each case. The reader is referred to the parent monograph for a more complete story.

One might suppose that under conditions of intense competition, the goals of the local civil rights movement might become more attuned to the national civil rights climate as competing leaders draw upon the idioms of the national movement for legitimation. This is partly true in cities where competition is individualized. In these cities the leadership goals have been set in an effort to bid for the support of the entire Negro community, hence the goals have been stated in the most diffuse way. In all three cities, the goals have stressed the elimination of *de facto* segregation and have been highly symbolic.[42] In the two cities with organized competition, the goals have been determined (it seems) by the need of the anti-establishment leaders to build a specific base in one sector of the community from which to wage war on the establishment. The result is that the stated goals have been set to meet the particular needs of only one part of the subcommunity. In both cases, the base was a racially changing neighborhood which developed a mixture of city-wide and local goals (and a mixture of symbolic and welfare goals) designed to encourage whites to stay in the area and to meet the most salient needs of the incoming Negroes. The two southern cities with organized competition have also shown a tendency toward a mixture of "symbolic" and "welfare" goals; this is particularly true in Jacksonville. The three cities without internal competition developed a set of goals which are in some ways more traditional. Although they were generally city-wide in orientation, they tended to be more specific; in Baltimore and Pittsburgh, focus was upon techniques for eliminating overcrowding by an integration plan; in Buffalo, the movement stressed integration of particular schools.

In the South, there is a narrower range of alternative goals available since the elimination of *de jure* segregation has been the main target. In the one city where there is competition between civil rights groups and a Negro political "establishment," the movement has adopted a heavy welfare orientation which led to a three-day boycott aimed at forcing the upgrading of Negro schools. As in the North, the movements with individual competition for leadership (New Orleans and Montgomery) have stated their goals in abstract terms, and have not paid much attention to specific goals or goals designed to benefit any particular sector or neighborhood of the Negro community. Thus, the data suggest that individualized competition leads to diffuse goals stressing symbolic issues, that cities with organized competition become welfare-oriented, while the cities with low competition tend to stress general and symbolic goals phrasing them in specific terms.

This is only a general tendency, and the data are confounded by three factors. First, the high-status city can be expected to develop more symbolic and diffuse goals since it tends to have an audience for mass-media exhortations, and (we assume) weaker neighborhood orientations. But, as we have discussed above, the high-status cities have individualized competition. Thus our correlation of individualized competition and diffuse goal orientation may be spurious. Secondly, the movements with low competition for leadership are better able to negotiate (since the school board knows who it has to negotiate with), a factor which probably affects the kinds of demands developed and made. And third, the willingness of the school system to meet the particular demands affects the goals of the movement. Since these extraneous factors are important, it is probably wisest to conclude that competition is not necessarily the most important factor in determining the goal orientation of the movement.

Competition also places great pressure on leaders to achieve results. However, in the case of northern school desegregation, the movement has relatively little impact on the degree to which the school board will acquiesce to the demands made.[43] Therefore there is some tendency for the movement to become means-oriented and evaluate its leaders by their ability to put together a good demonstration or boycott. Again, it is easy to exaggerate the importance of competition in determining level of activity. Much depends upon the amount of resources — especially manpower — available to the movement; and much depends upon whether the school system chooses to be resistant and invite demonstrations. However, with these two qualifications, we can suggest such a pattern. Within the northern sample, both cities with organized competition tend to have aggressive demonstrations, although they tend not to be able to sustain civil rights activity over a long period of time. There is almost an element of desperation in the style of militant groups in these cities. In St. Louis, for example, a blockade of school buses was agreed upon late the preceding evening, and final plans were not developed until a few hours before the blockade. However, it is difficult to sustain civil rights activity without complete support of the Negro community, and in both cities the presence of an organized opposition group eventually crippled the movement.[44] In the three cities with individualized competition, demonstrations have been sporadic, but have continued over a long period of time. In the noncompetitive cities, as expected, the decision to demonstrate is a purely tactical one; the demonstration is regarded as the ultimate weapon and is infrequently used.

The same general pattern seems to hold in the South, even though activity in connection with court-ordered desegregation is quite different from activity generated within a northern context. In the cities with organized competition (Atlanta and Jacksonville), there has been direct action in connection with the schools; there has not been such action in the other four cities. Accordingly, in these four cities, it is difficult to establish a relationship between competition and activity, although the civil rights action does seem more predictable when there is little competition.

The most important effect of competition in the civil rights movement has been to make negotiation with white leadership much more complex. In all northern cities, the movements with individualized competition have been more unpredictable. The San Francisco school superintendent has had to deal with nine civil rights groups. In another city the civil rights movement virtually forced the board to break off negotiations so that a boycott could be held. In the third city, the demands were so vague as to be perceived as merely antagonistic slogans.[45] In the two cities with organized competition, the main difficulty with negotiations is that the school board could not know how large an element of the Negro community was "represented" by a group of civil rights leaders vis-à-vis their opponents or competitors.[46] In contrast, the three cities with minimal competition have had much more orderly processes of negotiation — although in one case, the school board was so disorganized that the civil rights leaders didn't quite know with whom *they* should be talking.

Social Consequences of Competition: A Summary

Table 5 summarizes the data presented above. From this summary table we can clarify Walker's contention that competitive movements are more successful in achieving their goals.[47] It is probably true that organized competition is beneficial

Table 5: Style of Civil Rights Activity, by City Competition Level and Region

| Region | Level of Competition | Style of Civil Rights Activity | | |
		Goals	Action	Militancy
North	Individual	Symbolic, Diffuse, City-wide	Demonstration (sporadic)	Medium
	Minimal	Symbolic, Specific, City-wide	Bargain-table negotiation (extensive)	Low
	Organized	Welfare and Symbolic, Specific, Local and City-wide	Demonstration (intense, but short-lived)	Medium
South	Individual	Symbolic, City-wide	Court action (limited)	High
	Minimal	Symbolic, City-wide	Court action (extensive)	Medium
	Organized	Welfare and Symbolic, Diffuse, City-wide	Court action and demonstration (short-lived)	High

to a civil rights movement in that it stimulates the most intense (though sometimes short-lived) activity. On the other hand, individual competition, which produces a constant circulation of leaders, probably equips the movement best for sustained activity over a period of years. However, the city without competition is probably best able to carry out a tightly planned campaign to achieve specific goals, although in the process its small leadership may become stolid and lose the initiative to raise new issues or the courage to use ultimate sanctions.

Notes

[1] As an example of this diagnosis, see Daniel Bell, "Plea for a 'New Phase in Negro Leadership,' " *The New York Times Magazine,* May 31, 1964.

[2] William Kornhauser, *The Politics of Mass Society* (New York: The Free Press of Glencoe, 1959), pp. 230–231.

[3] Joseph Gusfield, *Symbolic Crusade: Status Politics and the American Temperance Movement* (Urbana: The University of Illinois Press, 1963). See especially "A Dramatistic Theory of Status Politics," chap. 7, pp. 166–188. See also "Mass Society and Extremist Politics," *American Sociological Review,* 27 (February 1962), pp. 19–30.

[4] James S. Coleman, *Community Conflict* (Glencoe, Illinois: The Free Press, 1957).

[5] William A. Gamson, "Rancorous Conflict in Community Politics," *American Sociological Review,* 31 (February 1966), pp. 71–81.

[6] See Anthony M. Orum, "A Reappraisal of the Social and Political Participation of Negroes," *American Journal of Sociology,* 72 (July 1966), pp. 32–46.

[7] For national data see William Brink and Louis Harris, *The Negro Revolution in America* (New York: Simon & Schuster, 1964), and for a local example (Durham, North Carolina) see M. Elaine Burgess, *Negro Leadership in a Southern City* (Chapel Hill: The University of North Carolina Press, 1962).

[8] Ralf Dahrendorf, *Class and Class Conflict in Industrial Society* (Stanford: Stanford University Press, 1959). See Part II, "Toward a Sociological Theory of Conflict in Industrial

Society," pp. 157–318. He writes that the integration theory of society "conceives of social structure in terms of a functionally integrated system held in equilibrium by certain patterned and recurrent processes; the other one, the *coercion theory* of society, views social structure as a form of organization held together by force and constraint and reacting continuously beyond itself in the sense of producing within itself the forces that maintain it in an unending process of change" (p. 159).

[9] *Ibid.,* p. 165.

[10] V. O. Key, *Southern Politics in State and Nation,* (New York: Alfred A. Knopf, 1949); Hugh D. Price, *The Negro and Southern Politics* (New York: New York University Press, 1957).

[11] For a comprehensive analysis of the data see Robert Crain, Morton Inger, and Gerald A. McWorter, *School Desegregation in New Orleans: A Comparative Study of the Failure of Social Control* (Chicago: National Opinion Research Center, 1966), pp. 15–106.

[12] James Q. Wilson, *Negro Politics: The Search for Leadership* (New York: The Free Press of Glencoe, 1960); and "Two Negro Politicians: An Interpretation," *Midwest Journal of Political Science,* 4 (November 1960), pp. 346–369.

[13] James Q. Wilson, *The Amateur Democrat* (Chicago: University of Chicago Press, 1962).

[14] Floyd Hunter, *Community Power Structure: A Study of Decision-Makers* (Chapel Hill: The University of North Carolina Press, 1954).

[15] Lester W. Milbrath, "Political Participation in the States," in Herbert Jacob and Kenneth Vines (eds.), *Comparative State Politics* (Boston: Little, Brown & Co., 1965).

[16] Robert E. Agger, Daniel Goldrich, and Bert Swanson, *The Rulers and the Ruled: Political Power and Impotence in American Communities* (New York: John Wiley & Sons, 1964).

[17] Robert E. Lane, *Political Life: Why People Get Involved in Politics* (Glencoe, Illinois: The Free Press, 1959).

[18] Donald R. Matthews and James W. Prothro, "Political Factors and Negro Voter Registration in the South," *American Political Science Review,* 57 (June 1963), pp. 355–367.

[19] Hunter, *op. cit.*

[20] Harold Pfantz, "The Power Structure of the Negro Sub-Community: A Case Study and Comparative View," *Phylon,* 23 (Summer 1962), pp. 156–166.

[21] Ernest Barth and Baha Abu-Laban, "Power Structure and the Negro Sub-Community," *American Sociological Review,* 24 (February 1959), pp. 69–76.

[22] Everett C. Ladd, *Negro Political Leadership in the South* (Ithaca: Cornell University Press, 1966).

[23] Lewis Killian and Charles Smith, "Negro Protest Leaders in a Southern Community," *Social Forces,* 38 (March 1960), pp. 253–257. Also see Tillman Cothran and William Phillips, "Negro Leadership in a Crisis Situation," *Phylon,* 22 (1961), pp. 107–118.

[24] Jacquelyn Johnson Clarke, "Standard Operating Procedures in Tragic Situations," *Phylon,* 22 (Winter 1961), pp. 318–328.

[25] Clarence E. Glick, "Collective Behavior in Race Relations," *American Sociological Review,* 13 (June 1948), pp. 287–294.

[26] Jack Walker, "The Functions of Disunity: Negro Leadership in a Southern City," *Journal of Negro Education,* 32 (1963), pp. 227–236.

[27] *Ibid.,* p. 228.

[28] For the case studies and an analysis of the data, see Robert Crain, with Morton Inger, Gerald A. McWorter, and James J. Vanecko, *School Desegregation in the North: Eight Comparative Case Studies of Community Structure and Policy Making* (Chicago: National Opinion Research Center, 1966), and Crain, Inger, and McWorter, *op. cit.*

[29] A key actor in St. Louis described this pattern: "Traditionally there have been certain Negroes who are recognized as leaders and they start off as militant, but somewhere along

the line they become part of the establishment. They first become militant, and this is caused by being anti-establishment, and then they become part of the establishment — they shift from one position to another. Of course, you can't remain a revolutionary as part of the establishment."

[30] A clear example of this in Jacksonville occurred during a recent three-day school boycott run by a militant NAACP-oriented leadership. On the second day of the boycott, a major establishment Negro politician appeared on television to appeal to the Negro community to return to normal and send the children back to school. However, his appeal was not legitimated by his political role, but by his "leadership in many areas, such as civil rights, etc." Further, while appearing on television a NAACP sign was visible in front of him. He warded off charges of fraudulent representation made by NAACP, local and national officials, by declaring that his life membership allowed him such prerogative.

[31] The data were collected prior to significant changes in the political involvement of Negroes in the South, particularly Atlanta. Our findings are essentially similar to those presented by Walker (see Walker, op. cit.). After reapportionment in Georgia, the summer primary and general elections added up to two Negro state senators, and five Negro state representatives including Attorney Ben Brown and Julian Bond, both former leaders of the Atlanta Student Movement during 1960–1961 sit-ins. What seems to have subsequently developed is the abdication of leadership by the two key figures (one died, one moved to New York), which in effect has turned over the power to the younger more militant cadre of leaders.

[32] Andrew F. Brimmer, "The Negro in the National Economy," in John P. Davis (ed.), *The American Negro Reference Book* (Englewood Cliffs, New Jersey: Prentice-Hall, 1966), see especially the section titled "Negroes as Entrepreneurs," pp. 291–321.

[33] The largest Negro-owned bank and insurance firm are both in Durham along with a large Ph.D.-granting Negro university. At times, Durham seems to have a pattern of civil rights competition resembling Atlanta's. For a detailed analysis of Durham see Burgess, op. cit.; E. Franklin Frazier, "Durham: Capital of the Black Middle Class," in Alain Locke (ed.), *The New Negro* (New York: A. and C. Boni, 1925); and on the early development of Atlanta see August Meier and David Lewis, "History of Negro Upper Class in Atlanta, Georgia, 1890–1958," *Journal of Negro Education* (Spring 1959), pp. 128–139.

[34] Brimmer, op. cit.

[35] For a more detailed analysis of this pattern of increasing militancy see Louis Lomax, *The Negro Revolt* (New York: Harper & Row, 1962); August Meier, "New Currents in the Civil Rights Movement," *New Politics* (Summer 1963), pp. 7–31; and August Meier and Francis L. Broderick (eds.), *Negro Protest Thought in the Twentieth Century* (Indianapolis: The Bobbs-Merrill Co., 1965).

[36] For a general interpretive discussion see Martin Luther King's *Stride Toward Freedom* (New York: Ballantine Books, 1960).

[37] Coleman, op. cit., p. 26.

[38] A possible fourth type, the community which maintains a stable elite but has no leadership roles, is almost an internal contradiction, and seems to be rare; but as we noted earlier Columbus, Georgia, comes close to this type.

[39] Detailed analysis can be found in Crain, Inger, McWorter, *School Desegregation in New Orleans . . . op. cit.*, and Daniel Thompson *The Negro Leadership Class* (Englewood Cliffs, New Jersey: Prentice-Hall, 1963).

[40] One can interpret leadership competition of the minority community as mechanisms of mobility. The northern pattern differs from the South in part because protest leadership is a functional alternative to established routes of leadership mobility, whereas in the South it is ofttimes the same as the total minority leadership. This is particularly true in cities without established political leadership; thus, the one Negro attorney in Columbus being elected to the Georgia House of Representatives following reapportionment was predicated on both his station in the Negro community and moderate acceptability to whites.

[41] The two items not cited above are (a) "Unless you dramatize an issue through mass protests and demonstrations it seems that there is scarcely any progress made," and (b) "It

is sometimes better to have white resistance to Negro requests, because then you have a basis for bringing the overall problem to the public's attention." Yules Q was used as a measure of association and produced the following matrix:

	2	3	4
1	.45	.73	.89
2	—	.62	.69
3	—	—	.54

[42] In this discussion of civil rights goals we have employed two axes of differentiation, status (symbolic) to welfare, and diffuse to specific. Wilson clearly states that the first basis of distinction is between tangible *things* (welfare) and intangible *principles* (status or symbolic). See Wilson, *Negro Politics: The Search for Leadership,* esp. pp. 185–199. The second dimension concerns the level of specificity of the goals, the extent to which the goals reflect a limited set of concrete propositions as compared to an ever expanding set of general claims.

[43] The major analysis of the parent study revealed that characteristics of the school board and its members so explained acquiescence that adding the effect of civil rights activity did not appreciably add to the predictability. Moreover, the explanatory relationship is opposite this, i.e., the initial reaction or acquiescence of the school board is a cause of civil rights activity rather than being caused by it.

[44] Related to a movement's resource needs for sustaining activity, there is probably an inverse relationship between the number of "troops" needed and the intensity/quality of commitment. But an opposition group affects both factors by drawing off some troops and immobilizing others, and providing alternative gratification which depletes the urgency of the initial controversy.

[45] Killian poses one explanation for cases when ". . . the Negro leader-agent takes the white agent's arguments as the rationalizations of a prejudiced person rather than the tactics of a bargaining agent. When he reiterates his demands, almost as slogans, rather than countering the tactics, he appears either unintelligent or unreasonable. This leads the white agent, in turn, into the psychodynamic fallacy, and he breaks off the negotiations on the ground that the Negro is simply an agitator who makes impossible demands for the sake of 'stirring up trouble.' " See Lewis Killian, "Community Structure and the Role of the Negro Leader-Agent," *Sociological Inquiry,* 35 (Winter 1965), pp. 69–79.

[46] School boards have normally faced the representation question with regard to teachers' unions and parent groups. But civil rights leaders face different problems because the above two are more easily defined constituencies, with longer traditions of negotiating with school boards, and are working within the context of a clearer uncontroversial set of legal guidelines.

[47] Walker, *op. cit.*

On the Role of
Martin Luther King

August Meier

The phenomenon that is Martin Luther King consists of a number of striking paradoxes. The Nobel Prize winner is accepted by the outside world as *the* leader of the nonviolent direct action movement, but he is criticized by many activists within the movement. He is criticized for what appears, at times, as indecisiveness, and more often denounced for a tendency to accept compromise. Yet, in the eyes of most Americans, both black and white, he remains the symbol of militant direct action. So potent is this symbol of King as direct actionist, that a new myth is arising about his historic role. The real credit for developing and projecting the techniques and philosophy of nonviolent direct action in the civil rights arena must be given to the Congress of Racial Equality which was founded in 1942, more than a dozen years before the Montgomery bus boycott projected King into international fame. And the idea of mass action by Negroes themselves to secure redress of their grievances must, in large part, be ascribed to the vision of A. Philip Randolph, architect of the March on Washington Movement during World War II. Yet, as we were told in Montgomery on March 25, 1965, King and his followers now assert, apparently without serious contradiction, that a new type of civil rights strategy was born at Montgomery in 1955 under King's auspices.

In a movement in which respect is accorded in direct proportion to the number of times one has been arrested, King appears to keep the number of times he goes to jail to a minimum. In a movement in which successful leaders are those who share in the hardships of their followers, in the risks they take, in the beatings they receive, in the length of time they spend in jail, King tends to leave prison for other important engagements, rather than remaining there and suffering with his followers. In a movement in which leadership ordinarily devolves upon persons who mix democratically with their followers, King remains isolated and aloof. In a movement which prides itself on militancy and "no compromise" with racial discrimination or with the white "power structure," King maintains close relationships with, and appears to be influenced by, Democratic presidents and their emissaries, seems amenable to compromises considered by some half a loaf or less, and often appears willing to postpone or avoid a direct confrontation in the streets.

King's career has been characterized by failures that, in the larger sense, must

August Meier, "On the Role of Martin Luther King," *New Politics,* IV, Winter 1965, pp. 52–59.

be accounted triumphs. The buses in Montgomery were desegregated only after lengthy judicial proceedings conducted by the NAACP Legal Defense Fund secured a favorable decision from the U.S. Supreme Court. Nevertheless, the events in Montgomery were a triumph for direct action, and gave this tactic a popularity unknown when identified solely with CORE. King's subsequent major campaigns — in Albany, Georgia; in Danville, Virginia; in Birmingham, Alabama; and in St. Augustine, Florida — ended as failures or with only token accomplishments in those cities. But each of them, chiefly because of his presence, dramatically focused national and international attention on the plight of the Southern Negro, thereby facilitating overall progress. In Birmingham, in particular, demonstrations which fell short of their local goals were directly responsible for a major Federal Civil Rights Act. Essentially, this pattern of local failure and national victory was recently enacted at Selma, Alabama.

King is ideologically committed to disobeying unjust laws and court orders, in the Gandhian tradition, but generally he follows a policy of not disobeying Federal Court orders. In his recent Montgomery speech, he expressed a crude, neo-Marxist interpretation of history romanticizing the Populist movement as a genuine union of black and white common people, ascribing race prejudice to capitalists playing white workers against black. Yet, in practice, he is amenable to compromise with the white bourgeois political and economic Establishment. More important, King enunciates a superficial and eclectic philosophy and by virtue of it he has profoundly awakened the moral conscience of America.

In short, King can be described as a "Conservative Militant."

In this combination of militancy with conservatism and caution, of righteousness with respectability, lies the secret of King's enormous success.

Certain important civil rights leaders have dismissed King's position as the product of publicity generated by the mass communications media. But this can be said of the successes of the civil rights nonviolent action movement generally. Without publicity it is hard to conceive that much progress would have been made. In fact, contrary to the official nonviolent direct action philosophy, demonstrations have secured their results not by changing the hearts of the oppressors through a display of nonviolent love, but through the national and international pressures generated by the publicity arising from mass arrests and incidents of violence. And no one has employed this strategy of securing publicity through mass arrests and precipitating violence from white hoodlums and law enforcement officers more than King himself. King abhors violence; as at Selma, for example, he constantly retreats from situations that might result in the deaths of his followers. But he is precisely most successful when, contrary to his deepest wishes, his demonstrations precipitate violence from Southern whites against Negro and white demonstrators. We need only cite Birmingham and Selma to illustrate this point.

Publicity alone does not explain the durability of King's image, or why he remains for the rank and file of whites and blacks alike, the symbol of the direct action movement, the nearest thing to a charismatic leader that the civil rights movement has ever had. At the heart of King's continuing influence and popularity are two facts. First, better than anyone else, he articulates the aspirations of Negroes who respond to the cadence of his addresses, his religious phraseology and manner of speaking, and the vision of his dream for them and for America. King has intuitively adopted the style of the old fashioned Negro Baptist preacher and transformed it into a new art form; he has, indeed, restored oratory to its place among the arts. Second, he communicates Negro aspirations to white America more effectively than anyone else. His religious terminology and manipulation of the Christian symbols of love and non-resistance are partly responsible for his appeal among whites. To talk in terms of Christianity, love, nonviolence is reassuring to the mentality of white America. At the same time, the very superficialities of his philosophy — that rich and eclectic amalgam of Jesus, Hegel, Gandhi and others as outlined in his *Stride Toward Freedom* — makes him appear intellectually profound to the superficially educated middle-class white American. Actually, if he were a truly profound religious thinker, like Tillich or Niebuhr, his influence would of necessity be limited to a select audience. But by uttering moral cliches, the Christian pieties, in a magnificent display of oratory, King becomes enormously effective.

If his success with Negroes is largely due to the style of his utterance, his success with whites is a much more complicated matter. For one thing, he unerringly knows how to exploit to maximum effectiveness their growing feeling of guilt. King, of course, is not unique in attaining fame and popularity among whites through playing upon their guilt feelings. James Baldwin is the most conspicuous example of a man who has achieved success with this formula. The incredible fascination which the Black Muslims have for white people, and the posthumous near-sanctification of Malcolm X by many naive whites (in addition to many Negroes whose motivations are, of course, very different), must in large part be attributed to the same source. But King goes beyond this. With intuitive, but extraordinary skill, he not only castigates whites for their sins but, in contrast to angry young writers like Baldwin, he explicitly states his belief in their salvation. Not only will direct action bring fulfillment of the "American Dream" to Negroes but the Negroes' use of direct action will help whites to live up to their Christian and democratic values; it will purify, cleanse and heal the sickness in white society. Whites will benefit as well as Negroes. He has faith that the white man will redeem himself. Negroes must not hate whites, but love them. In this manner, King first arouses the guilt feelings of whites, and then relieves them — though always leaving the lingering feeling in his white listeners that they should support his nonviolent crusade. Like a Greek tragedy, King's performance provides an extraordinary catharsis for the white listener.

King thus gives white men the feeling that he is their good friend, that he poses no threat to them. It is interesting to note that this was the same feeling white men received from Booker T. Washington, the noted early 20th century accommodator. Both men stressed their faith in the white man; both expressed the belief that the white man could be brought to accord Negroes their rights. Both stressed the importance of whites recognizing the rights of Negroes for the moral health and well-being of white society. Like King, Washington had an extraordinary following among whites. Like King, Washington symbolized for most whites the whole program of Negro advancement. While there are important similarities in the functioning of both men vis-à-vis the community, needless to say, in most respects, their philosophies are in disagreement.

It is not surprising, therefore, to find that King is the recipient of contributions from organizations and individuals who fail to eradicate evidence of prejudice in their own backyards. For example, certain liberal trade union leaders who are philosophically committed to full racial equality, who feel the need to identify their organizations with the cause of militant civil rights, although they are unable to defeat racist elements in their unions, contribute hundreds of thousands of dollars to King's Southern Christian Leadership Conference (SCLC). One might attribute this phenomenon to the fact that SCLC works in the South rather than the North, but this is true also for SNCC which does not benefit similarly from union treasuries. And the fact is that ever since the college students started their sit-ins in 1960, it is SNCC which has been the real spearhead of direct action in most of the South, and has performed the lion's share of work in local communities, while SCLC has received most of the publicity and most of the money. However, while King provides a verbal catharsis for whites, leaving them feeling purified and comfortable, SNCC's uncompromising militancy makes whites feel less comfortable and less beneficent.

(The above is not to suggest that SNCC and SCLC are responsible for all, or nearly all, the direct action in the South. The NAACP has actively engaged in direct action, especially in Savannah under the leadership of W. W. Law, in South Carolina under I. DeQuincy Newman, and in Clarksdale, Mississippi, under Aaron Henry. The work of CORE — including most of the direct action in Louisiana, much of the nonviolent work in Florida and Mississippi, the famous Freedom Ride of 1961 — has been most important. In addition, one should note the work of SCLC affiliates, such as those in Lynchburg, Virginia, led by Reverend Virgil Wood; in Birmingham led by Reverend Fred Shuttlesworth, and in Savannah, by Hosea Williams.

(There are other reasons for SNCC's lesser popularity with whites than King's. These are connected with the great changes that have occurred in SNCC since it was founded in 1960, changes reflected in the half-jocular epigram circulating in SNCC circles that the Student Nonviolent Coordinating Committee has now become the "Non-Student Violent Non-Coordinating Committee." The point is, however, that even when SNCC thrilled the nation in 1960–1961 with the student sit-ins that swept the South, it did not enjoy the popularity and financial support accorded to King.)

King's very tendencies toward compromise and caution, his willingness to negotiate and bargain with White House emissaries, his hesitancy to risk the precipitation of mass violence upon demonstrators, further endear him to whites. He appears to them a "responsible" and "moderate" man. To militant activists, King's failure to march past the State Police on that famous Tuesday morning outside Selma indicated either a lack of courage, or a desire to advance himself by currying Presidential favor. But King's shrinking from a possible bloodbath, his accession to the entreaties of the political Establishment, his acceptance of face-saving compromise in this, as in other instances, are fundamental to the particular role he is playing, and essential for achieving and sustaining his image as a leader of heroic moral stature in the eyes of white men. His caution and compromise keep open the channels of communication between the activists and the majority of the white community. In brief: King makes the nonviolent direct action movement respectable.

Of course, many, if not most, activists reject the notion that the movement should be made respectable. Yet, American history shows that for any reform movement to succeed, it must attain respectability. It must attract moderates, even conservatives, to its ranks. The March on Washington made direct action respectable; Selma made it fashionable. More than any other force, it is Martin Luther King who impressed the civil rights revolution on the American conscience and is attracting that great middle body of American public opinion to its support. It is this revolution of conscience that will undoubtedly lead fairly soon to the elimination of all violations of Negroes' constitutional rights, thereby creating the conditions for the economic and social changes that are necessary if we are to achieve full racial equality. This is not to deny the dangers to the civil rights movement in becoming respectable. Respectability, for example, encourages the attempts of political machines to capture civil rights organizations. Respectability can also become an end in itself, thereby dulling the cutting edge of its protest activities. Indeed, the history of the labor movement reveals how attaining respectability can produce loss of original purpose and character. These perils, however, do not contradict the importance of achieving respectability — even a degree of modishness — if racial equality is ever to be realized.

There is another side to the picture: King would be neither respected nor respectable if there were not more militant activists on his left, engaged in more radical forms of direct action. Without CORE and, especially, SNCC, King would appear "radical" and "irresponsible" rather than "moderate" and "respectable."

King occupies a position of strategic importance as the "vital center" within the civil rights movement. Though he has lieutenants who are far more militant and "radical" than he is, SCLC acts, in effect, as the most cautious, deliberate and "conservative" of the direct action groups because of King's leadership. This permits King and the SCLC to function — almost certainly unintentionally — not only as an organ of communication with the Establishment and majority white public opinion, but as something of a bridge between the activist and more traditionalist or "conservative" civil rights groups, as well. For example, it appears unlikely that the Urban League and NAACP, which supplied most of the funds, would have participated in the 1963 March on Washington if King had not done so. Because King agreed to go along with SNCC and CORE, the NAACP found it mandatory to join if it was to maintain its image as a protest organization. King's identification with the March was also essential for securing the support of large numbers of white clergymen and their moderate followers. The March was the brainchild of the civil rights movement's ablest strategist and tactician, Bayard Rustin, and the call was issued by A. Philip Randolph. But it would have been a minor episode in the history of the civil rights movement without King's support.

Yet curiously enough, despite his charisma and international reputation, King thus far has been more a symbol than a power in the civil rights movement. Indeed his strength in the movement has derived less from an organizational base than from his symbolic role. Seven or eight years ago, one might have expected King to achieve an organizationally dominant position in the civil rights movement, at least in its direct action wing. The fact is that in the period after the Montgomery bus boycott, King developed no program and, it is generally agreed, revealed himself as an ineffective administrator who failed to capitalize upon his popularity among Negroes. In 1957, he founded SCLC to coordinate the work of direct action groups that had sprung up in Southern cities. Composed of autonomous units, usually led by Baptist ministers, SCLC does not appear to have developed an overall sense of direction or a program of real breadth and scope. Although the leaders of SCLC affiliates became the race leaders in their communities — displacing the established local conservative leadership of teachers, old-line ministers, businessmen — it is hard for an observer (who admittedly has not been close to SCLC) to perceive exactly what SCLC did before the 1960's except to advance the image and personality of King. King appeared not to direct but to float with the tide of militant direct action. For example, King did not supply the initiative for the bus boycott in Montgomery, but was pushed into the leadership by others, as he himself records in *Stride Toward Freedom*. Similarly, in the late Fifties and early Sixties, he appeared to let events shape his course. In the last two years, this has changed, but until the Birmingham demonstrations of 1963, King epitomized conservative militancy.

SCLC under King's leadership called the Raleigh Conference of April 1960 which gave birth to SNCC. Incredibly, within a year, the SNCC youth had lost their faith in the man they now satirically call "De Lawd," and had struck out on their own independent path. By that time, the Spring of 1961, King's power in the Southern direct action movement had been further curtailed by CORE's stunning Freedom Ride to Alabama and Mississippi.

The limited extent of King's actual power in the civil rights movement was illustrated by the efforts made to invest King with the qualities of a Messiah during the recent ceremonies at the State Capitol in Montgomery. Reverend Abernathy's constant iteration of the theme that King is "our Leader," the Moses of the race, chosen by God, and King's claim that he originated the nonviolent direct action movement at Montgomery a decade ago, are all assertions that would have been superfluous if King's power in the movement was very substantial.

It is, of course, no easier today than it has been in the past few years to predict the course of the Negro protest movement, and it is always possible that the current state of affairs may change quite abruptly. It is conceivable that the ambitious program that SCLC is now projecting — both in Southern voter registration and in Northern urban direct action programs — may give it a position of commanding importance in civil rights. As a result of the recent demonstrations in Selma and Montgomery, King's prestige is now higher than ever. At the same time, the nature of CORE and NAACP direct action activities at the moment has created a programmatic vaccuum which SCLC may be able to exploit. Given this convergence of circumstances, SCLC leaders may be able to establish an organizational base upon which to build a power commensurate with the symbolic position of their president.

It is indeed fortunate that King has not obtained a predominance of power in the movement commensurate with his prestige. For today, as in the past, a diversity of approaches is necessary. Needed in the movement are those who view the struggle chiefly as a conflict situation, in which the power of demonstrations, the power of Negroes, will force recognition of the race's humanity and citizenship rights, and the achievement of equality. Equally needed are those who see the movement's strategy to be chiefly one of capitalizing on the basic consensus of values in American society by awakening the conscience of the white man to the contradiction between his professions and the facts of discrimination. And just as necessary to the movement as both of these are those who operate skillfully, recognizing and yet exploiting the deeply held American belief that compromise among competing interest groups is the best *modus operandi* in public life.

King is unique in that he maintains a delicate balance among all three of these basic strategy assumptions. The traditional approaches of the Urban League (conciliation of the white businessmen) and of the NAACP (most preeminently appeals to the courts and appeals to the sense of fair play in the American public), basically attempted to exploit the consensus in American values. It would of course be a gross oversimplification to say that the Urban League and NAACP strategies are based simply on attempting to capitalize on the consensus of values, while SNCC and CORE act simply as if the situation were purely a conflict situation. Implicit in the actions of all civil rights organizations are both sets of assumptions — even where people are not conscious of the theoretical assumptions under which, in effect, they operate. The NAACP especially encompasses a broad spectrum of strategies and types of activities, ranging from time-tested court procedures to militant direct action. Sophisticated CORE activists know very well when a judicious compromise is necessary or valuable. But I hold that King is in the middle, acting in effect as if he were basing his strategy upon all three assumptions described above. He maintains a delicate balance between a purely moral appeal and a militant display of power. He talks of the power of the bodies of Negro demonstrators in the streets, but unlike CORE and SNCC activists, he accepts compromises at times that consist of token improvements, and calls them impressive victories. More than any of the other groups, King and SCLC can, up to this point at least, be described as exploiting all three tactical assumptions to an approximately equal degree. King's continued success, I suspect, will depend to a considerable degree upon the difficult feat of maintaining his position at the "vital center" of the civil rights movement.

Viewed from another angle King's failure to achieve a position of power on a level with his prestige is fortunate because rivalries between personalities and organizations remain an essential ingredient of the dynamics of the movement and a precondition for its success as each current tries to outdo the others in effectiveness and in maintaining a good public image. Without this competitive stimulus, the civil rights revolution would slow down.

I have already noted that one of King's functions is to serve as a bridge between the militant and conservative wings of the movement. In addition, by gathering support for SCLC, he generates wider support for CORE and SNCC, as well. The most striking example is the recent series of demonstrations in Selma where SNCC had been operating for nearly two years with only moderate amounts of publicity before King chose that city as his own target. As usual, it was King's presence that focused world attention on Selma. In the course of subsequent events, the rift between King and SNCC assumed the proportions of a serious conflict. Yet people who otherwise would have been hesitant to support SNCC's efforts, even people who had become disillusioned with certain aspects of SNCC's policies during the Mississippi Summer Project of 1964, were drawn to demonstrate in Selma and Montgomery. Moreover, although King received the major share of credit for the demonstrations, it seems likely that in the controversy between King and SNCC, the latter emerged with more power and influence in the civil rights movement than ever before. It is now possible that the Administration will, in the future, regard SNCC as more of a force to be reckoned with than it has heretofore.

Major dailies like the *New York Times* and the *Washington Post,* basically sympathetic to civil rights and racial equality, though more gradualist than the activist organizations, have congratulated the nation upon its good fortune in having a "responsible and moderate" leader like King at the head of the nonviolent action movement (though they overestimate his power and underestimate the symbolic nature of his role). It would be more appropriate to congratulate the civil rights movement for *its* good fortune in having as its symbolic leader a man like King. The fact that he has more prestige than power; the fact that he not only criticizes whites but explicitly believes in their redemption; his ability to arouse creative tension combined with his inclination to shrink from carrying demonstrations to the point where major bloodshed might result; the intellectual simplicity of his philosophy; his tendency to compromise and exert caution, even his seeming indecisiveness on some occasions; the sparing use he makes of going to or staying in jail himself; his friendship with the man in the White House — all are essential to the role he plays, and invaluable for the success of the movement. It is well, of course, that not all civil rights leaders are cut of the same cloth — that King is unique among them. Like Randolph, who functions very differently, King is really an institution. His most important function, I believe, is that of effectively communicating Negro aspirations to white people, of making nonviolent direct action respectable in the eyes of the white majority. In addition, he functions within the movement by occupying a vital center position between its "conservative" and "radical" wings, by symbolizing direct action and attracting people to participate in it without dominating either the civil rights movement or its activist wing. Viewed in this context, traits that many activists criticize in King actually function not as sources of weakness, but as the foundations of his strength.

By Any Means Necessary

2

Status Discrepancy and the Radical Rejection of Nonviolence

Inge Powell Bell

In his *Anatomy of a Revolution,* Brinton[1] describes the typical revolutionary group as one whose status along certain dimensions is rising while their claims to other, parallel types of status are being frustrated. Usually, the revolutionary group has been rising economically while being denied commensurate political power and/or social recognition. Such groups have a high revolutionary potential because, as their status rises along one dimension, their expectations along all dimensions rise more rapidly than their actual advance, thus producing a steadily increasing level of relative deprivation. At the same time, the fact that they have attained certain economic, educational, or other advantages gives them the self-confidence and practical means with which to attack the established order.

Other sociologists have pointed to a parallel phenomenon on the individual level: the fact that status discrepancy may drive individuals to question the social order. Lenski[2] shows that when status is held constant, persons with lower status crystallization tend disproportionately to favor liberal measures such as government health insurance, price controls, and extension of government powers. He suggests that persons who have poorly crystallized statuses are exposed to rebuff and unpleasantness from persons of higher status. This leads to self-defensive attacks on the higher status levels and is easily turned into leftwing criticism of the whole social order. He shows that persons with discrepant statuses tend to withdraw from contact with those of solidly high status, thus confirming the theory that they suffer from rebuff.

Particularly relevant for our purposes is Lenski's finding that, though all patterns of status inconsistency show a positive asssociation with liberalism, low ethnic status combined with high income and education shows the closest association. Also relevant to our respondents is Goffman's[3] finding that status inconsistency produces

Inge Powell Bell, "Status Discrepancy and the Radical Rejection of Nonviolence," *Sociological Inquiry,* Vol. 38, Winter 1968, pp. 51–63. Reprinted by permission of *Sociological Inquiry.*

the greatest desire for change in the highest stratum because at high occupational levels people find it most difficult to separate social from job contacts and are hence unable to protect themselves against strain by segregating their various status dimensions into separate social roles.

In this study, we shall examine interview material from Negro members of the Congress of Racial Equality, made during the summers of 1962 and 1963. During this period, CORE was one of the three nationwide groups organizing direct action for civil rights and dedicated to a policy of nonviolence.[4] We shall divide the respondents into three ideological types, corresponding to three different degrees of radicalism with particular attention to the radical rejection of nonviolence. We shall examine the social background and socio-economic characteristics of the CORE activists, and show that status discrepancy is associated with a high degree of radicalism.

How the Data Were Gathered

Loosely structured interviews averaging two and a half hours in length were conducted with Negro members of CORE [the Congress of Racial Equality]. Respondents were chosen in equal numbers from five chapters designated as "Southern" by virtue of the general social atmosphere with regard to segregation (Miami, New Orleans, Baton Rouge, Jackson and Louisville), and six chapters designated as "Northern" (St. Louis, Seattle, Oakland, Berkeley, San Jose and Los Angeles).

Due to practical difficulties, the respondents were not drawn by systematic sampling methods. Rather, the interviewer obtained a general picture of each chapter's make-up with regard to race, age, occupation, and education by visiting meetings and interviewing chapter chairmen. On the basis of this picture an attempt was made to complete interviews with social types representative of the chapter's composition. Almost all members of local CORE chapters were very highly involved in terms of time, responsibility, and participation in direct action and civil disobedience. The respondent group tends to be particularly skewed in the direction of high involvement, since no special effort was made to hunt up persons carried on official membership lists but not attending meetings and projects. The group, then, is roughly representative of those who organized and carried through the headline-getting direct action activities of CORE on the local level.

A methodological weakness of this paper is the small size of the sample interviewed. CORE and the civil rights movement as a whole were undergoing such rapid changes during the period under study, that it would have been impossible to follow up the initial study with a subsequent survey designed to prove the points developed here with a larger sample. A year after these data were gathered, while the study was still being written, both the composition and the ideology of the movement had changed so drastically that an almost totally new analysis would have been necessary to encompass the new developments. The reliability of the present analysis must rest to some extent on the in-depth knowledge of the investigator. Analysis of the interview cases specifically cited in tables has been made in the context of insight derived from two years of intimate acquaintance with CORE, including many informal contacts with CORE members; observation of local chapter meetings; attendance at national conventions and workshops; and participant observation in many action projects.

Dimensions of Radicalism

Respondents were questioned extensively about their opinion of the policy of nonviolence as practiced by CORE and allied direct action organizations. Of the 27 Negro respondents who answered this question, 10 (37%) indicated that they felt an absolute moral commitment to nonviolence, by such statements as "violence never accomplishes anything," or "no other way is imaginable for the movement." Seven (26%) indicated that while they felt that nonviolence was definitely the best tactic for the movement, they did not regard it as a moral commitment. The tenor of some of these remarks in fact indicated a marked lack of understanding of true nonviolence as envisioned by Gandhi or Martin Luther King. So, for example, one respondent approved nonviolence because "it really stumps them (white hoodlums). They can't figure out what you're going to do next." Others merely emphasized a purely tactical orientation: "It's the best way because it helps us win allies." Five (19%) questioned the commitment to nonviolence and suggested that under some circumstances or conditions it might not be the best policy. Another five (19%) rejected the movement's adherence to nonviolence. These respondents felt that "violence is the only way of moving the white man" and "nonviolence is just another way of letting Negroes get kicked around."[5]

By itself, this distribution does not tell us much about the general radicalism of the respondents. If we define radicalism as a rejection of generally accepted social norms, then absolute pacifism of the Gandhian or Christian pacifist type may be more radical than a willingness to use some kinds of violence in the integration movement. The meaning of these opinions must be assessed within the context of the respondent's broader ideological orientation. Were those who accepted nonviolence consistent pacifists in their political judgments and personal lives and, conversely, were those who rejected nonviolence rejecting it in favor of some more common alternative viewpoint, for example, that of "realpolitik"?

Among the 17 persons who supported nonviolence as a moral commitment or technique, only six reported having read anything beyond CORE leaflets on the subject of nonviolence. In response to the question, "Do you consider nonviolence a personal ethic or 'way of life' as well as something to be followed in the movement?" only three of our respondents answered in the affirmative. Only one of these three appeared to have sufficient intellectual understanding of the doctrine to have applied the ethic to themselves in anything resembling the spirit in which it is understood by Gandhi or Martin Luther King. In the other two cases the investigator had occasion to observe that the respondents did not, in fact, adhere to a strict spirit of nonviolence when off the direct action line. Ambivalence with regard to the spirit of nonviolence was generally evident, in the "off-stage" deliberations and activities of CORE groups.

Since the existence of a deep, philosophically consistent commitment to nonviolence was not operating here, and since the type of violence discussed in the interviews was usually in self-defense, a right which has traditionally been granted in American society, the suspicion arises that adherence to nonviolence was an expression of ideological conservatism, i.e., that it arose out of the inability of the respondents to reject the society's pervasive double standard with regard to Negro rights and the means regarded as legitimate for obtaining those rights.

One question in the interview is particularly relevant to this hypothesis. Respondents were asked whether they felt nonviolence could or should be applied to problems of national defense — i.e., war and peace. Usually, the respondent was pressed to say whether he would be willing to use force in behalf of the U.S. in the event of war. On the basis of their answers, respondents were divided into two types: First, those who took a strict pacifist position plus those who took an intermediate position, being uncertain about conscientious objection but supporting disarmament, opposing militarism, etc. The second group consisted of those who expressed the prevailing norms with regard to war: "nonviolence can't be applied to war because the Communists would take us over," etc. Of 22 Negro respondents who gave answers on this question, 15 (68%) fell in the first group and seven (32%) fell into the second group.

Let us now look at a cross-classification of answers on these two questions: support for nonviolence in the integration movement and support for nonviolence in international affairs. If those who supported nonviolence in the movement also expressed pacifist sentiment with regard to international affairs, their beliefs might be said to express a general pacifist tendency, no matter how shallow or inconsistent. If, however, no such relationship or an inverse relationship exists, the hypothesis that nonviolence in the movement was an expression of relative conservatism will be considerably strengthened.[6]

Table 1 shows a slightly inverse relationship between support for nonviolence in the two different types of situations. Excluding the two exceptional persons who supported violence in both instances, the table suggests the existence of three ideological types.

At the conservative extreme were the seven respondents who would not defend themselves against white segregationists but would fight against enemies of the country. These persons accepted prevailing values to the extent of doubting the

Table 1: Combined Frequencies on Attitudes toward Nonviolence in the Movement and Nonviolence in National Defense, Negro Core Members*

	For Nonviolence in the Movement	Against or Questioning Nonviolence in the Movement
For Nonviolence in National Defense (Pacifist)	7	7
Against Nonviolence in National Defense	7	2

* We omit from this combined table those who do not have definite positions on both variables.

Negro's right to use culturally accepted methods of self-defense, while accepting the popular view that everyone has a duty to defend his country from those conventionally defined as enemies. We shall refer to these persons as "moderates."

At the opposite extreme were the seven radical persons who would consider the use of violence in the movement but reject their obligation to use force in national defense. The third type, those who support nonviolence in both situations, may represent either a genuine commitment to pacifist ideology or a position which is simply intermediate between the other two on a simple radical-conservative dimension. Previously cited material suggests the latter alternative. But let us look at some further material before characterizing this "nonviolent" type.

For each interview, a count was made of negative and positive evaluative statements about American society in general. Negative statements included criticisms of the economic system, U.S. foreign policy, American militarism, and American culture generally. Praise of Cuba, Communists and others conventionally defined as enemies were also counted as criticisms. With regard to the racial situation, only criticisms referring clearly to the whole nation or the Federal government were counted. Those expressly confined to one region were excluded, since the common Southern pattern of condemning the South while expressing confidence in the nation or the national government appeared to be at least neutral as far as general radicalism is concerned. Positive statements included praise of the Federal government's role in civil rights; confidence in the possibility of solving the race problem within the general framework of American institutions; support of the U.S. against conventionally defined enemies; and identification with American traditions and heroes. One positive point was given if the respondent did not mention the American system during the interview. This procedure was followed because respondents were not probed on this score, but remarks came up spontaneously during the interview. Since the overwhelming majority of remarks about the American system were negative, it was felt that no mention at all indicated a positive attitude, at least by comparison with other respondents.

Each respondent was given a score constructed by counting up negative and positive expressions and subtracting one from the other. The scores run from plus one (a preponderance of one positive over any negative mentions) to minus ten (a preponderance of ten negative over any positive mentions).

The association between our typology and the degree of anti-American criticism supports the contention that a radical-moderate dimension underlay the respondents' attitudes toward the use of nonviolence in the civil rights movement (see Table 2). The nonviolent respondents were between the two extreme types but much

Table 2: Radical, Nonviolent, and Moderate Types by Evaluations of the American System

Typology	+1	−1 to −5	−5 to −10
Radical	—	3	4
Nonviolent	4	3	—
Moderate	5	2	—

closer to the moderates. Their criticisms did not differ in kind from those of the other two groups. If their commitment to nonviolence had reflected a radical pacifism, grounded in Gandhian and/or Christian pacifist tradition, one would have expected numerous criticisms of America along pacifist lines: objection to the prevalence of coercion in domestic and foreign affairs, objection to materialism and competitiveness, etc. The absence of such a pacifist ideology coupled with the general lack of critical attitudes strengthens the conclusion that the support of the nonviolent types for nonviolence in the civil rights movement reflected relative conservatism.

Southern Moderates and Northern Radicals

At the outset of the paper we suggested that radicalism is a function of relative deprivation, i.e., the gap between expectation and reality, and that relative deprivation is increased by status discrepancy situations where some high statuses arouse high expectations which are blocked by a low component of status. We are now ready to look at the social background and socio-economic status of our three types to determine whether these factors were operating.

The most striking fact about our respondents is the association between the region in which the individual lived and his ideological type. All seven of the moderates were members of Southern chapters and all seven were born and brought up in the South. Only one of these persons had ever visited outside the South. Among the seven radicals, by contrast, five were from Northern chapters and two of these were also raised in the North. The nonviolent types fall between with three Southern and four Northern chapter members.

The gap between official policy and social reality with regard to race is infinitely greater in the North than in the South. Official philosophy and popular belief both have it that the North is the land of equality. The phrase "regardless of race, creed, or color" is officially stamped on every major Northern institution, while being widely ignored in actual practice. The North, then, raises the highest possible expectations of equality among Negroes, while failing to a very large extent to deliver on this promise. Particularly is this true among Northern Negroes from middle-class homes who are frequently shielded from the worst realities of discrimination during their formative years and consequently enter upon adult life with a very high level of expectation. Southern barriers to mobility, although objectively much greater, create less sense of deprivation and frustration because they are "out in the open" and officially recognized and consistent. They are taken into account from the beginning. This factor was well illustrated in the following account of a Southern born respondent who came North after finishing college in order to take advantage of greater employment opportunities.

In the South there was the feeling that nothing could be done. There were some jobs you knew you couldn't apply for — you'd just get kicked out of the office — no hopes there while the attitude is this way. I will admit that I hated the implications of the thing at the time but there was nothing you could do about it. We felt you could go North to improve things. That was my own reason — that I thought employment opportunity here would be held in fair play — in which I was deceived and this was a main reason for joining the civil rights group. I was out here one summer while I was still in school — looking around. At that time, they all said they couldn't do anything for me because I didn't have my degree — but when I came out here after finishing school the story had changed. I went to a private employment agency and was told to come back — and I would come back. I always did dress properly . . . and I was shaved and combed and neat. And I saw white men who come in there with their collars open and seen them sent out to jobs that were advertised for management trainees — I've even seen the people there send these guys home for a tie — but they would tell me to come back all the time. At another agency they took me in the back room and sort of patted me on the shoulder and said they didn't care if I was green or gray or black but the companies keep them in business, so they couldn't go against their wishes. I felt worse about this discrimination than about what was so obvious in the South — open segregation in employment because there you knew for a fact it exists.

In terms of the concept of relative deprivation, this respondent clearly shifted his reference group from Negroes to whites upon coming North, thus increasing his level of expectation far in excess of the objective increase in employment opportunity.

The typical Southern Negro respondent lived in comparative isolation from whites. The contacts he had involved great social distance maintained by sharply defined roles characterized by impersonality or by superiority and subordination. The Northern Negro, on the other hand, came in constant contact with whites. These contacts were often highly ambiguous. There was no clear structuring in terms of subordination. Many of them were of a primary or semi-primary group kind. The high status, Northern Negro had constantly to test his white associates for prejudice and had frequently to take chances on whites and suffer disappointment. On the job or at school, for example, he might have congenial personal relations with white associates to the point of joining them for lunch and coffee breaks but find himself excluded from dinners and parties shared by others in the group. Again, he might attend parties and socialize with white women who would chat with him or dance with him but who would refuse to date him. He might be on good terms with a boss who had decided that it would be unwise to promote him.

These experiences, because they were daily and inescapable and because they reached into the individual's deepest feelings and most intimate relationships, created a peculiar type of bitterness and frustration.

One other difference between the two regions must be taken into account here. It may be safe to assume that, given the same initial psychological make-up an increase in repression and frustration will increase expressed hostility toward the society. There is evidence, however, that persons raised under repressive conditions may develop a psychological incapacity to express or even to consciously experience hostility.

Karon has gathered evidence to show that the Southern environment tends to develop a Negro personality which is well equipped to "swallow" frustration and ill equipped to fight frustration openly, whether on the level of individual rebellion or political action — of direct aggression or ideological rebellion. After giving several groups of Southern and Northern Negroes and Northern whites a psychoanalytic projective test designed to test ability to deal with aggression, Karon concludes that Southern Negroes have a much greater tendency than Northern Negroes to "deny" aggressive situations, i.e., to fail to perceive aggression when it occurs, and much less capacity to express counter-aggression on any level. The Northern Negro personality resembled the northern white personality quite closely on these characteristics and differed sharply from the passivity characteristic of the Southern Negro.[7]

If we look at the deviant cases of the two Southern radicals, we see that they were strikingly different from the other respondents. Both of them were extremely light-skinned, one being light enough to pass easily.[8] It is no accident that our two Southern Negro radicals were exceptionally light. Skin color has a strong bearing on self-confidence and constitutes a high status characteristic which conflicts sharply with other low status characteristics typical of the Southern Negro's position. The lightest of these two respondents related that he always enjoyed fooling whites by passing for white and entering places which excluded Negroes. Once, while travelling on a train, he became obviously friendly with a white girl and spent the day sitting with his arm around her winking at Negro employees who spotted him as Negro and enjoyed sharing the joke with him. The other respondent reported that he and his whole family knew themselves to be closely related to the leading former slave-owning white family in his home town.

My great-grandfather was a white plantation owner. Grandfather used to tell me how he deserted my mother. My grandfather was a carpenter — he founded a town in Louisiana which is named after him. . . . Miscegenation brought about changes all over the world. Pinchback in Louisiana was a mulatto; Beethoven and Dodds in France were mulattos. . . .

These two radical Southerners also had exceptionally high status fathers. One was the son of an independent contractor and had himself become partner in the family business. The other was the son of a skilled worker and was himself a student with the aspiration of becoming a psychiatrist. All but one of the other Southern respondents were children of unskilled workers or farmers.

Frequently associated with region of origin and residence, but an additional and independent factor, is socio-economic and educational status. The child first forms his views of his own status by learning what status his family is accorded in the community. Parental status is especially important to us since many of our respondents were students who had not yet attained firm positions of their own. As expected, we find that the moderate types came predominantly from low status families. Five were children of unskilled workers or farmers. Only two had fathers in the categories of skilled worker, white collar, proprietor, or professional. The radicals again represent the opposite extreme with six of the seven fathers in the above listed high status occupations. The nonviolent types are intermediate with four low status and three high status fathers. Fathers of moderates had 7.3 mean years of education; fathers of nonviolent types had 9.6; and fathers of radicals, 10.3 mean years of education.

Despite the fact that 10 of our 21 respondents were still in process of getting their education, it is likely that the amount of education attained at the time of the interviews influenced self-image and self-confidence. A doctoral candidate will have higher expectations of equal treatment than a college sophomore, even if that sophomore expects to go on to a doctoral degree. The differences in average education of respondents again shows the association of high status with radicalism. Moderates had 12.4 mean years of education; nonviolent types had 12.8; and radicals show the astonishingly high mean of 16.3 years.

A word of caution is in order here. To say that the most politically militant people were drawn from this group is not to say that middle-class Negroes in general are radical. The bulk of the black bourgeoisie is, as Frazier has pointed out, apolitical and overconformist.[9] Militancy is an alternative reaction which is characteristic of only a small minority. It is beyond the scope of this paper to discuss the factors which determine such a reaction.[10] Important here is that it was predominantly this type of relatively acculturated, high status Negro who became an ideological radical during the early years of the direct-action movement.

Another factor, associated with those just discussed, but worthy of separate consideration, is exposure to radical ideas. The emotional strains created by relative deprivation were not directly translated into ideological radicalism, even by members of direct-action groups. There also had to be access to analyses of society which justified a very negative position vis-à-vis "America" and which legitimated great militancy with regard to the tactics of the movement.

Most of our respondents had previously belonged to the NAACP and other integration groups more moderate that CORE. None of the moderates had ever participated in any group to the left of NAACP. Among the nonviolent types, two had belonged to Democratic party groups. These are moderate relative to the range of opinion under discussion, but they may indicate a certain amount of stimulation along political lines and some increased contact with radical ideas. One nonviolent respondent had previously belonged to SNCC — a group similar to and slightly more militant than CORE.

Among the radicals the picture changes quite drastically. Five of the seven radicals belonged to groups of a similar or greater radicalism than CORE. Included were: The Independent Progressive Party, the Socialist Party, Turn Toward Peace, The Southern Educational Fund, Young People's Socialist League, The Jack London Club (left-wing Marxist) and the Du Bois Club. All of these respondents had absorbed Marxist, pacifist, and other radical ideologies to varying degrees.

Table 3 summarizes the various characteristics which have been found to be associated with radicalism.

To give the reader a more intimate picture of how these factors interacted in particular cases to produce radicals and moderates, we shall give two case histories of a "typical" Northern radical and a "typical" Southern moderate.

Table 3: Summary of Characteristics Associated with Ideological Types

	Moderate	Nonviolent	Radical
Region of Residence:			
South	7	3	2
North	0	4	5
Father's Occupation:			
Unskilled worker, farmer	5	3	1
Skilled worker, white collar, proprietor, professional	2	4	6
Father's Mean Education (in years)	7.3	9.6	10.3
Respondent's Mean Education (in years)	12.4	12.8	16.3
Number with previous membership in radical organizations	0	1	5

George: A Radical Northern Negro

George was an exceptionally handsome young man of twenty-five whose cynicism was softened by a personally warm, charming manner. He was obviously very bright, though given to disconcerting little lapses of attention during which he seemed to withdraw suddenly and completely into some inner reverie. He described his family as "middle class and light skinned, the typical 'Black Bourgeois' pictured in Frazier's book." The family laid great stress on their light complexion and objected to his dating girls much darker than himself. "Looking back on our attitudes," said George, "I'd say we were trying very hard to be white though not admitting it."

Born and raised in a large Northern city, he attended a predominantly white high school and college. He was fairly well accepted by his white associates on the basis of "not being like those other Negroes." He described the typical whites with whom he came in contact during these years as:

People who say things like 'some of my best friends are Negroes,' and talk about how terrible the South is — and then they tell me how I'm different than all those other Negroes. The more liberal part of them will say, 'of course we wouldn't mind having a Negro neighbor — but he should be chosen very carefully.' They mean they wouldn't mind living next to Ralph Bunche. The conservative type would mind, but only because of the threat to property values. . . .

After earning his master's degree, George spent a year in Europe. Here it became clear to him just how dissatisfied and uncomfortable he had always felt at home and he thought seriously of becoming an expatriate and escaping the race problem forever by settling in Europe. But he returned instead to the States and enrolled as a graduate student in a large Northern university. Here he ran into two former white acquaintances from his old college and became friendly with them. These two friends had become quite radical and were members of a Marxist study group and of CORE and SNCC. Through them, George got his first exposure to political ideas and activities. Up to this time he had been very apolitical.

It's hard for me to reconstruct my previous feelings now. Of course, I had opinions on civil rights — I was in favor of it, but I had no idea of doing something — not even the NAACP. Joining anything was kind of repugnant to me — like it was a public admission that I was a Negro. After I got into this political circle here through H and J I began to make a conscious effort to get out of this standard black bourgeois feeling that if I don't do anything about civil rights and don't join anything, maybe nobody will think I'm a Negro — you know, like maybe they'll think I'm white — so I'll just disassociate myself from the people in the Ghetto.

Eventually George joined CORE and SNCC while continuing his close association with members of the Marxist study group. It is important to note that at the same time that these associations increased the respondent's ability and willingness to formulate radical opinions, they also functioned to decrease his general sense of alienation from the country and his frustrations about his own identity. He reported that:

About the time I joined CORE the idea of being a Negro began to be more acceptable to me. It's hard to say which came first, the involvement in politics or the change in feeling. I suppose I got involved partly because I wanted to change my feelings.

Heretofore, he had never felt completely comfortable about his relationship to any whites. His attitude toward the white world was deeply ambivalent; he admired it and wished to emulate it; he saw himself by virtue of education and social position inevitably immersed in it; yet, he felt an underlying bitterness because of the impossibility of finding genuine acceptance of his total identity — including his inescapable identity as a Negro. Now he discovered a group of whites who met him on an entirely different level.

When I first picketed with CORE it gave me the feeling that I could do something — and also that I was being a Negro and acting like it — not being ashamed of it. At the same time I felt I was being part of a movement of doing things that were strongly approved of by people whose opinion was important to me. I felt that I could do this with the group and simultaneously feel accepted and like my acceptance was not based on the fact that 'you're different, you're not the same as all those other Negroes' — I didn't have to be somebody's 'best friend' — the exception everybody approved of — which meant being white, really. . . . Looking back I realize that I was in this position with my white friends at school and college all the time. I was always winning approval and respect from them based on how little Negro I was. The people I met here — they were committed to civil rights struggle — it was evident that it was possible to identify with the Negroes in the slums and in the South and still feel that I hadn't lost the respect of these people.

Having found whites who were solidly on his side relieved his ambivalence and frustration and, on the other hand, increased and clarified his dislike and opposition toward the "wishy-washy liberals" with whom he was previously in contact. Of these, he said:

They refuse to get committed. They believe in having an open mind — which means a vacant mind — they talk about extremists of the left. They are for integration but opposed to the 'haste that creates deep scars.'

Ambivalence and alienation toward the country as a whole had been transformed by participation in the movement into a feeling of involvement on the one
hand, but a clear demand for rapid change "or else" on the other.

When I went to Europe I thought in terms of running away from the whole
problem — moving to another country. But since I joined CORE, that's one thing
it has done for me, I feel much more like I am part of the country and I feel more
like staying here and working on the issue. I find some of my identity in being part
of the movement. It's an identity with the masses and with myself as a Negro and
having some reason to be proud of that fact. It's the general atmosphere of people
being committed to revolution — like the American Revolution — it has heroic
overtones of manly virtues and bravery.

Being now part of the nation he was prepared to berate it strongly for its
shortcomings. He saw American society as "in fact an Anglo-Saxon culture and
not this fictitious melting pot people talk about." It has always demanded complete
conformity as the price of admission. Of the Negro it demands that he become as
white as possible. From an economic and political viewpoint there is more wrong
with the country than just segregation. Before the race problem can be solved, the
respondent felt, there will have to be economic planning, public works programs
and much greater commitment to welfare. A minimum standard of living and the
right to work will have to be guaranteed to everyone. The country would have to
decide to spend more on its citizens and less on war, missiles and space racing. To
accomplish this, George saw the need for a drastic political realignment:

. . . any solutions to the problem would now be politically unrealizable with the
present power distribution — not to be Marxist about it, but I think power will have
to be shifted to the working class and to Negroes — to the people being hurt by
the situation. . . .

The respondent's position vis-à-vis the Black Muslims was complex and reveal-
ing. He berated them from a radical viewpoint as being really bourgeois: "Their
greatest wish is for a chain of Howard Johnson's from coast to coast — only all
black." He felt that Black Nationalism gave a lot of Negroes he knew an excuse
for doing nothing concrete while talking a lot about how radical they were. On the
other hand, he found obvious satisfaction in the militancy and outspokenness of
the Muslims while being unable to accept their unqualified racism:

It is a relief to hear the Muslims speak out. Like when they say, 'I'm going to look
the white man in the eye and call him a liar every time he opens his mouth.' All
of which is true — everything they say about whites except for their racist insistence
that all whites are inherently evil.

With regard to nonviolence, he said:

I'm not interested in it. I suppose it is generally the best tactic because 90% of the country is white. But to me nonviolence isn't a panacea. I don't know whether it can work in the deep South where the forces of law are lawbreakers themselves. There I think you have to have a right of self-defense.

Although he admitted to a natural middle class abhorrence of becoming involved in violence personally, the respondent freely expressed vicarious satisfaction with Negro violence elsewhere.

Maybe it's pointless, but there was a feeling of release when that Muslim in Mississippi killed the gas owner. This has a real appeal that, damnit, we're going to pay it back — I remember the description of the scene — how the guy turned a hose on him and he calmly went to his car and got out a gun and very calmly shot the guy — just emptied the gun into him and the guy dragged himself into the gas station and the Negro went back to the car and reloaded the gun and emptied it into the guy again and then drove away. . . . I tie up racial pride with things like rebellions in Angola and thinking abut raising money for the invasion of South Africa — I wish the U.S. Government would train African troops for the invasion of the South — the way some Southern newspapers claim.

A Moderate Southern Negro

Our Moderate respondent was a twenty-seven year old widow with four young children. Her husband was a small retailer and left her a little money on which she had been supporting her family. Her health was very poor and she required much medical attention. This had made it impossible for her to earn an income of her own. Sarah was raised on a farm by her grandparents, neither of whom had more than a third-grade education. Their greatest claim to status was that the grandmother was a licensed mid-wife. The respondent herself finished high school.

The respondent moved in a solidly Negro world. She had no white friends and has only passing acquaintances with whites at CORE conventions. Few whites belonged to her local CORE chapter. She knew none of them well and seemed uninterested and unconcerned about them.

Sarah thoroughly approved of nonviolence as a tactic for the movement. Significantly enough she misunderstood the question, "Will there be violence on the part of integrationists in future years?" to mean "Will there be more violence against integrationists?" When I clarified that I meant violence from CORE members, she said, "No, never!" This inability to imagine any other tactic stemmed partly from the self-evident validity which the nonviolent course of action had for her; and, even more, from that general inability to speculate beyond present realities which is typical of minimally educated persons who have never been exposed to such intellectual exercises.

In recounting her direct action experiences, Sarah gave vent to a good deal of undisguised hostility. But nonviolence seemed to be an adequate vehicle for its expression because her conception of nonviolence was rudimentary enough to keep her from seeing any contradictions between her hostility and the tactic, and because her hostility was of a type most easily expressed through "passivity with a slight bite." Of nonviolence she said:

I think you can't fight it. If you don't hit back and you don't talk back, well then they're just gonna stand around looking stupid — they can't do nothin'. One time we had some hoodlums come up ready to attack us. Well we didn't say anything — we just referred them to our spokesman. Well, that was really a ghastly lookin' thing. They was just standin' around not knowing what to do.

She remembered some direct action victories with rather vengeful satisfaction.

When we opened the theatres we worked on it a long time. There was this ticket lady there — she said she'd rather die than sell us tickets. So one night she had to sell us nine tickets and you should have seen her face. I got the biggest kick out of seeing her red face. She told me earlier I could have gotten in by myself if I wasn't with those other people (she is quite light-skinned) and I said we were together and we were all going in together — and in the end we did and she had to sell us the tickets.

Although this respondent was optimistic about the movement's chances of attaining most of its goals, she felt that whites and Negroes would probably never socialize or intermarry and accepted this as natural.

I think they (whites and Negroes) will put on an act, they aren't really going to accept each other — just like the Jews and Italians — they get mad if their children want to marry somebody different.

Sarah had high hopes that the movement would open better job opportunities for herself and her children. Indeed, worry about her children's future was one of her main reasons for participating in CORE. But her level of aspiration for both herself and her children was relatively modest, and she certainly did not feel presently deprived because of overqualification relative to the possibilities which were then open or would probably be open in the near future.

There's great improvement to be had in the employment field and I know that it's gonna affect my children. If they don't all get to college — well they could come out of high school and get a job typing any place — like white girls — a clean job, like sales lady. I wouldn't mind my daughter being a sales lady. That's not a bad job and you can work up in it — even if she hadn't been to college, she could work up to be a buyer. . . . CORE's been talking about getting the phone company as next phase. I'm very interested in that because I'd like a job as an operator myself. I'm a physical wreck and I've got to get a sitting down job. They have on-the-job training with pay; it's a good deal.

With respect to the overall problem of integration, she saw Negroes as having to take further steps into the middle-class world before they would be wholly accepted. She predicted that integration would help Negroes become more "cultured." Among other things, it should improve Negro speech.

. . . they'll be exposed to better speech and it'll rub off — won't be so many 'aints' and 'caints' — like what rubbed off on us.

She is willing to allow for the fact that whites will need time to "get used to seeing colored kids in the schools — and seeing us around everywhere."

But while she did not resent the need for such adjustments, neither was she willing to tarry while they were made. She was determined to enroll her own children in white schools as quickly as possible.

During the interview Sarah made no critical remarks about American culture, the Federal Government, the economic system, white culture, etc. Probing failed to elicit from her any desire for social changes other than those having to do strictly with the race problem. On the subject of pacifism, her views may be described as "ordinary patriotic."

Pacifism doesn't make sense to me. I mean, you could never fight a war that way. There's too much territory involved. And I mean the Communists, they say they're against violence, but they really use it. It's not even common sense. I mean if a war started, they're going to start by dropping a bomb — so what's that except violence?

Conclusion

The great majority of Negro members of CORE were either middle class or in process of transition from working-class backgrounds to middle-class status. We have seen that, within this group, it was the Northern, higher status Negroes who were most inclined toward a radical rejection of nonviolence. We have suggested that the pattern of status discrepancy characterized by low racial and high socio-economic status produced a high level of relative deprivation which, when combined with access to radical ideas, almost inevitably led to ideological radicalism.

In view of the recent outbreaks of violent insurrection in ghettos, a word must be said about the relationship between this lower-class violence and the type of radicalism found among high status Northern Negroes in CORE. The relationship is by no means as clear-cut as is maintained either by those who blame Negro radicals for fomenting and organizing riots, or by those who claim that the riots are strictly lower-class and have no connection with political organizations or ideologies.

The type of radicalism discussed in this article is exclusively verbal. None of the respondents reported committing or planning any acts of violence. The impression was rather that they would be extremely unlikely ever to engage in such behavior. Typical was the response of one young graduate student who strongly defended the Negro's right to strike back if attacked on a picket line. When asked whether he thought that he, himself, would respond to an attack by hitting back, he grinned at his own inconsistency and said, "No, I guess I probably wouldn't. I'm too middle class."

Middle-class persons have too much to lose in engaging in such behavior. More importantly, they are not practiced in violence and their whole upbringing has created strong inhibitions against it. Underlying the rejections of nonviolence expressed in the interviews was an unexpressed but pervasive distinction between the criminal and the political. The high status radical was engaging in the intellectual pursuit of ideology-building, and the acts of violence he envisioned were political acts, devoid of criminal connotations. In the actual urban insurrection, gang-fighting behavior, looting, drinking and other non-political activities are inextricably tied to acts of political insurrection. This is not a setting in which one can easily imagine our radicals participating.[11]

Yet educated Negro radicals have recently taken outspoken stands in defense of ghetto insurrections. At its 1966 convention, CORE drastically revised its official position on nonviolence and asserted the natural right of self-defense. This change was aimed mainly at legitimizing self-defense organizations in Southern communities and the right of demonstrators to defend themselves when attacked. By the summer of 1967, however, CORE's executive director, Floyd McKissick, was implying approval of the Detroit insurrection by stating that the old-style civil rights tactics were out of date and that the insurrection heralded a new era in the Negro revolution. Radical Negro leaders in other organizations were even more outspoken in their support of the insurrectionists. Indeed, the impression is inescapable that some leaders have tried to put themselves in the forefront of developments which, in fact, they neither organized nor controlled.

The crucial connection between these leaders and the lower-class insurrectionists is not organizational but ideological. The radicals have provided the unemployed youth of the ghetto with an ideology which legitimates and glorifies violent struggle. Ideology has raised the level of expectation in the ghetto and increased the sense of frustration. It has helped to develop racial consciousness and unity. In many instances, groups which are basically fighting gangs have begun to absorb a combination of Black Nationalism and left-wing political radicalism. Such groups are in a process of transition from non-ideological asocial gangs to politically conscious, revolutionary groups.

It is beyond the scope of this paper to assess the extent to which radical ideology has increased the tendency toward violent outbreaks. The effect may not be linear. Political organization and ideological sophistication are, in part, middle-class characteristics which conflict with lower-class patterns of spontaneous violence. It may be that at some point such influences begin to mitigate the potential for violence among lower-class youth. We can do no more here than to suggest the general nature of the connection.

Notes

[1] Crane Brinton, *The Anatomy of a Revolution,* New York: Vintage-Random House, 1952, p. 279.

[2] Gerhard E. Lenski, "Status Crystallization," *American Sociological Review,* 19 (August, 1954), pp. 405–413; and "Social Participation and Status Crystallization," *American Sociological Review,* 21 (August, 1956), pp. 458–464.

[3] Irwin W. Goffman, "Status Consistency and Preference for Change in Power Distribution," *American Sociological Review,* 22 (June, 1957), pp. 275–281.

[4] The other two were the Student Nonviolent Coordinating Committee and Martin Luther King's Southern Christian Leadership Conference.

[5] This distribution indicates a less consistent commitment to nonviolence than might be inferred from journalistic accounts of the movement or from the literature put out by CORE and similar organizations during these years.

[6] *Conservatism* is here defined as (a) a tendency to accept prevailing values of the dominant white culture, particularly the double standard by which violence by Negroes is condemned while similar instances of violence by whites is at least partially condoned; and (b) the general approval of violence in the defense of national interest, together with the conviction that all Americans have a duty to take part in such wars. *Radicalism* is defined as the tendency to reject both of these judgments. In this case, the values substituted are those of black nationalism which denies that the Negro owes loyalty to the country, and those of the old and new left which identifies with socialist and anti-colonialist movements and sees the United States as a dangerous imperialist power. Persons tending toward the latter view often implicitly sanctioned the use of force by leftist and anti-colonialist movements. However, at the time of this study, they seldom did so openly, and their sympathy with conventionally defined "enemies" took the form of opposing American militarism and refusing to serve in the armed forces.

[7] Bertram P. Karon, *The Negro Personality,* New York: Springer, 1958.

[8] Among the Negroes classed as moderate or nonviolent, only one was similarly light-skinned and this was a respondent raised in a rural Southern background and having low education and low occupational status and aspirations, so that in this case the effect of light skin was cancelled out by other factors.

[9] E. Franklin Frazier, *Black Bourgeoisie,* New York: The Free Press of Glencoe, 1957.

[10] Social background data on 88 Negro CORE members on whom interview or question-

naire data are available, indicate that most of them fell into one of two types: first, those from high status, usually professional, homes who had themselves moved from Negro middle-class circles into predominantly white, liberal or left-wing intellectual circles; and second, those who had moved into middle-class jobs from unskilled workingclass or farm families. Comments in the interviews suggest that the latter type, who were also predominantly dark-skinned, were not completely accepted in Negro middle-class circles because of their family background and racial characteristics. Thus, it may be that the "middle-class" Negroes who joined CORE were really either "post-bourgeois" in the sense of having moved out of bourgeois into intellectual circles, or "pre-bourgeois" in the sense of not having attained full social acceptance within the Negro middle class.

[11] It is perhaps conceivable that educated radicals might, under extreme circumstances, engage in some highly organized form of self-defense or even terrorism.

The Disintegration of the Negro Non-violent Movement

Donald von Eschen
Jerome Kirk
Maurice Pinard

Introduction

A major problem in the theory of non-violence is to determine its empirical limits both in terms of when an oppressed group will be willing to use it and when it will be effective. In this paper we probe these limits by asking why blacks in the U.S., after adopting non-violent tactics in 1960, abandoned them only 6 years later, in spite of the fact that such tactics had brought significant gains. That such gains had occurred is undeniable. The non-violent boycotts, picketing, 'sit-ins,' 'wade-ins,' marches, and the like *opened public facilities* that had long been closed to blacks, often through the passage of public accommodations laws, and compelled the federal government to *enforce voting rights* in the Deep South.[1] That non-violence was abandoned, however, is equally clear. In spite of its successes, by 1966 the non-violent movement began to dissolve. CORE leaders began to speak of the right of self-defense; SNCC leaders glorified as rebellions the riots that had started in 1964. Within a few years the remaining non-violent leaders found themselves largely without followers.[2] What accounts for this? Why should a movement, once so successful, so quickly have dissolved? By answering this question, we should gain considerable insight into the limits on non-violent action.

Our approach shall be as follows. We shall argue that once one understands the *circumstances* under which the non-violent movement succeeded, one can then understand at least part of the reason for its subsequent dissolution. By circumstances, we mean here such things as the movement's size, its social composition, the problems and dynamics of recruitment, its methods, and the responses of friends and opponents. Thus, in the next section of the paper, we shall develop a theory,

Donald von Eschen, Jerome Kirk, and Maurice Pinard, "The Disintegration of the Negro Non-violent Movement," *Journal of Peace Research,* Issue No. 3, 1969, pp. 216–34. Reprinted by permission of the publisher and authors.

based on data, about how (i.e., the circumstances under which) the movement succeeded; then in section 3, we shall use this theory to explain, at least *in part*,[3] why the movement dissolved.

Our theory about how it succeeded will be based primarily on three empirical studies: (1) A study we carried out of the Maryland movement from 1961–64, based on interviews and questionnaires from demonstrators, participant observation within the movement, and documents.[4] (2) A study of the movement in Nashville, Tennessee, during these same dates, carried out by Lyle Yorks in which he reconstructed the history of that movement by interviewing all available participants, including those *against* whom the movement was aimed.[5] (3) An interview study by Killian and Grigg of bi-racial committees in Florida.[6] In addition, we shall use whatever other information can be gleaned from journalistic reports, unsystematically gathered accounts by participants and leaders, documents, and the like.

How Then Did the Movement Succeed?

The Movement Did Not
Depend for Success on Large Numbers

A common image of the movement is that it overcame its opponents largely through the sheer weight of its numbers. This image is suggested by: (1) Newspaper reports and publications of civil rights organizations which describe massive demonstrations — for instance, CORE, in its July, 1963, CORE-LATOR, reported that 'from 2 to 4,000 students marched daily into . . . [Greensboro, N.C.] joined by hundreds of adults.'[7] (2) Counts of the number of people who have participated in the movement made by survey organizations — in polls, for instance, up to 8% of the eligible Negro population claimed that they had participated in the sit-ins,[8] a figure rising to 15% for Negro students in southern schools[9] — and by such organizations as the Southern Regional Conference, which reported that about 70,000 Negroes and whites had demonstrated in over 100 communities in the first year and a half of the movement.[10]

Nevertheless, evidence indicates that this image is false, that data of this sort are highly misleading.

Participation was low   In both the Maryland and Nashville studies, where data consisted, instead, of interviews, questionnaires, and/or participant observation, the finding was one of *low* participation. From a vantage point *inside* the movement, the most *frequent* experience was one of great difficulty in assembling enough people to carry out a demonstration of any significant size. Almost always the number of demonstrators fell far short of the numbers hoped for. This was true in spite of the fact that newspaper accounts or survey data, etc., would have given a contrary impression.

The reports of large demonstrations carried in the newspapers and elsewhere were misleading for three reasons:

1. Such demonstrations were *atypical.* It is true that, on occasion, the movement was able to get hundreds of people out on the streets. So, for example, some 800 Negro college students in Maryland demonstrated in a massive assault against a segregated movie theater near their campus, and in Nashville hundreds demonstrated in similar actions against theaters there. But although such demonstrations established an image of widespread participation, they were not representative. Most demonstrations were small. Usually, a few days after a large demonstration it was impossible to put together one of any noticeable size whatsoever.

2. Demonstrations were large often only because they involved considerable numbers of *outsiders.* Thus, in one of the biggest demonstrations, the Route 40 Freedom Ride, a majority of participants were from out of state. This concentration in one place of demonstrators from a wide geographic area made the movement seem larger than it in fact was. Its actually smaller size was revealed by the fact that only rarely could it stage newsworthy demonstrations in more than one or two localities simultaneously. Thus, in Maryland, a CORE official explained to reporters that demonstrations had been unusually small that weekend because a demonstration was going on in New York at the same time.

3. As we shall explain in more detail later, many non-members (i.e. *bystanders,* friendly or hostile) were mistakenly enumerated by the press and TV as participants, thus exaggerating the movement's actual size.

Similarly, survey data would have greatly exaggerated participation. It is probable, for instance, that over a third of the student body of the Negro college in Maryland mentioned above participated in the theater demonstrations. A survey would thus have revealed high participation. Yet these figures would have been misleading. What counts in a sustained drive for social change is not the number of people who have participated at one time or another, but the number who can be assembled for particular demonstrations. These were not the same. Firstly, participation tended to be *sporadic;* and secondly, the *turnover* in participation was high, each demonstration seeing both many new participants and the 'drop out' of many old ones. As a result, in no more than a few demonstrations were there more than a dozen or two students from that Negro college.

In short, in spite of widespread impression to the contrary, participation in Maryland and Nashville was low.

Can we generalize these findings of low participation to the movement elsewhere? This seems likely for several reasons:

1. In terms of importance, as measured by media coverage and the like, the Maryland and Nashville movements were among the major ones in the U.S. during this period. Participation in them, then, should have been as great as in *most* other instances.[11]

2. The data used to support the idea of massive participation elsewhere we now know to be suspect. With respect to reports of large demonstrations, such demonstrations may have been atypical; outsiders were clearly involved in some of the most important of them (in Selma, for instance); and bystanders were clearly mistaken at times for participants, as we shall indicate shortly. Similarly, with respect to counts, if participation was as *sporadic* as it was in Maryland and if *turnover* was as high, the impact of the numbers reported would be severely diluted.[12]

3. Random accounts of participants also suggest low participation. Organizers in the South have, at times, complained about the difficulty of mobilizing Negroes. Furthermore, SNCC organizers have claimed that the large demonstrations led by Martin Luther King in the South were *sporadic*, lasting only the length of his stay.[13]

4. The recruitment processes which led in Maryland to low participation almost certainly were at work elsewhere.

Participation was low because it required socially contradictory characteristics This was shown by questionnaire data collected from Maryland demonstrators.[14] These indicated that *active* participation required, first of all, sufficient deprivation so that the person would have a strong reason to be active in the movement. At the same time, it required characteristics particularly rare among highly deprived people: a sense of political efficacy so that participation might appear worthwhile, *or* organizational involvement so one might be dragged through one's social connections into activity. In short, it required characteristics that, in the real world, are rarely found in the same persons. This limited participation in two ways: (1) It *limited the numbers* available to the movement. Because the most deprived are the least likely to possess a sense of efficacy or high organizational involvement, the movement was by and large denied access to them. (2) It meant that *participation was sporadic*. Because the movement was forced to recruit from among the less deprived, those with less reason to participate, participation was inconstant.

Evidence and argument for these propositions has been presented in detail elsewhere.[15] The essence of the data, however, is this:

1. *Deprivation is necessary for high participation.* This is shown in Table 1, where it can be seen that, *among* the demonstrators, activity in the movement (measured by how often a person went out on demonstrations) was highest among those of lower social status and of downward social mobility. The same was true for those dissatisfied with their jobs, those whose job aspirations greatly exceeded their expectations, etc. On the other hand, the less deprived showed a lower rate of participation.

Table 1: The Most Deprived Were the Most Active Participants
(% More Active*)

	Negroes %	N	Whites %	N	Both %	N
Socio-economic status** (all R's)						
High	32	(28)	49	(76)	44	(104)
Medium	44	(63)	59	(108)	54	(171)
Low	67	(27)	83	(18)	73	(45)
Social mobility*** (non-students only)						
Upward	42	(12)	61	(23)	54	(35)
Stable	46	(11)	67	(12)	56	(23)
Downward	100	(2)	80	(15)	82	(17)

* % who reported to have been out on demonstrations 3 times or more, in answer to the question: 'How many times have you been out on demonstrations before today?'
** Socio-economic status: determined by North and Hatt scores for occupations given in response to the question: 'What job are you training for in school?' (students), or 'What is your job?' (non-students). A high status corresponds to a score of 85 or above; a low status, to a score of 71 or below. (Notice that many low status participants had at most a lower-middle class occupational level, i.e. below, approximately, the status of an undertaker, a grade school teacher, or a reporter.)
*** Social mobility: comparison, for non-students, of their socio-economic scores with that of their fathers ('What is your father's main occupation?'). The scores were broken into four classes (less than 72; 72–74; 75–84; 85 or more) and differential positions in these four classes were taken to measure social mobility.

2. *Participation requires characteristics rare among the highly deprived.* Although the most deprived were the most active, the movement was made up predominantly of the less deprived. Thus, virtually all the students involved were training for high-status professional and managerial occupations; while of the older, non-student demonstrators, 81% of the whites and 60% of the Negroes already occupied such positions. Similarly, Table 2 shows that the demonstrators came from the higher reaches of the class system.

Table 2: Participants over 25 Years Old Had a Much Higher Educational Level Than Did the Population of Maryland As a Whole

Education	White Freedom Riders	White Maryland Population	Negro Freedom Riders	Negro Maryland Population
College graduates	74%	10%	47%	4%
Some college	22	9	34	4
High school graduates	4	24	6	12
Some high school	0	19	9	20
Grade school or less	0	38	4	61
	100%	100%	100%	101%
	(N = 55)		(N = 47)	

* Maryland figures from 1960 census.

How may we explain this paradox? Analytically, the answer lies in Tables 3 and 4 which show that, although the most deprived were the most active *once they were in the movement,* they were among the last to join. Thus, although deprivation was necessary for intense activity, it inhibited joining.

Table 3: The Most Deprived, in Terms of Socio-Economic Status,
Were Among the Latest Recruits
(% Early Joiners*)

Socio-economic Status:**	High		Medium		Low	
	%	N	%	N	%	N
Total sample	27	(97)	36	(161)	27	(45)
Negro non-students	43	(7)	44	(18)	18	(17)
Negro students	35	(20)	40	(42)	30	(10)
White non-students	40	(5)	42	(40)	33	(18)
White students	22	(65)	26	(61)	—	(0)

* % who first participated prior to 1961.
** Socio-economic status: as in Table 1.

Table 4: The Most Deprived, in Terms of Social Mobility, Were Among
the Latest Recruits
(% Early Joiners*)

	Negroes		White		Both	
	%	N	%	N	%	N
Social mobility** (non-students only)						
Upward	25	(12)	41	(22)	35	(34)
Stable	50	(10)	33	(12)	41	(22)
Downward	0	(2)	29	(14)	25	(16)

* As in Table 3.
** Social mobility: as in Table 1.

But why were the most highly deprived late joiners? We suggest it is because other attributes are necessary for participation besides deprivations. Two major ones are these: (1) A *belief in the efficacy of political action.* People are not likely to join a movement if they do not believe it will be effective.[16] This is indicated in Tables 5 and 6. Table 5 indicates that those highly pessimistic about the chances of desegregating restaurants in Baltimore, a major goal of the movement at that time, were late joiners. Table 6 indicates that, among Negroes, a *general* lack of faith in political activity, i.e. political alienation, led to late joining (the relation was different for whites, for reasons too complicated to go into here).[17] On the other hand, if demonstrators did have faith in the possibilities of political action, they were able to join early. One such group were ideologues whose beliefs embodied a deep conviction that history was on their side. They were among the earliest joiners, as is indicated in Table 7. (2) *Organizational involvement.* Previous studies have indicated that organizations function to drag people into political activity.[18] That the sit-ins were no exception is indicated in Table 8. Not only were those involved in civil rights organizations more likely to join early, but so *also* were those involved in *other* organizations.

Thus, a sense of efficacy and organizational involvement are two additional

Table 5: Deep Pessimism Inhibits Early Joining

	Deeply Pessimistic*		Somewhat Pessimistic		Not Pessimistic	
	%	N	%	N	%	N
% active**	55	(22)	42	(84)	43	(210)
% early joiners***	10	(21)	31	(81)	33	(202)

* Deeply pessimistic are those who *strongly* disagreed with the statement: 'Baltimore restaurants will be desegregated by the middle of 1962.' Somewhat pessimistic are those who disagreed, but not strongly. Not pessimistic are those who agreed with the statement.
** As in Table 1.
*** As in Table 3.

Table 6: Politically Alienated Negroes Were Late Joiners

	Politically Alienated* (Blacks Only)		Not Politically Alienated (Blacks Only)	
	%	N	%	N
% active**	55	(31)	40	(80)
% early joiners***	17	(29)	38	(76)

* Those who agreed that 'there is really little difference between the Republican and Democratic Parties,' and did not strongly feel that 'letters are a good way for a citizen to make his voice count in public policy.' The same relations hold for the item, 'All politicians are corrupt,' when a control is made for ideology.
** As in Table 1.
*** As in Table 3.

Table 7: Ideologues Were Early Joiners

	Socialists		Non-socialists	
	%	N	%	N
% active*	76	(59)	47	(245)
% early joiners**	41	(58)	29	(237)

* As in Table 1.
** As in Table 3.

factors necessary for active participation. But we know from numerous studies, that such characteristics are particularly rare among the highly deprived.[19] Here, then, is an explanation for their late joining. Additional evidence is given in Table 9. This shows that where lower status persons *do* possess a belief in the possibilities of action — for instance, when they possess an ideology whose belief system guarantees success — they are early, rather than late, joiners. Unfortunately, due to a lack of sufficient case bases, we cannot make similar controls for either political alienation or organizational involvement. However, in a later study of recruitment to another social movement, sufficient cases did exist. When feelings of hopelessness and non-

Table 8: Those Involved in Alienating Organizations Were Early Joiners Even When the Organizations Were Not Civil Rights Organizations

Civil Rights Organizations Only

Number of Alienating Organizations into Which Respondent Reported Himself Integrated*

	≥ 2 Alienating		1 Alienating		No Organizations	
	%	N	%	N	%	N
% early joiners**	75	(4)	36	(28)	32	(165)
% more active***	100	(4)	68	(28)	49	(181)

Non-Civil Rights Organizations Only

Number of Alienating Organizations into Which Respondent Reported Himself Integrated

	≥ 2 Alienating		1 Alienating		No Organizations	
	%	N	%	N	%	N
% early joiners	71	(7)	40	(20)	32	(165)
% more active	86	(7)	65	(20)	49	(181)

* Alienating organizations are those with goals in opposition to the larger society, but with little power. For further explication, see Von Eschen, *et al.*: 'Organizations and Disorderly Politics,' cited in Note 2.
** As in Table 1.
*** As in Table 3.

Table 9: Ideology Permitted a Lower Status Person to Join Early
(% Early Joiners*)

Party Preferences	Left of Mother** (Ideologues)		Not Left of Mother (Non-ideologues)	
	%	N	%	N
Socio-economic status***				
High	29	(28)	29	(49)
Medium	38	(61)	34	(71)
Low	43	(14)	18	(22)

* As in Table 3.
** Based on a comparison of respondent's and his mother's party preference. The reason the socialist-non-socialist distinction is not used in this table is that the case base among those of low status was too small. Instead, we are using a wider measure of ideology. The purpose of the comparison of respondent's with mother's preference is to separate those who have consciously adopted their political positions from those only weakly committed to them. We did this because we found *no relation* between ideology and participation for those who inherited their politics. We used left of mother rather than father because of the absence of data on father's political preference for many participants and because in those cases where parents were split politically, most participants agreed with their mothers. As about half of those classified as 'left of mother' were socialists and most of the rest independents who were left of the Democratic and Republican parties, this group is not only 'left of mother,' but left politically as well.
*** As in Table 1.

involvement in organizations were controlled in this study, class differences in joining disappeared.[20]

3. *The consequence of these processes was low participation.* Active participation required socially contradictory characteristics: deprivation on the one hand; and a sense of efficacy on the other. Thus: (1) The numbers available to the movement for recruitment were limited. It had to draw on that relatively narrow stratum possessing *both* characteristics to some degree. This accounts for the curvilinear relations in Tables 3 and 4. The highly deprived did not possess the sense of efficacy or organizational involvement necessary to join; while the least deprived while possessing these, did not possess sufficient deprivation. The movement was, thus, denied access both to the bulk of the Negro population — working class Negroes (see Tables 2 through 4 again) — and to the Negro upper class. Its numbers were, thus, restricted. (2) Because it, therefore, had to recruit from those only moderately deprived, participation was sporadic; for the moderately deprived were less motivated to participate intensely (see Table 1 again).

Were these processes operating outside Maryland? This seems almost certain. Matthews and Prothro found in their study of Negro students in the South that joining was disproportionately low among those attending the poorer schools and coming from the least advantaged social backgrounds.[21] The same was found by Searles and Williams in their study of Negro students in Greensboro and Raleigh, N.C.[22] In addition, both sets of investigators found that joining was inversely related to *pessimism* about the probable resistance of whites.[23] Finally, Searles and Williams found that those who joined the sit-ins were more likely to have participated in *previously* established organizations,[24] i.e. had a higher level of organizational involvement. Also an examination of data on the composition of *all* movements for which such data could be gathered showed that, without exception, the most deprived were under-represented even though, for many of these movements, they would have had the most reason to participate.[25] Thus, such processes seem to be universal.

We, therefore, have further reason to think participation was low everywhere. But, if this is true, how then did the movement succeed?

The Movement Depended for Success on the Creation of Disorder

Although the movement was itself non-violent, disorder frequently followed in its wake. The intense racist sentiments of the whites led them violently to attack demonstrators; and, in response, Negro *non*-members of the movement often retaliated by rioting.

That such disorder was essential to the movement's success is clear. Except when accompanied by a boycott, demonstrations had an impact only when they generated, or at least threatened, disorder. This was clear in all three studies:

Maryland. (1) In 1960 and 1961, numerous peaceful demonstrations were carried out in Baltimore with virtually no impact. A close examination of the newspapers during this period shows practically no coverage given to these demonstrations; and, as far as can be discerned from the few accounts that do appear, the targets of the demonstrations gave them equally scant attention. What was missing was disorder. It was finally provided by the violent reaction of racists, not in Baltimore, but in Birmingham and Anniston, toward the Freedom Riders. After these events, when CORE announced a demonstration on Route 40 in Maryland, the mood communicated by the newspapers was one of hysteria. The inevitably selective attention of the media was focused on images of burning buses, uncontrollable mobs, and the like. The elites now began to respond. Restauranteurs said they would desegregate. Political elites began to pay attention to the movement. In short, only when the demonstrations appeared to threaten disorder did they get attention. (2) A similarly striking example occurred later on Maryland's Eastern Shore, where sentiments similar to those in the Deep South are prevalent. For some time demonstrations had been held in this area, yet with little effect. Subsequently, however, peaceful demonstrations led to violent racist attacks until finally some of the less sophisticated (and, therefore, difficult to organize) elements of the Negro population began to lash back violently at their opponents in Cambridge, a small Eastern Shore community. The impact was startling. Towns around Cambridge began desegregating at a rapid rate as soon as civil rights groups announced proposed demonstrations in these towns. Again, only with disorder was attention, and sometimes capitulation, given to the movement.

Nashville. The Nashville movement occurred in two major waves. In the first, demonstrations combined with a nearly complete boycott desegregated lunch counters in the downtown department stores. In the second, a drive was made to desegregate all restaurants. Here, a boycott could not be effective, as these restaurants did not depend on Negro clientele. For almost two years, a series of peaceful demonstrations failed to bring any progress whatsoever. The turning point finally came when the movement leaders hit on the idea of recruiting high school students. When these students entered the picket lines, the whole character of the demonstrations changed. These students and their friends who came to watch were unwilling to practise non-violence in the face of the attacks of white racists. Rioting ensued. The movement, nevertheless, continued to hold demonstrations, each generating more disorder than the last. Within the week, the leaders of the community had called a general meeting and persuaded restauranteurs to make a settlement.

Florida. The importance of disorder was also indicated in Killian and Grigg's investigation. In their study of a bi-racial committee, they wrote that, 'in the absence of issues raised through the application of power (in this case, the failure of Negroes to hold a wade-in at the nearby beach, an action that would have brought mob violence), the committee not only failed to act, but ceased to meet.'[26]

Why disorder was so important is not hard to determine:

Disorder mobilized friends and sanctioned opponents   Although many whites in powerful positions were favorable to Negro equality, in general they did not act strongly on these beliefs. They had other goals that consumed their time and energies, often the realization of these goals was dependent on those unsympathetic to Negro rights, etc. Thus, for example, northern liberal Senators often compromised their commitment to civil rights to gain the support of southern Senators for other pieces of liberal legislation. One function of disorder was to force these liberals, by creating a *crisis*, to set Negro rights over their other goals.

Secondly, disorder brought *economic* and *political* sanctions. For example, in Cambridge, Maryland, tourist trade was severely injured after the riots there. In Nashville, one reason financial leaders gave for their attempts to persuade restauranteurs to settle after the disorders was their fear that industry would not locate in a town torn by riots. In a Florida city studied by Killian and Grigg, Negro demonstrators:

. . . demonstrated their ability to invoke the sanctions of notoriety upon the community, as national newspapers, radio and television broadcast descriptions of mob violence on the city's main streets. A group of economically powerful white leaders became convinced that this sort of notoriety could be extremely harmful to the city's industrial growth, as the experience of Little Rock had demonstrated.[27]

Finally, the Southern Regional Conference put out a general report documenting the adverse economic consequences of demonstrations throughout the South.

Disorder brought *political* sanctions as well. Both the public and elected officials regard the maintenance of order as a primary function of government. Thus, officials not only feel responsible for maintaining order, but they know that if they do not succeed, the public may hold them accountable. In addition, politically, disorder is a symptom of politicization in the population. Such a process, if not discouraged, may increase mass interest in politics, bringing new forces into the political arena and threatening the position of established politicians. Thus, in Cambridge, Maryland, the moderate leaders were replaced with extreme conservatives after the racist masses had been activated by the disturbances. The same phenomenon occurred elsewhere in the South.

Disorder could be created by small numbers   Given the intense reaction of white racists and the resentment of the Negro community, even a handful of demonstrators could spark disorder. For instance, only a few dozen demonstrators were sufficient to generate violence in Cambridge after the situation there had become intense.

This fact was of utmost importance to the movement. It meant that it could have an impact despite its small numbers. In a sense, the necessary numbers were supplied by its opponents and by Negro bystanders who were caught up in the ensuing melee. For example, in Baltimore the media gave great attention to a mob that surrounded only a handful of demonstrators in Little Italy. In speaking of the Birmingham demonstrations that figured so importantly in the national movement, an aide of King told Robert Penn Warren:

And here we are at the mercy of — they don't do it with malice — the white press corps, they can see it only through white eyes. They can't distinguish between Negro spectators. All they know is Negroes, and most of the spectacular pictures printed in *Life* and in television clips had the commentary 'Negro demonstrators' when they were not that at all. I could go through reams of pictures.

On the first Sunday of the demonstration, we had twenty-three demonstrators in the march. But people began to stand around, and it swelled to about fifteen hundred, and they followed us twenty-three down the street, and when UPI took pictures they said: fifteen hundred demonstrators, twenty-two arrested. Well, that was all we had.

So we devised the technique, we'd set the demonstration up for a certain hour and then delay it two hours and let the crowd collect. This is a little Machiavellian, and I don't know whether I ever discussed this with Dr. King. It was the spectators following upon whom the dogs turned. It wasn't until three weeks later that the hoses were actually used on demonstrators.[28]

Not only were few numbers necessary to create disorder, but once disorder had been created, it was no longer necessary to use even these few. As any demonstration came to have, for whites, a violent potential, in time it was necessary only to announce a demonstration to get effects. Thus, in Maryland, certain areas on the Eastern Shore were partially desegregated through threats of demonstrations, rather than by actually carrying them out. This tactic was consciously used by a leader of one of the major civil rights organizations in the state. The importance of *not* having to demonstrate cannot be underestimated in a situation where the movement organizations involved had trouble mobilizing people for action.

Thus, disorder was essential to the movement's success. But, of course, it was not sufficient. Confronted with disorder, elites had at least two alternatives open to them — capitulation to demands or suppression of the demonstrators. Why was suppression not used? The answer specifies the other conditions for the movement's success.

The Movement Depended for Success on the Prior Existence of a Dilemma

American values stress equalitarianism, while the subordinate position of the Negro in U.S. society conflicts grossly with these norms. In short, there is, in Gunnar Myrdal's terms, a dilemma.[29] Thus, as Hyman and Sheatsley have shown through the use of public opinion polls, from 1944 to 1963 the public became increasingly sympathetic with the plight of the Negro.[30] By the time national legislators were confronted in 1963 with demands for open accommodations and protection of voting rights, a majority of whites were at least somewhat sympathetic.[31] Thus:

The dilemma meant that elements among the white population were willing to work for legislation supporting the movement's goals and to agitate against suppression The importance of this cannot be underestimated. Had there not been this sympathy, suppression would surely have been the alternative chosen. This can be seen by examining what happened in the Deep South where the white population was nearly uniformly *against* Negro demands. Here, at the local level, attempts at repression was the response. Even the mass demonstrations of SCLC in Birmingham, Albany, and the like, seem to have brought little change locally. That the civil rights movement was not totally destroyed in these areas was due to the fact that northern sentiment inhibited total repression and that the issue was finally settled outside the Deep South by federal legislation sponsored by national elites with constituencies either in favor of or, at worst, indifferent to Negro demands.

The impact of the dilemma was heightened by its concentration among the elite Public opinion polls have universally shown that the higher the education of a person, the more likely he is to favor civil rights for Negroes.[32] That is, sensitivity to the dilemma is greatest among the more powerful. This meant that the impact of the dilemma could be greater than its average acceptance in the population might suggest — particularly important in those Border State areas where the majority of whites were opposed to Negro rights. Thus, in Maryland, referendums and a George Wallace primary held late in the conflict revealed that whites, in general, opposed public accommodations. Elite sentiment minimized the impact of this fact. During the struggle for a public accommodations law, ministers, Young Democrats, junior members of the Bar, editors of one of the major newspapers, and the like, all spoke out in its favor. The result was to create a climate of opinion in which it was illegitimate among established leaders, whatever their private opinions, publicly to oppose equal public accommodations. In short, no established leader dared to agitate the segregationist masses. Thus, even those who voted against the public accommodations law in the Baltimore City Council and in the State Assembly, refused, in general, to make speeches defending their beliefs. This meant that the masses were left without leadership throughout most of the conflict and, therefore, remained disorganized and ineffective.

Still, we have not yet arrived at the whole answer. Public or elite sympathy for the movement's goals does not entirely account for capitulation rather than suppression. Since the means used by the movement were illegitimately non-routine, opponents could have used this issue as a way of publicly opposing the movement without having to appear segregationist. And, in fact, it was common to hear opponents say that they did not oppose integration, but that it should not be brought about by picketing and the like. That this was not a successful or widely used tactic was due to two additional factors.

The Movement Depended for Success on Using
Means Less Illegitimate than Those of Its Opponents

The movement chose the least illegitimate of all non-routine means — non-violence. This minimized not only its illegitimacy, but also the danger that the disorder so necessary for the movement's progress would be attributed directly to the movement and its organizations. Had the violence arising from demonstrations been advocated by the movement, or even informally encouraged by it, there would have been far less hesitation in suppressing its activity. This choice of non-violence, it should be added, was closely related to the small size of the movement. Few people have the sophistication and self-control both to see the necessity of non-violence and to live by that principle. The very smallness of the movement made it possible to behave in a disciplined and even self-sacrificing manner.

Almost always the behavior of the opposition was more illegitimate than that of the movement. Throughout the Maryland demonstrations, the movement never departed from non-violent means. The opponents on the other hand engaged in numerous illegitimate acts, from beating the grandson of a distinguished public servant (in front of a TV camera, it might be added) to kicking a pregnant woman in the stomach. The same was true for the movement in other areas. When the movement picketed, its enemies screamed and jeered; when the movement sang freedom songs, it was squirted with mustard, spat on, and beaten. The result of this behavior on the part of the segregationists was to make the movement appear extremely virtuous; indeed, it made the system of segregation appear far more brutal than it had prior to the demonstrations. It meant that the illegitimacy of the movement's methods was greatly outweighed by that of the opposition's. It meant that it was very difficult for established leaders outside the Deep South to ally themselves in any way with the lawless opposition. The movement owed no little of its success to the Jim Clarks and 'Bull' Conners.

The Movement Depended
for Success on Concentration

Because of the movement's small size, it was forced to concentrate its effort geographically. In Maryland, for instance, either the demonstrations were being held in Baltimore, or in the county, or on the Eastern Shore, but rarely in all places at the same time. The effect of this was striking. First, areas that had not yet been attacked tended to criticize the resistance of areas under siege. Apparently they were willing to refer the issue to their abstract values of equality. Second, after an area had been attacked and had capitulated, it tended to support the movement in other areas. There seem to have been a number of reasons for this. First, an ideological one — once an area had done what was right, even if forced to do it, it felt virtuous. Second, there were material reasons: businessmen feared that if only their area were desegregated, customers might go elsewhere. Concentration had similar effects on the national movement. Again, partly because of limited resources, the movement tended to concentrate on the South. This permitted the North to refer the issue to its abstract values, to feel superior, to offer support. The potency of concentration can perhaps be seen in the deep resentment expressed by northern whites in those few instances where civil rights leaders publicly stated that conditions in the North were just as bad as in the South.

In sum, the movement did not depend on large numbers for success. It could not, for *active* participation required the participant to be highly deprived, but such persons were held out of the movement by feelings of low political efficacy. Instead, the movement relied on the creation of disorder — disorder which could mobilize friends and sanction opponents, and which could be created by small numbers. That this method did not lead to suppression was due to several factors: that there existed in the society a dilemma, a dilemma to which the most powerful were the most sensitive; that the movement chose the least illegitimate of all non-routine means while its opponents responded without restraint; and that, because of its small numbers, the movement was forced to concentrate its efforts geographically, permitting most people to refer the issue to their abstract values rather than their self-interest.

Why Did the Movement Dissolve?

This understanding of the circumstances under which the non-violent movement succeeded permits us to arrive at a *partial* explanation of why, despite these successes, it shortly thereafter dissolved. In brief, these circumstances were such that (a) the will of blacks to use non-violence inevitably weakened, and (b) the conditions for effective non-violent action inevitably became attenuated, so that, even had the will persisted, a viable movement would no longer have been possible.

Dissolution of the Will to Use Non-violence[33]

First, because the movement used disorder as a major sanction, it was inevitable that many of the later participants would draw the conclusion that violence works, failing to perceive the more subtle conditions under which such violence can be effective (e.g., the use of means less illegitimate than those of one's opponents, the necessity of a dilemma, etc.)

Second, the need for and the dynamics of recruitment inevitably pushed the movement away from non-violence:

As we have seen, the movement during its non-violent phase was not large: its core, in fact, was small. This smallness was one of the major features permitting the use of non-violence. Only those committed to non-violence were likely to participate intensely, leaders could reach each member for training in non-violence, and small groups were easy to discipline. But the movement, inevitably, could not remain small. For reasons given below, larger numbers were necessary and, being necessary, the movement actively sought them. Also, the movement, by demonstrating success, was bound to break down a major inhibition to participation — pessimism about its potentialities — and increased recruitment was bound to follow. But as the movement, for these two reasons, became larger, selectivity, discipline and training inevitably weakened. This was evident in the Chicago housing demonstrations of 1966 where a segment of the movement refused to obey King's order to cease demonstrating in order to prevent violence.

Also, as we have seen, the movement was heavily middle class. This probably aided non-violence in that such an ethic, requiring a sophisticated theory of its effects and strong self-discipline, is more congenial to middle class personality and cognitive development.[34] But the movement could not remain solely middle class, for two reasons. The shift to welfare goals, mentioned below, meant that the movement would have less appeal to middle class individuals and that, therefore, if it were to maintain even the numbers it had before, it would have to extend its roots into the working class. Second, the success of the movement would remove a major barrier to working class participation, belief that action is not effective. That the movement did, in time, begin to attract more working class individuals was indicated in the Maryland study, where, in some of the later demonstrations, considerable numbers of working class individuals did begin to participate. This is also evident in the questionnaire data above where lower status individuals reported themselves as having recently joined the movement.

The dependence of the movement on its small, middle class character for non-violence is indicated in this quote from Robert Penn Warren:

Stokeley Carmichael, of Snick, tells me that in some of the demonstrations in Cambridge, Maryland, only a few Negroes were willing to enter a non-violent demonstration, but that when Snick demonstrators, committed to non-violence, moved into the street they were followed by a crowd of the local people who had refused to demonstrate. Then when the Snick demonstrators confronted the police, the local people behind the screen, threw bricks and bottles at the police.[35]

In short, the mass of the population, most of whom were working class, were not committed to non-violence. One consequence of this in Cambridge was that when they did become fully involved in the struggle, a riot ensued in which a number of people sustained serious injuries.

Dissolution of the Conditions
Necessary for Successful Non-violent Action

Even had the will to use non-violence persisted, the conditions for its effectiveness were bound to disappear.

First, the dilemma inevitably had to weaken. The movement initially sought goals with the most legitimacy in the eyes of the public — open public accommodations, and voting rights. This was not because these were the highest goals of the leaders: on the contrary, in Nashville, for instance, the leaders were primarily interested in jobs and welfare. This was, instead, due to recruitment requirements. A movement needs victories. Movements, thus, seek easily obtainable goals first, to demonstrate to those inhibited from joining by feelings of political futility that action is, in fact, not futile; and thereby ease the difficult process of recruitment. But this meant that once the initial goals were obtained, the movement had to move on to less legitimate ones: ones where the dilemma would be less strong.

This did in fact happen. The movement shifted to two new sets of goals:

1. Welfare goals. In summer 1966, Martin Luther King led a drive to end housing discrimination in Chicago. But public opinion polls showed that integrated housing did not have the legitimacy that open public accommodations had, surely one of the reasons why resistance to King's drive was so great and the results so meager.[36] The movement also began to press for compensatory hiring and education: and again, goals stressing special benefits rather than equalization had less legitimacy.

2. Acceptance of the legitimacy of black culture. Assimilation of ethnic groups in the U.S. has always consisted more of legitimizing than of erasing the culture of the group assimilated, and one of the mechanisms of collective social mobility has been pride in the knowledge that the group culture is shared from childhood. By 1966, some Negro leaders began to ask whether Negroes should be required to give up their culture. But this idea is not highly legitimate to most whites. As most Negroes are not far from the culture of the Delta and the slum, U.S. Negro culture represents poverty, symbolizing total failure to most Americans, as well as expressive behavior and immediate gratification. This runs counter to the whole moral burden of child socialization in the U.S., and Negroes arguing that there may be elements of dignity in this culture are latently suggesting that the devil of America's secular ethic be permitted to walk the street.

Second, concentration of the dilemma among the elite inevitably had to become less important.

Although sensitivity to the dilemma by elite elements may make it initially difficult for the masses, being thus deprived of leadership, to make their views heard politically, this is clearly a temporary situation. If established elites will not represent a popular view, new leadership which does will *in time* be developed. This happened in Maryland toward the end of the public accommodations struggle, when previously unknown individuals began to organize a counter movement, and later in 1966 when George Mahoney, once regarded as a near amateur in political circles, ran on a platform of opposition to open housing.

In addition, the masses may act through referendums. Although masses must act normally through elites if their voice is to be heard, where referendums exist, they may *in time* bypass elite unresponsiveness. Ultimately, therefore, concentration of the dilemma matters little. Thus, in Maryland, by the third year of the movement and after a public accommodations bill had been passed by the state legislature, a referendum was held in which the majority of whites voted against open accommodations. In California, whites, through a referendum, voted down a law integrating housing. The importance of referendums in permitting masses to bypass elites is seen by the following quote: 'Despite the support of most clergymen, prominent citizens, of most leaders of both parties, the new housing law was overwhelmingly repealed by the voters.'[37]

Third, the *comparative* legitimacy of the movement's means to those used by its opponents was bound to change.

The response of the movement's opponents was bound to become less extreme. For one thing, a movement is a school in which the movement and its opponents learn by trial and error the most appropriate moves. Thus, much of the success of the movement had depended on the untutored, emotional responses of the southern police. In time, however, authorities learned that such responses were counter-productive. In some areas, authorities learned responses sufficiently appropriate to deny the movement its instrument of disorder and to totally disorganize its leadership. In Maryland, for instance, Mayor McKeldin responded to CORE's announcement that Baltimore was to become CORE's target city with a warm welcome and an offer of aid, and the temporary chief of police, Gelston, used highly sophisticated tactics to defuse CORE's strategies.[38] In addition, the shift to goals where discrimination was far more subtle than in the case of public accommodations and voting meant a shift to geographical areas where the population was less likely to respond in a violently racist manner. Thus, when the movement tried in New York to press for desegregation of *de facto* segregated schooling, whites responded not by violence, as they had in the South, but by peaceful picketing, a tactic both legal and less disruptive than staying away from school, the means used by the Negroes.

Simultaneously, the *perceived* means of the movement were bound to become less legitimate. We do not refer here to the fact that many in the movement, for reasons given above, were bound to become less committed to non-violence, as in Chicago where demonstrators asserted the right of self-defense and responded to white attacks by throwing bottles back at their tormentors. Even had this not occurred, even if the movement had remained entirely non-violent, its means would have come to appear less legitimate. For one thing, under the religious leadership of Martin Luther King, the non-violent means used by the movement between 1960 and 1965 generally employed a rhetoric of moral persuasion, an emphasis *overtly* on morally converting one's opponents. This meant that the movement had the tone of non-violently *asking* whites to *give* greater status and power to blacks. Of all types of non-violent action, this is likely to appear the most legitimate. But such *moral* non-violence was inevitably unstable. As the movement was forced to shift to new and harder goals, as leadership developed among the white masses, as whites learned to respond without creating disorder, it became necessary for the movement to recruit greater numbers. Only larger numbers were likely to bring gains in the face of this greater, but more subtle resistance. As we have shown, however, recruitments is difficult, inhibited by feelings of low political efficacy. One way to overcome this barrier is, as Table 9 indicated, to propagate an ideology stressing the possibilities of action. It was inevitable, therefore, that 'Black Power' or some similar ideology should have been developed by the movement.[39] Among other things, 'Black Power' attempts to break down feelings of low efficacy by emphasizing to the Negro his potential political power. But such an ideology, while functional for recruitment, no longer creates in the minds of whites an image of a movement that is *asking* them to *give* it concessions. 'Black Power' *tells* whites that blacks are going to *take* what is due. This may be done, of course, non-violently, through such actions as bloc voting, massive economic sanctions (boycotts), etc. But such non-violence, emphasizing in rhetoric not moral persuasion but coercion, appears less legitimate. In addition, the previous *successes* of the movement through *disorder* inevitably led working class members of the Negro community to engage in rioting.[40] As such rioting by people *not* in the movement became ever more frequent, as it occurred more and more on the heels of non-violent demonstrations carried out by the movement, and as movement members themselves increasingly made 'Black Power' statements, it became harder and harder for the public to distinguish the riots from the actions of the movement itself. This meant that the non-violent means of the movement, by becoming merged in the public mind with the riots, came to appear less and less legitimate.

Fourth, the advantages of concentration inevitably had to be lost. This was true for at least two reasons: (1) Insofar as the previous successes of the movement aided recruitment, the movement gained the ability to carry on demonstrations in many areas at once. (2) Even had the movement tried to concentrate its efforts, as was done when King made Chicago and CORE made Baltimore their target cities, the movement had no control over rioting which broke out everywhere.

In sum, the *will* to non-violence declined as blacks concluded correctly that disorder works, and as the inevitable expansion and changing composition of the movement brought in people whose life styles were inconsistent with non-violent action. Simultaneously, the conditions for *effective* non-violent action attenuated as the movement was forced to shift to new goals where the dilemma was less strong; as the segregationist masses developed their own leadership or gained political access through referendums; as both they and the authorities began to respond in less disorder-creating ways; as the perceived means of the movement became less legitimate; and as the movement lost the advantages of concentration. All these changes were largely inevitable. The result was the disintegration of the movement. The loss of potential effectiveness made the creation of a viable movement exceedingly difficult. When combined with the loss of will, the movement dissolved.

Conclusion

What, then, is the future of non-violence in the Negro movement? It is clear that non-violence as we have known it in the past is dead; few leaders now espouse a non-violent ideology. Yet, it can be argued that, in some sense, the actions of certain of these leaders is still non-violent. Some are presently engaged in the attempt to create parallel institutions: i.e. to develop black-controlled businesses, black-controlled schools, and even, in the case of one leader, fully black communities. This action is clearly non-violent, although quite different from the previous non-violent action, for it does *not* attempt to throw off oppression by *confrontation* with whites. Instead it attempts to withdraw from such confrontation and establish peacefully the same bases of power-capital, educational systems, community institutions — now predominantly in the hands of whites. *If* these efforts succeed, a new and perhaps more powerful non-violent method will have been found.

Notes

[1] For background information of the history of the non-violent movement, see e.g. Donald R. Matthews & James W. Prothro: *Negroes and the New Southern Politics* (New York: Harcourt, Brace and World, 1966), pp. 407 ff, or Louis Lomax: *The Negro Revolt* (New York: Signet Books, 1963).

[2] For documentation of this abandonment of non-violence, see Chapter 10 ('Weakness of the Non-violent Commitment'), and the Epilogue ('End of Non-violence') in Inge Powell Bell: *CORE and the Strategy of Non-violence* (New York: Random House, 1968). CORE stands for the Congress on Racial Equality and SNCC for the Student Non-violent Coordinating Committee, two of the major groups leading the non-violent movement of that period. The third was SCLC, the Southern Christian Leadership Conference, the group led by Martin Luther King. This organization has not abandoned non-violence.

[3] It must be emphasized that we are not in this paper trying to give a complete explanation of why non-violence was abandoned. Rather, we are delineating *only* those reasons implied by our understanding of the circumstances under which the movement succeeded in attaining its initial goals. Other reasons, supplementing ours, are given in Bell, *op. cit.*

[4] Maurice Pinard, Jerome Kirk & Donald Von Eschen: 'Processes of Recruitment in the Sit-In Movement,' *Public Opinion Quarterly* (forthcoming); Von Eschen, Kirk, & Pinard: 'The Conditions of Direct Action in a Democratic Society,' *Western Political Quarterly* (forthcoming); Von Eschen, Kirk, & Pinard: 'Organizations and Disorderly Politics,' paper read at the 1964 meetings of the American Sociological Association; Kirk, Pinard, & Von Eschen: 'The Revolutionary Movement as a Political Organization,' paper read at the 1964 meeting of the American Sociological Association.

[5] Lyle Yorks & Donald Van Eschen: 'The Micro-Dynamics of the Civil Rights Movement, 1960–1964: The Case of Nashville,' paper read at the 1968 meeting of the Southern Sociological Association.

[6] Lewis Killian & Charles Grigg: *Racial Crisis in America* (Englewood Cliffs, N.J.: Prentice-Hall, 1964).

[7] CORE-LATOR (New York City: 38 Park Row), July 1963, Issue Number 101.

[8] William Brink & Louis Harris: *The Negro Revolution in America* (New York: Simon and Schuster, 1964), p. 67.

[9] Matthews & Prothro, *op. cit.,* p. 413.

[10] *Ibid.,* p. 408.

[11] This is not to say that no local movements experienced higher participation, only that *most* probably did not.

[12] The impact of some of this data is diluted even before interpreting it in terms of our Maryland and Nashville findings. For instance, the claim by the Southern Regional Conference that 70,000 persons participated in over 800 sit-ins in over 100 cities during the first year and one half of the movement indicates that, *on the average, only* 700 persons participated per city carrying out *only* an average of 8 or so sit-ins per city or an average of one every two months throughout the period. When our Maryland and Nashville findings are applied to this data, it becomes even less impressive. Assume, as is plausible in light of these findings, that, say, out of every eight demonstrations, one was large and seven small, and that, on the average, most people (excluding the hard core of activists) participated in one large and two small demonstrations. This would mean that each city, on the average, experienced one demonstration of 700 people and seven of 200 (instead of eight of 700 people). Of course, there were probably many small demonstrations which the Southern Regional Conference failed to report. But this is precisely our point. Most demonstrations were, in fact, small.

[13] See Robert Penn Warren: *Who Speaks for the Negro* (New York: Vintage, 1965), pp. 367–368, for reports of complaints by student activists in the South about the complacency and apathy of their fellow students. Data about the attitudes of SNCC workers toward King's demonstrations were gathered by Louis Goldberg in summer 1965 (personal communication).

[14] The data were collected from participants in one of the major demonstrations in Maryland, the 'Route 40 Freedom Ride.' African diplomats, in their travels between the UN in New York and their embassies in Washington, D.C., had been denied service in restaurants along the major route between these two centers, Route 40. In December 1961, some 500 to 600 members of CORE and other civil rights organizations drove along the Maryland section of the route requesting service at restaurants previously known to be segregated, variously sitting-in, picketing, or submitting to arrest if service was refused. By passing out questionnaires at the Baltimore terminal of the ride we obtained data from 386 of the participants (i.e. 60 to 80%). The reason why some participants did not fill out the questionnaire is that they either did not arrive at the Baltimore terminal or, more often, were organized into groups leaving for a demonstration before they could complete it. While the sample is, thus, not random, so that confidence or significance measures cannot be applied, we have been unable to discern any source of systematic non-response bias and we feel satisfied that these data present an undistorted picture of the group.

[15] See the reference cited in Note 4.

[16] The importance of a sense of efficacy for participation in *routine* politics has been shown in many studies. See, for instance, Angus Campbell *et al.: The American Voter* (New York: John Wiley, 1960), pp. 104–105.

[17] See, however, Von Eschen, *et al.:* 'The Conditions of Direct Action in a Democratic Society.'

[18] See, for example, Seymour Lipset, Martin Trow, & James Coleman: *Union Democracy* (Glencoe, Illinois: Free Press, 1956), especially pp. 69–105; or William Erbe, 'Social Involvement and Political Activity: A Replication and Elaboration,' *American Sociological Review,* Vol. 29, No. 2 (April, 1964), pp. 198–215.

[19] For data showing that feelings of political efficacy are *much* lower among those toward

the bottom of the stratification system, see, for instance, Angus Campbell, *et al.:* 'Sense of Political Efficacy and Political Participation,' in Heinz Eulau *et al.,* (eds.): *Political Behavior* (Glencoe, Illinois: Free Press, 1956), pp. 172–173. Note that such feelings are particularly absent among Negroes as compared with whites. For data that high organizational involvement is much less frequent among those at the bottom of the stratification system, see, for instance, William Erbe, *op. cit.,* p. 207. Also see Arnold Rose: *The Power Structure* (New York: Galaxy, 1967), p. 22, where Rose surveys the literature on social class and organizational involvement.

[20] Maurice Pinard, *The Rise of a Third Party: The Social Credit Party in Quebec in the 1962 Federal Election* (Englewood Cliffs: Prentice-Hall, forthcoming). Chapter 8, 'The Response of the Poor,' contains the tables controlling for feelings of hopelessness. Chapter 11, 'Mass Society and Social Credit,' contains the tables controlling for organizational involvement. Maurice Pinard, 'Poverty and Political Movements,' *Social Problems,* Vol. 15, No. 2 (Fall, 1967) is a condensed version of Chapter 8.

[21] *Op. cit.,* p. 419 and p. 426.

[22] Ruth Searles & J. A. Williams, 'Negro College Students' Participation in Sit-ins,' *Social Forces,* Vol. 40 (March, 1962), p. 219.

[23] Matthews & Prothro, *op. cit.,* pp. 421–422; Searles & Williams, *loc. cit.*

[24] Searles & Williams, *loc. cit.*

[25] See Maurice Pinard, *The Rise of a Third Party,* section in Chapter 8 entitled, 'The Poor in Other Movements.' Among these movements were the socialist C. C. F. party in Saskatchewan, Canada, the Social Credit Party in Quebec, Canada, the Poujadist movement in France, and the popular rebellions of the 18th century in France.

[26] *Op. cit.,* p. 75.

[27] *Ibid.,* p. 137.

[28] Warren, *op. cit.,* p. 226.

[29] Gunnar Myrdal: *An American Dilemma* (New York: Harper, 1944).

[30] Herbert Hyman & Paul Sheatsley: 'Attitudes Toward Desegregation,' *Scientific American,* Vol. 211. No. 1 (July, 1964).

[31] A Louis Harris poll published in *Newsweek* on October 21, 1963, showed that a majority of whites favored equal accommodations.

[32] See, for instance, the Louis Harris poll reported in the *Washington Post* of August 13, 1966, in which 57% of 'affluent' whites, but only 24% of 'low-privileged' whites 'backed' Negro protest.

[33] For additional reasons why blacks lost the will to use non-violence, see Bell, *op. cit.*

[34] Bell, *ibid.,* also makes this point. See pp. 15 and 80.

[35] *Op. cit.,* p. 214.

[36] In the 1966 Louis Harris poll, cited in note 32, only 16% of whites objected to sitting next to a Negro in a restaurant, while most objected to living next door to a Negro.

[37] Bell, *op. cit.,* p. 177.

[38] An excellent account of the successful strategies used by McKeldin and Gelston to 'tame' CORE in Baltimore is given by Louis Goldberg, 'Cops and CORE: The Case of Baltimore,' unpublished manuscript, Department of Sociology, McGill University, 1968.

[39] The ideology of 'Black Power' is well laid out in Stokely Carmichael & Charles V. Hamilton: *Black Power, The Politics of Liberation in America* (New York: Vintage, 1967).

[40] The way in which riots were generated by the non-violent movement is more complicated than indicated in this sentence. Essentially, the non-violent movement (1) raised the expectations of blacks, (2) showed them that disorder works, and (3) that sanctions were not as likely to be meted out as might have been anticipated, protest having become legitimate. As a result, when it became clear that hopes (expectations) were not going to be quickly realized, blacks engaged in acts (disorder in the form of riots) which sanctioned whites without being prohibitively costly to blacks.

From Civil Rights to Black Power: The Case of SNCC, 1960–1966

Allen J. Matusow

The transformation of black protest in the 1960's from civil rights to black power has seemed in retrospect an inevitable development. When the inherent limitations of the civil rights movement finally became apparent and when the expectations that the movement created met frustration, some kind of militant reaction in the black community seemed certain. However predictable this development may have been, it tells little about the concrete events that led to the abandonment of the civil rights program and to the adoption of a doctrine that is in many ways its opposite. For black power was not plucked whole from impersonal historical forces; nor was its content the only possible expression of rising black militancy. Rather, black power both as a slogan and a doctrine was in large measure the creation of a small group of civil rights workers who in the early 1960's manned the barricades of black protest in the Deep South. The group was called the Student Nonviolent Coordinating Committee (SNCC). Through its spokesman, Stokely Carmichael, SNCC first proclaimed black power and then became its foremost theoretician. Others would offer glosses on black power that differed from SNCC's concept, but because SNCC had contributed so much to the civil rights movement, no other group could speak with so much authority or command a comparable audience. Although SNCC borrowed freely from many sources to fashion black power into a doctrine, the elements of that doctrine were in the main the results of SNCC's own history. An examination of that history reveals not only the roots of black power but also the sad fate of the whole civil rights movement.

Founded in 1960, SNCC was an outgrowth of the historic sit-in movement, which began in Greensboro, North Carolina, on February 1 of that year. Four freshmen from a local Negro college attempted to desegregate the lunch counter at a Woolworth's five and ten store. The example of these four sent shock waves through the black colleges of the South and created overnight a base for a campaign

Allen J. Matusow, "From Civil Rights to Black Power: The Case of SNCC, 1960–1966," in Barton J. Bernstein and Allen J. Matusow, eds., *Twentieth Century America: Recent Interpretations,* Harcourt Brace Jovanovich, 1969, pp. 531–536. Reprinted by permission of the author.

of massive civil disobedience. The new generation of black students seemed suddenly unwilling to wait any longer for emancipation at the hands of the federal courts and in the next months supplied most of the recruits for the nonviolent army of 50,000 that rose spontaneously and integrated public facilities in 140 Southern cities. For the students on the picket lines, the prophet of the sit-in movement was Dr. Martin Luther King, the leader of the successful Montgomery bus boycott of 1955–56. The students found in King's nonviolent philosophy a ready-made ethic, a tactic, and a conviction of righteousness strong enough to sustain them on a sometimes hazardous mission.[1] It was King's organization, the Southern Christian Leadership Conference (SCLC), that first suggested the need for some central direction of the sit-in movement. At the invitation of SCLC's executive secretary, some 300 activist students from throughout the South met in Raleigh, North Carolina, in April 1960, to discuss their problems. The students agreed to form a coordinating body, which became SNCC, and in May 1960, hired a secretary and opened an office in Atlanta. In October the organization decided to become a permanent one, and 235 delegates approved a founding statement inspired by King's philosophy:

We affirm the philosophical or religious ideal of nonviolence as the foundation of our purpose, the presupposition of our belief, and the manner of our action. . . . Through nonviolence, courage displaces fear. Love transcends hate. Acceptance dissipates prejudice; hope ends despair. Faith reconciles doubt. Peace dominates war. Mutual regards cancel enmity. Justice for all overwhelms injustice. The redemptive community supersedes immoral social systems.[2]

In truth, the Christian rhetoric of SNCC's founding statement was not appropriate. The author of the statement was James Lawson, a young minister who never actually belonged to SNCC.[3] Most of the students who rallied to the sit-ins in 1960 accepted King's teachings more out of convenience than conviction and respected his courage more than his philosophy. For while King believed that Christian love was an end in itself and that Negro nonviolence would redeem American society, the students preferred to participate in America rather than to transform it. Sociologists who examined the attitudes of protesters in the black colleges found not alienation from American middle-class values but a desire to share fully in middle-class life.[4] In a perceptive piece written for *Dissent,* Michael Walzer supported these findings from his own first-hand impressions of the sit-ins. Walzer concluded that the students were materialistic as well as moral, were "willing to take risks in the name of both prosperity and virtue," and had as their goal "assimilation into American society." As for nonviolence, Walzer wrote, "I was told often that 'when one side has all the guns, then the other side is non-violent.' "[5]

In the beginning, the philosophical inconsistencies of the sit-ins did not trouble SNCC, for it stood at the forefront of a movement whose ultimate triumph seemed not far distant. But within months, as mysteriously as it began, the sit-in movement vanished. By the spring of 1961 the black campuses had lapsed into their customary quiescence, their contribution to the civil rights movement at an end. As for SNCC, since October 1960, the student representatives from each Southern state had been meeting monthly to squander their energies trying to coordinate a movement that was first too amorphous and then suddenly moribund. SNCC's attempts in early 1961 to raise up new hosts of students proved ineffectual, and lacking followers, the organization seemed without a future.[6] Then in May 1961, the Freedom Rides restored a sense of urgency to the civil rights movement and gave SNCC a second life.

On May 14, 1961, members of the Congress of Racial Equality (CORE) began the Freedom Rides to test a Supreme Court decision outlawing segregation in transportation terminals. On May 20, after one of CORE's integrated buses was bombed near Anniston, Alabama, and another was mobbed in Birmingham, CORE decided to call off its rides. But amid sensational publicity, students from Nashville and Atlanta, many associated with SNCC, rushed to Birmingham to continue the journey to New Orleans. After mobs assaulted this second wave of riders, the Federal Government stepped in to protect them, and they were permitted to go as far as Jackson, where local authorities put them in jail for defying segregation ordinances. Throughout the summer of 1961 some 300 citizens from all over America took Freedom Rides that brought them to the jails of Jackson.[7] For SNCC the Freedom Rides provided a temporary outlet for activism and, more important, inspired radical changes in the structure and purpose of the organization.

Perhaps the most important result of the Freedom Rides for SNCC was to focus its attention on the Deep South. Most of the sit-ins had occurred in the cities and larger towns of the Upper South, and the victories there had come with relative ease. Now the magnitude of the task confronting the civil rights movement became clearer. As some in SNCC had already perceived, sit-ins to desegregate public places offered no meaningful benefits to poverty-stricken tenant farmers in, say, Mississippi. In order to mobilize the black communities in the Deep South to fight for their rights, sporadic student demonstrations would be less useful than sustained efforts by full time field workers.[8] In the summer of 1961, as SNCC was beginning to grope toward the concept of community action, the Federal Government stepped in with an attractive suggestion.

Embarrassed by the Freedom Rides, Attorney General Robert F. Kennedy moved to direct the civil rights movement into paths that, in his view, were more constructive. Kennedy suggested that the civil rights organizations jointly sponsor a campaign to register Southern black voters. Such a drive, its proponents argued, would be difficult for even extreme segregationists to oppose and eventually might liberalize the Southern delegation in Congress. When the Justice Department seemed to offer federal protection for registration workers and when white liberals outside the Administration procured foundation money to finance anticipated costs, the civil rights groups agreed to undertake the project.[9] Within SNCC, advocates of direct action fought acceptance of the project, but the issue was compromised and a threatened split was averted. SNCC's decision to mobilize black communities behind efforts to secure political rights decisively changed the character of the organization. It thereafter ceased to be an extracurricular activity of student leaders and became instead the vocation of dedicated young men and women who temporarily abandoned their careers to become full time paid workers (or "field secretaries") in the movement. Moreover, as SNCC workers drifted away from the black campuses and began living among Deep South blacks, they cast aside the middle-class goals that had motivated the sit-ins of 1960 and put on the overalls of the poor. Begun as middle-class protest, SNCC was developing revolutionary potential.[10]

In Mississippi the major civil rights groups (NAACP, SCLC, CORE, and SNCC) ostensibly joined together to form the Council of Federated Organizations (COFO) to register black voters. But in reality, except for one Mississippi congressional district where CORE had a project of its own, COFO was manned almost entirely by SNCC people. The director of COFO was SNCC's now legendary Robert Moses, a product of Harlem with a Masters degree in philosophy from Harvard, whose courage and humanity made him the most respected figure in the organization. Moses had entered Pike County, Mississippi, alone in 1961, stayed on in spite of a beating and a jail term, and in the spring of 1962 became COFO's director in charge of voting projects in Vicksburg, Cleveland, Greenwood, and a few other Mississippi towns.[11] Although SNCC also had registration projects in Arkansas, Alabama, and Georgia, it concentrated on Mississippi, where the obstacles were greatest.

Throughout 1962 and into 1963 SNCC workers endured assaults, offered brave challenges to local power structures, and exhorted local blacks to shake off fear and stand up for freedom. But SNCC scored no breakthroughs to sustain morale, and while its goals remained outwardly unchanged, its mood was turning bitter. To SNCC the hostility of local racists was not nearly so infuriating as the apparent betrayal that it suffered at the hands of the Justice Department. SNCC believed that in 1961 the Kennedy Administration had guaranteed protection to registration workers, but in Mississippi in 1962 and 1963, SNCC's only contact with federal authority consisted of the FBI agents who stood by taking notes while local policemen beat up SNCC members. SNCC and its supporters insisted that existing law empowered the Federal Government to intervene, but the Justice Department contended that it was in fact powerless. SNCC doubted the sincerity of the Government's arguments and became convinced that the Kennedys had broken a solemn promise for political reasons.[12] Thus by 1963 SNCC was already becoming estranged from established authority and suspicious of liberal politicians.

SNCC's growing sense of alienation cut it off even from other civil rights organizations and most importantly from Dr. King, who by 1963 had become a fallen idol for SNCC workers. They believed that King was too willing to compromise, wielded too much power, and too successfully monopolized the funds of the movement. Doubts about King had arisen as early as the Freedom Rides, when students turned to him for advice and leadership and received what they considered only vague sympathy. In fact, after CORE called off the first ride, King privately supported Robert Kennedy's plea for a "cooling-off" period. But much to SNCC's annoyance, when militant voices prevailed and the rides continued, the press gave King all the credit.[13] In Albany, Georgia, in December 1961, after SNCC aroused the black population to pack the local jails for freedom, King came to town, got arrested, monopolized the headlines, and almost stole the leadership of the Albany campaign from SNCC.[14] In SNCC's view, dependence on King's charisma actually weakened the civil rights movement, for it discouraged development of leadership at the grass-roots level. Why, SNCC asked, did King use his huge share of civil rights money to maintain a large staff in Atlanta, and why did he never account for the funds that he so skillfully collected?[15] As King lost influence on SNCC, dissenting attitudes about nonviolence, implicit since 1960, came to be frankly articulated. When Robert Penn Warren asked Robert Moses what he thought of King's philosophy, Moses replied,

We don't agree with it, in a sense. The majority of the students are not sympathetic to the idea that they have to love the white people that they are struggling against. . . . For most of the members, it is tactical, it's a question of being able to have a method of attack rather than to be always on the defensive.[16]

During the March on Washington in August 1963, the nation almost caught a glimpse of SNCC's growing anger. John Lewis, the chairman of SNCC and one of the scheduled speakers, threatened to disrupt the harmony of that happy occasion by saying what he really thought. Only with difficulty did moderates persuade Lewis to delete the harshest passages of his address. So the nation did not know that SNCC scorned Kennedy's civil rights bill as "too little and too late." Lewis had intended to ask the 250,000 people gathered at the Lincoln Memorial,

What is there in this bill to insure the equality of a maid who earns $5 a week in the home of a family whose income is $100,000 a year? . . . This nation is still a place of cheap political leaders who build their careers on immoral compromises and ally themselves with open forms of political, economic, and social exploitation. . . . The party of Kennedy is also the party of Eastland. The party of Javits is also the party of Goldwater. Where is *our* party? . . . We cannot depend on any political party, for the Democrats and the Republicans have betrayed the basic principles of the Declaration of Independence.

In those remarks that he never delivered, Lewis used both the language of Christian protest and images alive with the rage of SNCC field workers. "In the struggle we must seek more than mere civil rights; we must work for the community of love, peace, and true brotherhood." And, the time will come when we will not confine our marching to Washington. We will march through the South, through the heart of Dixie, the way Sherman did. We shall pursue our "scorched earth" policy and burn Jim Crow to the ground — non-violently. We shall fragment the South into a thousand pieces and put them back together in the image of democracy.[17]

The crucial milestone of SNCC's road to radicalism was the Freedom Summer of 1964. Freedom Summer grew out of a remarkable mock election sponsored by SNCC in the autumn of 1963. Because the mass of Mississippi's black population could not legally participate in choosing the state's governor that year, Robert Moses conceived a freedom election to protest mass disfranchisement and to educate Mississippi's blacks to the mechanics of the political process. COFO organized a new party called the Mississippi Freedom Democrats, printed its own ballots, and in October conducted its own poll. Overwhelming the regular party candidates, Aaron Henry, head of the state NAACP and Freedom Democratic nominee for governor, received 70,000 votes, a tremendous protest against the denial of equal political rights. One reason for the success of the project was the presence in the state of 100 Yale and Stanford students, who worked for two weeks with SNCC on the election. SNCC was sufficiently impressed by the student contribution to consider inviting hundreds more to spend an entire summer in Mississippi. Sponsors of this plan hoped not only for workers but for publicity that might at last focus national attention on Mississippi.[18] By the winter of 1963–64, however, rising militancy in SNCC had begun to take on the overtones of black nationalism, and some of the membership resisted the summer project on the grounds that most of the volunteers would be white.

Present from the beginning, by mid-1964 whites made up one-fifth of SNCC's approximately 150 full time field secretaries. Though whites had suffered their fair share of beatings, some blacks in SNCC were expressing doubts about the role of white men in a movement for black freedom. At a staff meeting at Greenville, Mississippi, in November 1963, a debate on the proposed Freedom Summer brought the issue of white-black relations into the open. In his book *SNCC: The New Abolitionists,* Howard Zinn, who attended this meeting, summarizes the views of the militants:

Four or five of the Negro staff members now urged that the role of whites be limited. For whites to talk to Mississippi Negroes about voter registration, they said, only reinforced the Southern Negro's tendency to believe that whites were superior. Whites tended to take over leadership roles in the movement, thus preventing Southern Negroes from being trained to lead. Why didn't whites just work in the white Southern community? One man noted that in Africa the new nations were training black Africans to take over all important government positions. Another told of meeting a Black Muslim in Atlanta who warned him that whites were taking over the movement. "I had the feeling inside. I felt what he said was true."

But Fannie Lou Hamer disagreed. Mrs. Hamer had been a time-keeper on a cotton plantation and was one of the local Mississippi blacks whom SNCC discovered and elevated to leadership. Speaking for the majority of the meeting, she said, "If we're trying to break down this barrier of segregation, we can't segregate ourselves." Thus in February 1964, SNCC sent an invitation to Northern college students to spend their summer vacation in Mississippi.[19]

In retrospect, the summer of 1964 was a turning point in the civil rights movement. When the summer began, SNCC was still operating within the framework of liberal America, still committed to integration and equal political rights for all citizens. But by the end of the summer of 1964, the fraying cords that bound SNCC to liberal goals and values finally snapped. In a sense, much of later black power thought was merely a postscript to SNCC's ill-fated summer project.

In June 1964, more than 700 selected students, judged by a staff psychiatrist at MIT to be "an extraordinarily healthy bunch of kids,"[20] came to Oxford, Ohio, for two week-long orientation sessions conducted by veteran SNCC workers. The atmosphere in Oxford, tense from the outset, became on June 22 pervaded with gloom. Robert Moses quietly told the volunteers that three workers had gone into Neshoba county in Mississippi the day before and had not been heard from since. One was Michael Schwerner, a CORE staff member; the second was James Chaney, a black SNCC worker from Mississippi; and the third was Andrew Goodman, a student volunteer who had finished his orientation in Ohio a few days before.[21] (In August the bodies of these three were discovered in their shallow graves near Philadelphia, Mississippi.)

The volunteers in Ohio had to face not only their own fear but also unanticipated hostility from the SNCC workers whom they had come to assist. Tensions between black workers and white volunteers seethed under the surface for some days and then finally erupted. One night SNCC showed a film of a grotesque voting registrar turning away black applicants. When the student audience laughed at the scene, six SNCC people walked out, enraged at what they considered an insensitive response. There followed an exchange between the workers and the volunteers, in which the students complained that the staff was distant, uncommunicative, and "looked down on us for not having been through what they had." A SNCC worker replied,

If you get mad at us for walking out, just wait until they break your head in, and see if you don't have something to get mad about. Ask Jimmy Travis over there what he thinks about the project. What does he think about Mississippi? He has six slugs in him, man, and the last one went right through the back of his neck when he was driving a car outside Greenwood. Ask Jesse here — he has been beaten so that we wouldn't recognize him time and time and time and time again. If you don't get scared, pack up and get the hell out of here because we don't need any favors of people who don't know what they are doing here in the first place.

The bitter words seemed to have a cathartic effect, and the meeting culminated in emotional singing. Said one volunteer a bit too optimistically, "The crisis is past, I think."[22]

From one perspective the story of the two months that followed is one of the human spirit triumphant. Though three more people were killed, eighty others were beaten, thirty-five churches were burned, and thirty other buildings bombed, few turned back; black and white together, the civil rights workers in Mississippi worked for racial justice.[23] The student volunteers taught in Freedom Schools, where 3,000 children were given their first glimpse of a world beyond Mississippi. They organized the disfranchised to march on county courthouses to face unyielding registrars. Most importantly, they walked the roads of Mississippi for the Freedom Democratic Party (FDP). Denying the legitimacy of the segregated Democratic party, COFO opened the FDP to members of all races and declared the party's loyalty to Lyndon Johnson. The goal of the FDP in the summer of 1964 was to send a delegation to the Democratic convention in Atlantic City to challenge the credentials of the regular Democrats and cast the state's vote for the party's nominees. To mount this challenge against the racist Democrats of Mississippi, COFO enrolled 60,000 members in the FDP and then organized precinct, county, and state conventions to choose 68 integrated delegates to go north. The FDP, in which tens of thousands of black Mississippi citizens invested tremendous hopes, was a true grass-roots political movement and the greatest achievement of Freedom Summer.[24]

Although the FDP brought to Atlantic City little more than a sense of moral outrage, it nevertheless managed to transform its challenge of the Mississippi regulars into a major threat to the peace of the national party. Mrs. Hamer helped make this feat possible by her electrifying (and televised) testimony before the credentials committee on how Mississippi policemen had beaten her up for trying to register to vote. As Northern liberals began rallying to the FDP, the managers of the convention sought a compromise that would satisfy the liberals and at the same time keep the bulk of the Southern delegations in the convention. President Johnson favored a proposal to seat all the Mississippi regulars who pledged their loyalty to the party, to deny any voting rights to the FDP delegates, but to permit them to sit on the floor of the convention. In addition, he proposed that at future conventions no state delegations chosen by racially discriminatory procedures would be accredited. But because this compromise denied the FDP's claims of legitimacy, the FDP and many liberals declared it unacceptable and threatened to take their case to the floor of the convention, a prospect that greatly displeased the President. Johnson then sent Senator Hubert Humphrey to Atlantic City to act as his agent in settling the controversy. Unsubstantiated rumors had it that if Humphrey's mission failed, the President would deny the Senator the party's vice-presidential nomination. In close touch with both the White House and the credentials committee, Humphrey proposed altering the original compromise by permitting two FDP delegates to sit in the convention as delegates at large with full voting rights. This was as far as Johnson would go, and at the time it seemed far enough. Though the

Mississippi white regulars walked out, no Southern delegations followed them, and, at the same time, most liberals felt that the Administration had made a genuine concession. Black leaders, including Dr. King, pleaded with the FDP to accept Humphrey's compromise. But the FDP denied that the compromise was in any sense a victory.[25] Angered at Humphrey's insistence that he alone choose the two at-large delegates, the FDP announced that it had not come to Atlantic City "begging for crumbs."[26] Mrs. Hamer, by now a minor national celebrity, said of Humphrey's efforts, "It's a token of rights on the back row that we get in Mississippi. We didn't come all this way for that mess again."[27]

To the general public the FDP appeared to be a band of moral zealots hostile to reasonable compromise and ungrateful for the real concession that the party had offered. The true story was more complicated. Aware that total victory was impossible, the FDP had in fact been quite willing to accept any proposal that recognized its legitimacy. At the beginning of the controversy Oregon's Congresswoman Edith Green offered a compromise that the FDP found entirely acceptable. Mrs. Green proposed that the convention seat every member of both delegations who signed a pledge of loyalty and that Mississippi's vote be divided between the two groups according to the number of seated delegates in each. Since only eleven members of the credentials committee (10 percent of the total) had to sign a minority report to dislodge the Green compromise from committee, the FDP seemed assured that its case would reach the convention floor, where many believed that the Green compromise would prevail over Johnson's original proposal. FDP's hopes for a minority report rested chiefly on Joseph Rauh, a member of the credentials committee, leader of the Democratic party in the District of Columbia, veteran of innumerable liberal crusades, and, happily, adviser and legal counsel of the FDP. But Rauh was also a friend of Hubert Humphrey and an attorney for Humphrey's strong supporter, Walter Reuther. After Humphrey came on the scene with his compromise, Rauh backed away from the minority report.

In his semi-official history of the Mississippi Summer Project, *The Summer That Didn't End,* Len Holt presents the FDP and SNCC interpretation of what happened. Presumably pressured by his powerful friends, Rauh broke a promise to the FDP and would not support the Green compromise. One by one the FDP's other allies on the committee backed away — some to protect jobs, others to keep alive hopes for federal judgeships, and one because he feared the loss of a local antipoverty program. In the end the FDP failed to collect the needed signatures, and there was no minority report. The angry rhetoric that the FDP delegates let loose in Atlantic City was in reality inspired less by Humphrey's compromise than by what the FDP regarded as its betrayal at the hands of the white liberals on the credentials committee. By the end of the Democratic convention SNCC was convinced that membership in the Democratic coalition held little hope for Southern blacks and that, lacking power, they would always be sold out by the liberals. In Atlantic City the phrase "white power structure" took on concrete meaning. Freedom Summer, which began with SNCC fighting for entrance into the American political system, ended with the radical conviction that that system was beyond redemption.[28]

In the end the Freedom Summer Project of 1964 not only destroyed SNCC's faith in the American political system; it also undermined its commitment to integration. Within the project racial tensions between white and black workers were never successfully resolved. Though many white volunteers established warm relationships with the local black families that housed them,[29] healthy communication between students and veteran SNCC workers proved difficult at best. Staff members resented the officious manner of better-educated volunteers and feared that the white students were taking over the movement. "Several times," one volunteer wrote, "I've had to completely re-do press statements or letters written by one of them."[30] Said a SNCC worker, "Look at those fly-by-night freedom fighters bossing everybody around."[31] SNCC people found it hard to respect the efforts of volunteers who they knew would retreat at the end of the summer to their safe middle-class world. One sensitive white female volunteer wrote that SNCC workers "were automatically suspicious of us, the white volunteers; throughout the summer they put us to the test, and few, if any, could pass. . . . It humbled, if not humiliated, one to realize that *finally they will never accept me.*"[32] By the end of the summer a spirit akin to black nationalism was rising inside the SNCC organization.

The overall failure of Freedom Summer administered a blow to SNCC's morale from which the organization almost did not recover. In November 1964, Robert Coles, a psychiatrist who had worked closely with SNCC, wrote about the tendency of veteran workers to develop battle fatigue. Even heroic temperaments, he said, could not escape the depression that inevitably results from long periods of unremitting dangers and disappointments. But by the fall of 1964 battle fatigue was no longer just the problem of individual SNCC members; it was pervading the entire organization. One patient told Coles,

I'm tired, but so is the whole movement. We're busy worrying about our position or our finances, so we don't do anything. . . . We're becoming lifeless, just like all revolutions when they lose their first momentum and become more interested in preserving what they've won than going on to new challenges. . . . Only with us we haven't won that much, and we're either holding to the little we have as an organization, or we get bitter, and want to create a new revolution. . . . You know, one like the Muslims want which is the opposite of what we say we're for. It's as if we completely reverse ourselves because we can't get what we want.[33]

Uncertain of their purpose, SNCC workers in the winter of 1964–65 grew introspective. Months were consumed in discussing the future of whites in the movement and the proper structure of the organization. Fresh from a trip to Africa where he met the black nationalist Malcolm X, John Lewis, Chairman of SNCC, spoke for the majority in early 1965 when he demanded that blacks lead their own movement.[34] At the same time, quarrels over organization almost tore SNCC apart. Some workers became "high on freedom" and advocated a romantic anarchism that rejected bureaucratic structure and leadership. Robert Moses, for instance, believed that SNCC workers should "go where the spirit say go, and do what the spirit say do." Moses was so disturbed by his own prestige in the movement that he changed his name, drifted into Alabama, and thereafter was only vaguely connected with SNCC. Meanwhile SNCC's field work tended to fall into neglect.[35]

In the summer of 1965 SNCC brought 300 white volunteers into Mississippi for its second and last summer project. The result was a shambles. Racial tensions caused some projects to break up and prevented serious work in others. Problems only dimly perceived a year before assumed stark clarity, and SNCC's resentment of the volunteers became overt and unambiguous. At staff meetings blacks would silence white students with such remarks as "How long have you been here?" and "How do you know what it's like being black?" and "If you don't like the way we do it, get the hell out of the state."[36] Not all the blame for the final breakdown of race relations in SNCC, however, belonged to the black staff. The questionable motivation of some of the white students led Alvin Poussaint, a black psychiatrist close to SNCC, to add a new neurosis to medical terminology — the white African Queen or Tarzan complex. The victim of this neurosis harbored repressed delusions of himself as an "intelligent, brave, and handsome white man or woman, leading the poor down-trodden and oppressed black men to freedom and salvation."[37]

But the most serious obstacle to healthy race relations inside SNCC was sex, and in this dimension, as really in all others, the villain was neither black worker nor white student, but rather the sad and twisted history of race relations in America. The white girl who came South to help SNCC found herself, according to Dr. Poussaint, "at the center of an emotionally shattering crossfire of racial tensions that have been nurtured for centuries."[38] In the summer of 1965 a veteran black civil rights worker in SCLC tried to warn white girls of the perils that awaited them in their dealings with black men in the movement:

What you have here is a man who had no possible way of being a man in the society in which he lives, save one. And that's the problem. The only way or place a Negro man has been able to express his manhood is sexually and so you find a tremendous sexual aggressiveness. And I say quite frankly, don't get carried away by it and don't get afraid of it either. I mean, don't think it's because you're so beautiful and so ravishing that this man is so enamoured of you. It's not that at all. He's just trying to find his manhood and he goes especially to the places that have robbed him of it. . . . And so, in a sense, what passes itself as desire is probably a combination of hostility and resentment — because he resents what the society has done to him and he wants to take it out on somebody who symbolizes the establishment of society.[39]

At the end of the summer a white girl spoke of her experiences:

Well, I think that the white female should be very well prepared before she comes down here to be bombarded. And she also has to be well prepared to tell them to go to hell and be prepared to have them not give up. . . . I've never met such forward men as I have in Mississippi.[40]

The problem was complicated by the jealousy of black girls toward their white rivals, and by neurotic whites who sought to ease their guilt by permitting blacks to exploit them sexually and financially.[41] On leaving their projects to go home, a few white girls told Poussaint, "I hate Negroes."[42] By the end of the summer of 1965 no one could any longer doubt that the blacks reciprocated the feeling.

The year 1965 was a lost one for SNCC. For the first time since its founding, it was no longer on the frontier of protest, no longer the keeper of the nation's conscience, no longer the driving force of a moral revolution. The civil rights acts of 1964 and 1965 brought the civil rights movement, for which SNCC had suffered so much, to a triumphant conclusion, but SNCC had lost interest in integrated public accommodations and equal political rights. SNCC seemed to be losing its sense of mission and after years of providing heroes for the black protest movement, it now needed a hero of its own. Significantly it chose Malcolm X, the black nationalist who had been assassinated by Muslim rivals in February 1965.[43] Only a few years before, SNCC and Malcolm X had seemed to occupy opposite poles of black protest. Thus while SNCC's John Lewis was toning down his speech at the March on Washington, Malcolm X was saying,

Who ever heard of angry revolutionists all harmonizing "We Shall Overcome . . . Suum Day . . ." while tripping and swaying along arm-in-arm with the very people they were supposed to be angrily revolting against? Who ever heard of angry revolutionists swinging their bare feet together with their oppressors in lily-pad park pools, with gospels and guitars and "I Have a Dream" speeches?[44]

While policemen were clubbing SNCC workers in Mississippi, Malcolm X was saying, "If someone puts a hand on you, send him to the cemetery."[45] While SNCC was pondering the meaning of Atlantic City, Malcolm X was saying, "We *need* a Mau Mau. If they don't want to deal with the Mississippi Freedom Democratic Party, then we'll give them something else to deal with." While black nationalists were still a minority in SNCC, Malcolm X was calling for black control of black politicians in black communities, black ownership of ghetto businesses, and black unity "to lift the level of our community, to make our society beautiful so that we will be satisfied in our own social circles and won't be running around here trying to knock our way into a social circle where we're not wanted."[46] This was the language that had made Malcolm X the hero of the urban ghetto, and it was the language appropriate in 1965 to SNCC's militant mood. In a certain sense Malcolm X was the link that connected SNCC with the black radicalism that was arising in the North.

Unlike SNCC, the ghetto masses never had to disabuse themselves of the colorblind assumptions of the civil rights movement. Trapped permanently in their neighborhoods, the poor blacks of the North have always been painfully conscious of their racial separateness. As Essien-Udom, a historian of black nationalism, has written, blackness "is the stuff of their lives and an omnipresent, harsh reality. For this reason the Negro masses are instinctively 'race men.' "[47] But the civil rights movement nevertheless had its consequences in the ghetto. The spectacle of Southern blacks defying their white tormentors apparently inspired among Northern blacks race pride and resurgent outrage at the gap between American ideals and black realities. Thus the civil rights movement had the ironic effect of feeding the nationalist tendency in the ghetto to turn inward, to separate, and to identify the white men outside as the enemy. SNCC's frustrations exploded intellectually in the formulation of black power doctrines, but ghetto rage took the form of riot.

The riot of August 1965, in Watts (the sprawling ghetto of Los Angeles) dwarfed the violent outbursts of the previous year and awakened America to the race crisis in her big cities. A social trauma of the first order, the Watts riot resulted in 35 deaths, 600 burned and looted buildings, and 4,000 persons arrested.[48] Above all it revealed the dangerous racial hatred that had been accumulating unnoticed in the nation's black ghettos. The official autopsy of Watts denied by implication that it was a revolt against white oppression. The McCone Commission (after its chairman, John McCone), appointed by California's Governor Pat Brown to investigate the riot, estimated that only 10,000 Watts residents, or 2 percent of the population in the riot area, had actually been on the streets during the uprising. This minor fraction, the Commission contended, was not protesting specific grievances, which admittedly existed in abundance, but was engaged in an "insensate rage of destruction" that was "formless, quite senseless."[49] Critics of the McCone report have ably challenged these findings. (For example, Robert Fogelson points out that "to claim that only 10,000 Negroes rioted when about 4,000 were arrested is to presume that the police apprehended fully 40 percent of the rioters.")[50] In reality, a rather large minority of the riot-age population in Watts was on the streets during the riot, and as one of the Commission's own staff reports revealed, the riot had significant support inside the ghetto, especially in the worst slum areas.[51]

On the crucial question of the riot's causes, observers on the scene agreed that the rioters were animated by a common anger against whites.[52] Robert Blauner, a staff member for the McCone Commission and its severest critic, has written,

Most of the actions of the rioters appear to have been informed by the desire to clear out an alien presence, white men, rather than to kill them. . . . It was primarily an attack on property, particularly white-owned businesses. . . . The spirit of the Watts rioters appears similar to that of anti-colonial crowds demonstrating against foreign masters.[53]

Said Bayard Rustin, a moderate black intellectual who was in Watts during the riot, "The whole point of the outburst in Watts was that it marked the first major rebellion of Negroes against their masochism and was carried on with the express purpose of asserting that they would no longer quietly submit to the deprivation of slum life."[54] Thus in 1965, for different reasons, both the ghetto masses and the members of SNCC were seized by militant anti-white feelings, and it was this congruence of mood that would shortly permit SNCC to appeal to a nation-wide black audience.

After a year on the periphery of the black protest movement, SNCC in 1966 moved again to the forefront. In May 1966, at a time when the organization was apparently disintegrating, 135 staff members (25 of them white) met in Nashville to thrash out their future. Early in the emotional conference, by a vote of 60 to 22, John Lewis, the gentle advocate of nonviolence, retained the chairmanship of SNCC by defeating the challenge of the militant Stokely Carmichael. But as the conference went on, the arguments of the militants began to prevail. When the staff voted to boycott the coming White House conference on civil rights, Lewis announced that he would attend anyway, and the question of the chairmanship was then reopened. This time SNCC workers chose Carmichael as their new leader by a vote of 60 to 12. The conference next issued a statement calling, among other things, for "black Americans to begin building independent political, economic, and cultural institutions that they will control and use as instruments of social change in this country."[55]

A few weeks later the full meaning of Carmichael's election became clear to the whole nation. The occasion was the famous Meredith march through Mississippi in June of 1966. James Meredith, the man who integrated the University of Mississippi in 1962 with the help of the United States Army, embarked on a 200-mile walk from Memphis to Jackson to show the black people of Mississippi that they could walk to the voting booths without fear. On June 6, 28 miles out of Memphis, a white man felled Meredith with buckshot. Erroneously believing that Meredith had been killed, civil rights leaders immediately flew to Mississippi to continue his walk against fear. So it was that arm in arm, Martin Luther King of SCLC, Floyd McKissick of CORE, and Stokely Carmichael of SNCC marched down U.S. Highway 51.

Early efforts of the three leaders to maintain surface unity rapidly broke down. Significantly, the first issue that divided them was the role of white people in the Meredith march. King's workers publicly thanked Northern whites for joining the procession. McKissick also thanked the Northerners but announced that black men must now lead the civil rights movement. And Carmichael mused aloud that maybe the whites should go home. As the column moved onto the back roads and Southern white hostility increased, the leadership of the march failed to agree on how to respond to violence. In Philadelphia, Mississippi, Dr. King conducted a memorial service for Goodman, Chaney, and Schwerner and told a crowd of 300 jeering whites that the murderers of the three men were no doubt "somewhere around me at this moment." Declaring that "I am not afraid of any man," King then delivered a Christian sermon. But after the service was over and local whites got rough, the marchers returned punch for punch.

The real spokesman for the march, it soon developed, was not King but Stokely Carmichael. In one town, after spending a few hours in jail, Carmichael told a crowd, "I ain't going to jail no more. I ain't going to jail no more," and he announced, "Every courthouse in Mississippi ought to be burned down to get rid of the dirt." Carmichael then issued the cry that would make him famous. Five times he shouted "Black Power!" and, the *New York Times* reported, "each time the younger members of the audience shouted back, 'Black Power.'" Informed of this new slogan, Dr. King expressed disapproval, and SCLC workers exhorted crowds to call not for black power but for "freedom now." Nevertheless, by the end of the Meredith march, black power had become a force to reckon with.[56]

At its inception in June, 1966, black power was not a systematic doctrine but a cry of rage. In an article in the *New York Times Magazine*, Dr. Poussaint tried to explain the psychological origin of the anger expressed in the new slogan:

I remember treating Negro workers after they had been beaten viciously by white toughs or policemen while conducting civil rights demonstrations. I would frequently comment, "You must feel pretty angry getting beaten up like that by those bigots." Often I received a reply such as: "No, I don't hate those white men, I love them because they must really be suffering with all that hatred in their souls. Dr. King says the only way we can win our freedom is through love. Anger and hatred has never solved anything."

I used to sit there and wonder, "Now, what do they really do with their rage?"

Poussaint reported that after a while these workers vented their mounting rage against each other.

While they were talking about being nonviolent and "loving" the sheriff that just hit them over the head, they rampaged around the project houses beating up each other. I frequently had to calm Negro civil rights workers with large doses of tranquilizers for what I can describe clinically only as acute attacks of rage.

In time the civil rights workers began to direct their anger against white racists, the Federal Government, and finally white people in the movement. Said Poussaint:

This rage was at a fever pitch for many months, before it became crystallized in the "Black Power" slogan. The workers who shouted it the loudest were those with the oldest battle scars from the terror, demoralization, and castration which they experienced through continual direct confrontation with Southern white racists. Furthermore, some of the most bellicose chanters of the slogan had been, just a few years before, examples of nonviolent, loving passive resistance in their struggle against white supremacy. These workers appeared to be seeking a sense of inner psychological emancipation from racists through self-assertion and release of aggressive angry feelings.[57]

In the months following the Meredith march, SNCC found itself at the center of a bitter national controversy and spokesman for an enlarged constituency. The anger implicit in the slogan "black power" assured SNCC a following in the ghettos of the North and ended its regional confinement. Through its leader, Stokely Carmichael, SNCC labored through 1966 and into 1967 to give intellectual substance to the black power slogan, seeking especially to frame an analysis that would be relevant to black Americans of all sections. Although his speeches were often inflammatory, Carmichael in his writing attempted serious, even restrained, argument suitable for an educated audience. But the elements of black power were not, in truth, derived from rational reflection but from wretched experience — from the beatings, jailhouses, and abortive crusades that SNCC veterans had endured for six years. SNCC had tried nonviolence and found it psychologically destructive. (The "days of the free head-whipping are over," Carmichael and his collaborator Charles Hamilton wrote. "Black people should and must fight back."[58]) SNCC, for example, had believed in integration and tried it within its own organization, but black and white together had not worked. (Integration, said Carmichael, "is a subterfuge for the maintenance of white supremacy" and "reinforces, among both black and white, the idea that 'white' is automatically better and 'black' is by definition inferior."[59]) SNCC had allied with white liberals in the Democratic party and had come away convinced that it had been betrayed. (In dealing with blacks, Carmichael said, white liberals "perpetuate a paternalistic, colonial relationship."[60]) SNCC had struggled for equal political rights but concluded finally that political inequality was less oppressive than economic exploitation. In 1966 SNCC felt it was necessary to go beyond the assertion of these hard conclusions and to attempt to impose on them systematic form. So it was that after years of activism divorced from ideology, SNCC began to reduce its field work and concentrate on fashioning an intellectual rationale for its new militancy. At a time when the black protest movement was floundering and its future direction was uncertain, SNCC stepped forward to contribute the doctrines of black power, which were really the culmination of its career. No history of SNCC would be complete, therefore, without some consideration of those doctrines.

According to Stokely Carmichael, the black masses suffer from two different but reinforcing forms of oppression: class exploitation and white racism. To illustrate this point, he relies on an analogy apparently inspired by Franz Fanon's *Wretched of the Earth,* a book with considerable influence in black power circles. The black communities of contemporary America, Carmichael says, share many of the characteristics of African colonies under European rule. Thus as Africa once enriched its imperialist masters by exporting valuable raw materials to Europe, so now do the American ghettos "export" their labor for the profit of American capitalists. In both Africa and America, white men own local businesses and use them to drain away any wealth somehow possessed by the subject population. As in Africa, there exists in the ghetto a white power structure that is no abstraction, but is a visible and concrete presence — the white landlords, for instance, who collect rent and ignore needed repairs, the city agencies and school systems that systematically neglect black people, the policemen who abuse black citizens and collect payoffs from white racketeers. By far the most insidious method devised by the white imperialists for perpetuating class exploitation has been the use of race as a badge of inferiority. Colonial masters, says Carmichael, "purposely, maliciously, and with reckless abandon relegated the black man to a subordinated, inferior status in society. . . . White America's School of Slavery and Segregation, like the School of Colonialism, has taught the subject to hate himself and deny his humanity." As the colonies of Africa have done, black Americans must undergo "political modernization," liberate their communities, and achieve self-determination. And like Africa, the ghetto must win the struggle by its own effort.[61]

For Carmichael, liberation begins with eradication of the effects of white racism. To overcome the shame of race bred in them by white men, blacks must develop a cultural identity, rediscover the rich African civilization from which they originally came, and learn from their history that they are a "vibrant, valiant people."[62] Freed of their damaging self-image, they can begin to challenge the capitalist values that have enslaved them as a class. The white middle class, says Carmichael, has fostered esteem for "material aggrandizement," is "without a viable conscience as regards humanity," and constitutes "the backbone of institutional racism in this country." Black men, however, will develop values emphasizing "the dignity of man, not . . . the sanctity of property," "free people," not "free enterprise."[63] "The society we seek to build among black people, then, is not a capitalist one. It is a society in which the spirit of community and humanistic love prevail."[64] To complete the process of liberation, black men will have to purge the ghetto of exploiting institutions and develop structures that conform to their new values.

The reconstruction of the black community, Carmichael contends, should be in the hands of black people in order to "convey the revolutionary idea . . . that black people are able to do things themselves." Among other acts of liberation that they can perform, ghetto blacks should conduct rent strikes against slum landlords and boycotts against the ghetto merchant who refuses to " 'invest' say forty to fifty percent of his net profit in the indigenous community." Governmental structures that have violated the humanity of blacks will have to be either eliminated from the ghetto or made responsive to their black constituency. The school system must be taken from professionals, most of whom have demonstrated "insensitivity to the needs and problems of the black child" and given to black parents, who will control personnel and curriculum. The indifference of the existing political parties to black people necessitates formation of separate (parallel) black organizations, both in the 110 Southern counties with black majorities and in the ghettos of the North.[65] According to Carmichael, it is simply naive to think that poor and powerless blacks have anything in common with the other components of the Democratic coalition. White liberals inevitably fall under the "overpowering influence" of their racist environment, and their demands for civil rights are "doing for blacks." Labor unions accept the existing order and, in the case of the AFL, even discriminate against black workers. Black political parties, Carmichael believes, will alone be devoted to real change and will in fact make possible emancipation from dominant American values and power centers.[66]

Carmichael professes to believe that black power is not really a departure from American practice. "Traditionally," he writes, "for each new ethnic group, the route to social and political integration into America's pluralistic society has been through the organization of their own institutions with which to represent their communal needs within the larger society."[67] Once in possession of power, blacks then could reenter the old coalitions for specific goals. But "let any ghetto group contemplating coalition be so tightly organized, so strong, that . . . it is an 'undigestible body' which cannot be absorbed or swallowed up." Given Carmichael's scheme for a radical reconstruction of American society, it is not surprising that the only group that he someday hopes to make his ally is the poor whites.[68]

As several critics have pointed out,[69] Carmichael's version of black power is hardly more than a collection of fragments, often lacking in clarity, consistency, and conviction. Thus, for example, Carmichael talks about the need for parallel institutions but offers only one example — black political organizations. He claims that these organizations can regenerate the entire political system but typically neglects to explain concretely how this regeneration is to be achieved. He calls for radical rejection of American values and institutions but at the same time portrays the black community as merely another ethnic group turning temporarily inward to prepare for later integration into American society. According to Carmichael, ghetto blacks are an exploited proletariat kept in bondage to enrich America's capitalist class; yet black workers seem more like a *lumpenproletariat* threatened with loss of economic function and forced to the margin of the American economy. Carmichael fails to reveal the mechanisms by which big business keeps the black man exploited, and indeed it seems doubtful that big business especially profits from the depressed condition of such a large group of potential consumers. But the real criticism of black power is not that as a body of thought it lacks coherence and sustained argument. Its greatest weakness is its failure to propose adequate solutions.

Carmichael began his argument by maintaining that black men suffer from two separate but related forms of discrimination — racial and economic. When Carmichael proposes ways for black men to undo the effects of racism, he makes good sense. Certainly black men should uncover their cultural roots and take pride in what has been of worth in their heritage. Certainly liberal paternalism is now anachronistic and black men should lead their own organizations. Nonviolence probably *was* psychologically damaging to many who practiced it, and integration into a hostile white society is not only an unrealistic goal but demeaning to a self-respecting people. Furthermore, some middle-class values, as Carmichael maintains, are less than ennobling, and elements of the black man's life style do have intrinsic merit. But it is doubtful whether black self-respect can ever be achieved without a solution of the second problem confronting ghetto blacks, and it is here that Carmichael's version of black power is most deficient.

Concerned primarily with humanizing social and governmental structures inside the ghetto, Carmichael has little to say about ending poverty in black America. Although more responsive policemen and schoolteachers and less dishonest slum lords and merchants will no doubt be a great step forward, these aspects of ghetto life are of less consequence than unemployment or poverty wages. Within the ghetto the resources for economic reconstruction are simply not available and since Carmichael rejects coalitions outside the ghetto, he is barred from offering a realistic economic strategy. It is this weakness that led the black intellectual and long-time civil rights leader Bayard Rustin to oppose black power. Pointing to the futility of separatist politics in a society in which the black man is a minority, Rustin calls for "a liberal-labor-civil rights coalition which would work to make the Democratic party truly responsive to the aspirations of the poor, and which would develop support for programs (specifically those outlined in A. Philip Randolph's $100 billion Freedom Budget) aimed at the reconstruction of American society in the interest of greater social justice."[70] Rustin's goals are considerably less apocalyptic than Carmichael's, but they are far more realistic. Carmichael's radical ruminations about a socialist alliance of poor whites and poor blacks seem fantasies irrelevant to American social realities. Although Carmichael's vision holds out hope for some distant time, it offers no meaningful proposals for the present.

The true significance of black power lies not in the doctrines into which it evolved but in the historical circumstances that gave it birth. The real message of black power is that after years of struggle to make America an open and just society, an important group of civil rights workers, instructed by the brute facts of its own history, gave up the fight. Black power was a cry of rage directed against white bigots who overcame righteous men by force, a cry of bitterness against white liberals who had only a stunted comprehension of the plight of the black poor, and a cry of frustration against gains that seemed meager when compared to needs. It is possible, however, that even rage can perform a useful function, and if the black power slogan brings about a constructive catharsis and helps rouse the black masses from apathy, then the intellectual shortcomings of black power doctrines may seem of little consequence, and what began as a cry of despair may yet play a creative role in the black protest movement. Therefore, whether the history of SNCC in this decade will be considered triumph or tragedy depends on events yet to occur.

Notes

[1] For accounts of the sit-ins see Howard Zinn, *SNCC: The New Abolitionists* (Beacon, 1965), Chapter 2; Jack Newfield, *A Prophetic Minority* (Signet, 1966), Chapter 3; August Meier, "The Successful Sit-Ins in a Border City: A Study in Social Causation," *The Journal of Intergroup Relations,* II (Summer, 1961), 230–37; Charles U. Smith, "The Sit-Ins and the New Negro Student," *ibid.,* 223–29; James Peck, *Freedom Ride* (Simon & Schuster, 1962), Chapter 6.

154 **By Any Means Necessary**

² Quoted in Newfield, *A Prophetic Minority,* p. 47.

³ Emily Schottenfeld Stoper, "Student Nonviolent Coordinating Committee: The Growth of Radicalism in a Civil Rights Organization," unpublished dissertation, Harvard University, 1968, pp. 35–36.

⁴ Ruth Searles and J. Allen Williams, Jr., "Negro College Students' Participation in Sit-Ins," *Social Forces* (Dec., 1966), 215–20.

⁵ Michael Walzer, "The Politics of the New Negro," *Dissent,* VII (Summer, 1960), 235–43.

⁶ Anne Braden, "The Southern Freedom Movement in Perspective," *Monthly Review,* XVII (July–Aug., 1965), 31–32; also James Howard Laue, "Direct Action and Desegregation: Toward a Theory of the Rationalization of Protest," unpublished dissertation, Harvard University, 1965, p. 128.

⁷ For accounts of the Freedom Rides, see Zinn, *SNCC,* Chapter 3; and Peck, *Freedom Ride,* Chapters 8 and 9.

⁸ Laue, "Direct Action and Desegregation," pp. 154, 160, 167–68.

⁹ On origins of the voter registration drive, see Pat Watters and Reece Cleghorn, *Climbing Jacob's Ladder* (Harcourt, Brace & World, 1967), pp. 44–59; and Louis Lomax, *The Negro Revolt* (Signet, 1963), pp. 246–50.

¹⁰ Braden, "Southern Freedom Movement," p. 36; Laue, "Direct Action and Desegregation," p. 171; Stoper, "The Student Nonviolent Coordinating Committee," pp. 6 and 8.

¹¹ For an account of Moses in Mississippi, see Zinn, *SNCC,* Chapter 4.

¹² See *ibid.,* Chapter 10; and Watters and Cleghorn, *Climbing Jacob's Ladder,* p. 58.

¹³ Laue, "Direct Action and Desegregation," pp. 179, 338.

¹⁴ Stoper, "The Student Nonviolent Coordinating Committee," p. 104; *New York Times* (Dec. 24, 1961), section IV, 5.

¹⁵ "Integration: Hotter Fires," *Newsweek,* LXII (July 1, 1963), 19–21.

¹⁶ Robert Penn Warren, *Who Speaks for the Negro* (Random House, 1965), p. 91.

¹⁷ Quoted in Watters and Cleghorn, *Climbing Jacob's Ladder,* pp. xiv–xv.

¹⁸ On freedom ballot, see Len Holt, *The Summer That Didn't End* (William Morrow, 1965), pp. 35–36, 152–53.

¹⁹ Zinn, *SNCC,* pp. 8–9, 186–88; see also Calvin Trillin, "Letter from Jackson," *New Yorker,* XL (Aug. 29, 1964), 80–105.

²⁰ Quoted in James Atwater, "If We Can Crack Mississippi . . . ," *Saturday Evening Post,* CCXXXVII (July 25, 1964), 16.

²¹ Sally Belfrage, *Freedom Summer* (Viking, 1965). p. 11.

²² Elizabeth Sutherland, ed., *Letters from Mississippi* (McGraw-Hill, 1965), pp. 5–6.

²³ Watters and Cleghorn, *Climbing Jacob's Ladder,* p. 139.

²⁴ Holt, *The Summer That Didn't End,* Chapter 8; Zinn, *SNCC,* p. 251.

²⁵ Holt, *The Summer That Didn't End,* pp. 16–17; Watters and Cleghorn, *Climbing Jacob's Ladder,* pp. 290–92; *New York Times* (Aug. 25, 1964), 23.

²⁶ William McCord, *Mississippi: The Long Hot Summer* (Norton, 1965), p. 117.

²⁷ Mrs. Hamer is quoted in Holt, *The Summer That Didn't End,* p. 174.

²⁸ *New York Times* (Aug. 25, 1964), 23; Holt, *The Summer That Didn't End,* pp. 171–78; see also Zinn, *SNCC,* pp. 251–56; and Stoper, "The Student Nonviolent Coordinating Committee," pp. 74, 77–79, 81.

²⁹ See, for instance, Sutherland, *Letters from Mississippi,* p. 48.

³⁰ Quoted in *ibid.,* p. 202.

³¹ Quoted in Pat Watters, *Encounter with the Future* (Southern Regional Council, May, 1965), p. 32.

³² Belfrage, *Freedom Summer,* p. 80.

[33] Robert Coles, "Social Struggle and Awareness," *Psychiatry,* XXVII (Nov., 1964), 305–15.

[34] Watters, *Encounter with the Future,* pp. 29–31; see also Lerone Bennett, Jr., "SNCC, Rebels with a Cause," *Ebony,* XX (July, 1965), 146–53.

[35] For the Moses quote, see Gene Roberts, "From Freedom High to 'Black Power,' " *New York Times Magazine* (Sept. 25, 1966), 21; see also Bruce Payne, "The Student Nonviolent Coordinating Committee: An Overview Two Years Later," *The Activist* (Nov., 1965), 6–7; and Stoper, "Student Nonviolent Coordinating Committee," pp. 126–27.

[36] These quotations are from transcripts of informal taped interviews conducted in the South in 1965 by students of Stanford University. The tapes are stored at Stanford.

[37] Alvin F. Poussaint, "Problems of White Civil Rights Workers in the South," *Psychiatric Opinion,* II (Dec., 1966), 21.

[38] Alvin F. Poussaint, "The Stresses of the White Female Worker in the Civil Rights Movement in the South," *American Journal of Psychiatry,* CXXIII (Oct., 1966), 401.

[39] Taped by Stanford students in 1965.

[40] *Ibid.*

[41] Poussaint, "Problems of White Civil Rights Workers in the South," 20–21.

[42] Poussaint, "Stresses of the White Female Worker," 404.

[43] On influence of Malcolm X on SNCC, see Stoper, "The Student Nonviolent Coordinating Committee," p. 181.

[44] *The Autobiography of Malcolm X* (Grove Press, 1966), pp. 280–81.

[45] *Malcolm X Speaks: Selected Speeches and Statements* (Merit, 1965), p. 12.

[46] *Ibid.,* 38–39.

[47] E. U. Essien-Udom, *Black Nationalism* (Univ. of Chicago Press, 1962), p. 3.

[48] A Report by the Governor's Commission on the Los Angeles Riot, *Violence in the City — An End or a Beginning?* (Dec. 2, 1965), pp. 1–2. (Referred to hereafter as the McCone Report.)

[49] McCone Report, pp. 1,4–5.

[50] Robert M. Fogelson, "White on Black: A Critique of the McCone Commission Report on the Los Angeles Riots," *Political Science Quarterly;* LXXXII (Sept., 1967), 345.

[51] E. Edward Ransford, *Attitudes and Other Characteristics of Negroes in Watts, South Central, and Crenshaw Areas of Los Angeles* (a staff study prepared for the McCone Commission), p. 2.

[52] See, for instance, Robert Conot, *Rivers of Blood, Years of Darkness* (Bantam Books, 1967), p. 204.

[53] Quoted in Robert Blauner, "Whitewash over Watts: The Failure of the McCone Commission Report," *Transaction,* III (March–April, 1966), 9.

[54] Bayard Rustin, "The Watts 'Manifesto' and the McCone Report," *Commentary,* XLI (March, 1966), 30.

[55] This account of Carmichael's election and the quotations from SNCC's statement are from Newfield, *A Prophetic Minority,* pp. 75–77.

[56] For the Meredith march, see *New York Times,* June 7, 1966, p. 1; June 8, pp. 1 and 26; June 9, p. 1; June 12, pp. 1 and 82; June 17, p. 1; June 21, p. 30; June 22, p. 25.

[57] Alvin F. Poussaint, "A Negro Psychiatrist Explains the Negro Psyche," *New York Times Magazine* (Aug 20, 1967), 55 ff.

[58] Stokely Carmichael and Charles V. Hamilton, *Black Power: The Politics of Liberation* (Vintage, 1967), p. 52.

[59] Stokely Carmichael, "What We Want," *New York Review of Books* (Sept. 22, 1966), 6.

[60] Carmichael and Hamilton, *Black Power,* p. 65.

[61] For the colonial analogy, see *ibid.*, Chapter 1.

[62] *Ibid.*, pp. 37–39.

[63] *Ibid.*, pp. 40–4.

[64] Carmichael, "What We Want," 7.

[65] Carmichael and Hamilton, *Black Power*, Chapter 8 and p. 166.

[66] *Ibid.*, pp. 60–66.

[67] Stokely Carmichael, "Toward Black Liberation," *The Massachusetts Review*, VII (Autumn, 1966), 642.

[68] Carmichael and Hamilton, *Black Power*, pp. 80, 82.

[69] For critiques of black power, see, for instance, Paul Feldman, "The Pathos of 'Black Power,'" *Dissent* (Jan.–Feb., 1967), 69–79; Bayard Rustin, "'Black Power' and Coalition Politics," *Commentary*, XLII (Sept., 1966), 35–40; Christopher Lasch, "The Trouble with Black Power," *New York Review of Books*, X (Feb. 29, 1968), 4 ff.

[70] Bayard Rustin, "'Black Power' and Coalition Politics," 36.

The Meanings of Black Power: A Comparison of White and Black Interpretations of a Political Slogan

Joel D. Aberbach
Jack L. Walker

Introduction

Angry protests against racial discrimination were a prominent part of American public life during the 1960's. The decade opened with the sit-ins and freedom rides, continued through Birmingham, Selma, and the March on Washington, and closed with protests in hundreds of American cities, often punctuated by rioting and violence. During this troubled decade the rhetoric of protest became increasingly demanding, blanket charges of pervasive white racism and hostility were more common, and some blacks began to actively discourage whites from participating either in protest demonstrations or civil rights organizations. Nothing better symbolized the changing mood and style of black protest in America than recent changes in the movement's dominant symbols. Demonstrators who once shouted "freedom" as their rallying cry now were shouting "black power" — a much more provocative, challenging slogan.

The larger and more diverse a political movement's constituency, the more vague and imprecise its unifying symbols and rallying cries are likely to be. A slogan like black power has no sharply defined meaning; it may excite many different emotions and may motivate individuals to express their loyalty or take action for almost contradictory reasons. As soon as Adam Clayton Powell and Stokely Carmichael began to use the phrase in 1966 it set off an acrimonious debate among black leaders over its true meaning. Initially it was a blunt and threatening battle cry

Joel D. Aberbach and Jack L. Walker, "The Meanings of Black Power: A Comparison of Black and White Interpretations of a Political Slogan," *American Political Science Review,* LXIV, June 1970, pp. 367–88. Reprinted by permission of The American Political Science Association.

meant to symbolize a break with the past tactics of the civil rights movement. As Stokely Carmichael put it in one of his early speeches:

The only way we gonna stop the white men from whippin' us is to take over. . . . We've been saying freedom for six years and we ain't got nothin'. What we gonna start saying now is black power, . . . from now on when they ask you what you want, you know to tell them: black power, black power, black power![1]

Speeches of this kind not only were a challenge to the white community; they also were attacks on the currently established black civil rights leaders, especially those who had employed more accommodating appeals or had used conventional political and legal channels to carry on their struggle. Carmichael's speeches brought a swift, negative response from Roy Wilkins:

No matter how endlessly they try to explain it, the term black power means anti-white power. . . . It has to mean going it alone. It has to mean separatism. Now separatism . . . offers a disadvantaged minority little except a chance to shrivel and die. . . . It is a reverse Mississippi, a reverse Hitler, a reverse Ku Klux Klan. . . . We of the NAACP will have none of this. We have fought it too long.[2]

Although not so adamant and uncompromising as Wilkins, Martin Luther King expressed the doubts of many moderate leaders when he said:

It's absolutely necessary for the Negro to gain power, but the term "black power" is unfortunate because it tends to give the impression of black nationalism. . . . We must never seek power exclusively for the Negro, but the sharing of power with the white people. Any other course is exchanging one form of tyranny for another. Black supremacy would be equally evil as white supremacy. My problem with SNCC is not their militancy. I think you can be militantly non-violent. It's what I see as a pattern of violence emerging and their use of the cry "black power," which whether they mean it or not, falls on the ear as racism in reverse.[3]

This disagreement over the implications of the black power slogan was caused partly by a clash of personalities and ambitions, but it was also the result of fundamental differences over the proper role of a black minority in a society dominated by white men. Should the ultimate goal be complete assimilation and the development of an essentially "color blind" society, or should blacks strive to build a cohesive, autonomous community, unified along racial lines, which would be in a stronger position to demand concessions and basic social changes from the whites? For American Negroes, who bear the brutal legacy of slavery and are cut off from their African heritage, this is a terribly difficult choice. As James Baldwin said when he compared himself with the lonely, poverty-stricken African students he met in Paris: "The African . . . has endured privation, injustice, medieval cruelty; but the

African has not yet endured the utter alienation of himself from his people and his past. His mother did not sing 'Sometimes I Feel Like a Motherless Child,' and he has not, all his life long, ached for acceptance in a culture which pronounced straight hair and white skin the only acceptable beauty."[4] The slogan black power raises all the agonizing dilemmas of personal and national identity which have plagued black Americans since the end of slavery; the current dispute over its meaning is echoed in the speeches of Frederick Douglass, Booker T. Washington, W. E. B. DuBois, and Marcus Garvey.

Those, like Harold Cruse,[5] interested in a comprehensive social theory to guide black development in the United States are not particularly impressed with the term black power because:

it is open to just as many diverse and conflicting interpretations [as the former abstractions Justice and Liberation]. While it tries to give more clarity to what forms Freedom will assume in America as the end-product of a new program, the Black Power dialogue does not close the conceptual gap between shadow and substance any more than it plots a course for the program dynamic.[6]

Cruse hopes for the development of a synthetic political ideology in the classic sense which brings together economic, cultural and political factors; black power, at this point in time, is a label for a series of ideas which fall far short of this goal.

Whatever interpretation may be given it, black power is a provocative slogan which causes excitement and elicits strong responses from people. Even though, as Charles Hamilton says, "in this highly charged atmosphere it is virtually impossible to come up with a single definition satisfactory to all,"[7] the definition an individual selects may tell us a great deal about how he defines himself politically in a society torn by racial strife. His definition is a way for him to bring together his view on leaders and events in the environment. If he agrees with Stokely Carmichael and Charles Hamilton, he sees black power as "a call for black people in this country to unite, to recognize their heritage, to build a sense of community."[8] He may also see it as a call for anything from "premeditated acts of violence to destroy the political and economic institutions of this country" to "the use of pressure-group tactics in the accepted tradition of the American political process."[9]

We know that community leaders have strong reactions to the black power slogan, but little is known of its impact on ordinary citizens, both black and white. As we shall demonstrate, for the white citizen the slogan usually provokes images of black domination or contemporary unrest which he cannot understand or tolerate. For the black citizen, it is more likely to raise subtle issues of tactics and emphasis in the racial struggle. In this essay we will examine how blacks and whites in a large urban center define black power, why they define it as they do, and whether their view of the slogan is part of a coherent set of interpretations and evaluations, a racial ideology, which they use to define the role of blacks as political and social actors in our society.

The Data

Our analysis is based on data gathered in a survey of Detroit, Michigan, completed in the fall of 1967. A total of 855 respondents were interviewed (394 whites and 461 blacks). In all cases whites were interviewed by whites, blacks by blacks. The total N came from a community random sample of 539 (344 whites and 195 blacks) and a special random supplement of 316 (50 whites and 266 blacks) drawn from the areas where rioting took place in July, 1967.[10] Since there are few meaningful differences between the distributions or the relationships of interest in the random and riot-supplement samples, we have employed the total N in the analysis so that a larger number of cases are available when controls are instituted.

A Profile of Community Opinion

Since there is such confusion and uncertainty over the meaning of black power among the writers, spokesmen and political leaders of both races, we might wonder if the slogan has had any impact at all on average citizens. The first questions we must ask are simply: do our respondents recognize the term, have they formed an elaborate reaction to it, and if so, what meaning do they give it?

Because of the lack of consensus among community leaders about the precise meaning of black power or even agreement on a common framework for discussing the slogan, we were reluctant to use a close-ended question to capture our respondents' interpretations of the term. In order to avoid the danger of biasing responses or eliciting a random choice we used a simple, open open-ended question: "What do the words 'black power' mean to you?" This has the advantage of permitting people to speak with a minimum of clues, but it also has disadvantages which we recognized. Respondents may not have given the term a great deal of thought and their answers may be unreliable indicators of their opinion (or lack of opinion). Use of the vernacular at times inhibited interpretation of the answers.[11] It was sometimes difficult to judge whether a respondent was sympathetic or unsympathetic to black power as he interpreted it. For example, a small number of Negro respondents (N = 3) could only define black power as "rebellion." We can guess their feelings about this word from the context of the interview, but this carries us a step away from their answers.

Fortunately, the answers were generally quite comprehensible and when we asked the same open-ended question of a subsample of the original respondents one year later (1968) we received answers consistent with their first response from a majority of the people.[12] In addition, in 1968 we supplemented the question on the meaning of black power with a close-ended item: "Do you approve or disapprove of 'black power'?" This provided a means of checking the criteria we developed in 1967 from the open-ended question for deciding whether respondents had a favorable or unfavorable view of the black power slogan. The correlation between our scoring as favorable or unfavorable of the 1968 respondents' interpretations of black power on the open-ended question and their own assessment, on the close-ended question, of their position was (Gamma) .99 for blacks and .97 for whites.[13]

Table 1 presents a simple profile of Detroit community responses to our question on black power. As noted above, since there were no appreciable differences for either race in the interpretations given by respondents in the riot or non-riot areas, we have included all our respondents in the analysis.[14]

Table 1: Black Power Interpretations, by Race

(Question: What do the words "black power" mean to you?)

Interpretation	Blacks	Whites
Unfavorable		
Blacks Rule Whites	8.5%	38.6%
Racism	3.9	7.3
Trouble, Rioting, Civil Disorder	4.1	11.9
"Nothing"	22.3	5.3
Negative Imprecise Comments (ridicule, obscenity, abhorrence)	6.5	11.7
Other*	4.3	5.9
	49.6	80.7
Favorable		
Fair Share for Black People	19.6	5.1
Racial (Black) Unity	22.6	5.6
	42.2	10.7
Don't Know, Can't Say	8.2	8.6
	100%	100%
	(N = 461)	(N = 394)

* "Other" responses were scattered and inconsistent, although generally negative. They include references to black power as communism, radicalism, a return to segregation and a sophisticated failure to define the concept because of a perception that it has contradictory meanings. The latter answer was given by one black and five white respondents.

Interpretations indicating a favorable or unfavorable attitude toward black power are marked off for the convenience of the reader. As we go through the various categories the reasons for our designations will be explained in detail.

Almost 40 percent of the whites believe black power means black rule over whites, while only 9 percent of the black respondents hold this view. This attitude of the whites is clearly *not* a function of a rational projection that the increasing black population in the city of Detroit (now about 40 percent) will soon elect a black mayor, but is an almost hysterical response to the symbolism of the slogan. White people in this category usually refer to blacks taking over the entire country or even the world:[15]

(white, male, 47, 12 grades) Nasty word! That the blacks won't be satisfied until they get complete control of our country by force if necessary.

(white, male, 24, 12 grades plus) Black takeover — Take over the world because that is what they want to do and they will. There's no doubt about it. Why should they care? I'm working and supporting their kids. In time they'll take over — look at how many there are in Congress. It's there — when they get to voting age, we'll be discriminated upon.

(white, female, 28, 12 grades plus) The colored are going to take over and be our leaders and we're to be their servants. Yes, that's exactly what it means.

(white, female, 28, 12 grades) They want the situation reversed. They want to rule everything.

(white, male, 32, 11 grades) The Negro wants to enslave the white man like he was enslaved 100 years ago. They want to take everything away from us. There will be no middle class, no advancement. He is saying, "If I can't have it neither can you." Everything will be taken away from us. We'll all be poor.

(white, female, 40, 12 grades) I don't like the sound of it. Sounds like something coming to take you over.

Most of our black respondents *do not* interpret black power in this way. Blacks who were coded in this category were usually also hostile to black power. For example:

(black, male, 28, 12 grades plus) It means dominating black rule — to dominate, to rule over like Hitlerism.

(black, female, 38, 11 grades plus) It means something I don't like. It means like white power is now — taking over completely.

(black, male, 29, no answer on education) It means to me that Negroes are trying to take over and don't know how.

A few others gave this answer because they have very vague ideas about the concept:

(black, female, 50, 9 grades) Sounds like they want to take over control.

There were only seven people in this group of 37 blacks who saw black domination over whites as the definition of black power and whose answers could possibly be interpreted as approval of this goal.

A small number of whites and blacks simply defined black power as racism or race hatred. The comments of blacks holding this view were especially scathing:

(black, female, 57, 11 grades) It's like the Ku Klux Klan and I don't like it.

(black, female, 38, 12 grades) It means something very detrimental to the race as a whole. This is the same tactic the whites use in discriminating.

The black power definitions of about 12 percent of the white population and 4 percent of the blacks sampled were directly influenced by the violence of the 1967 Detroit disorders. Terms like "trouble" and "rioting" were commonly used by these individuals, especially blacks in the riot areas and whites outside of it. Clearly, however, the vast majority of black people sampled do not see black power as a synonym for violence and destruction, racism or even black rule over whites, while 57.2 percent of the whites do.

Two views of black power predominate among our black respondents. One represents a poorly articulated negativism or opposition to the term and the other a positive or approving interpretation of the concept and its meaning. Roughly 23 percent of the black respondents indicated that the term meant "nothing" to them. This category was coded separately from the "Don't Know," "Can't Say," and "No Answer" responses because the word "nothing" is generally used as a term of derision, especially in the black community. Some examples of extended responses give the proper flavor:

(black, female, 39, 10 grades) Nothing! (Interviewer probe) Not a damn thing. (further probe) Well, it's just a word used by people from the hate school so it don't mean nothing to me.

(black, male, 52, 12 grades plus) It means nothing! (probe) A word coined by some nut. (further probe) There is only one power and that is God.

(black, female, 60, 5 grades) It doesn't mean nothing. (probe) Biggest joke in the 20th century.

It is, of course, possible that some people use "nothing" as a synonym for "I don't know." We have two major pieces of evidence which indicate that this is not so for the major proportion of blacks giving the response: (1) while direct expressions of ignorance ("don't know," "can't say," etc.) are a function of educational level, "nothing" is used in the same proportion by blacks no matter what their academic accomplishments; (2) blacks use the expression more than four times as often as whites (22 percent to 5 percent) in trying to express what black power means to them; and (3) almost 90 percent of the respondents who interpreted black power in this way in 1968 also expressed disapproval of the term on our close-ended question.[16]

There are other individuals who give less ambiguous, clearly negative interpretations of the term. A small proportion of our respondents (1.3 percent of the blacks and 0.7 percent of the whites) found profanity indispensable as the sole expression of their definition. Others (5.2 percent of the blacks and 11.0 percent of the whites) were slightly more articulate in their condemnation, although their definitions were still imprecise. Often, especially for the whites, they reflect a general abhorrence of power in any form:

(white, female, 52, 12 grades) I hate the expression because I don't like power. It's very domineering and possessive and (they) have only themselves in mind.

(white, male, 54, 4 grades) No more than the words white power mean. They should cut that word out.

(black, female, 37, 9 grades) Black power and white power means the same to me which is no good. Man should be treated as a man.

(white, female, 55, 12 grades) Disaster! You know what you can do with your black power.

(white, female, 53, 12 grades) Scare! Why should there be black power any more than white power? Don't the blacks agree that all races are equal?

The last remaining major category of answers clearly distinguishes the black from the white community in its view of black power. In their statements 42.2 percent of our black respondents as compared to 10.7 percent of the whites emphasized a "fair share for black people" or "black unity." We coded all those answers which stressed blacks getting their share of the honors and fruits of production in society, exercising equal rights, bettering their living conditions or gaining greater political power into our "fair share" categories. Definitions stressing black unity or racial pride were coded separately.[17] Since only 7 blacks and 2 whites mentioned racial pride specifically, we will refer in the text to "black unity" or "racial unity" only. We felt that a definition of black power in terms of black people gaining political power in areas where blacks are in the majority fell under our fair share concept, but there were only two statements of this type. This definition may be implicit in the statements made (or in some of our black unity interpretations), but virtually all references are to justice and equity rather than exclusive control of a geographical area.

Fair share answers were given by almost twenty percent of our black respondents. People whose responses fall into this category see the black power slogan as another statement of traditional Negro goals of freedom, equality and opportunity. Respondents often take pains to reject notions of blacks taking advantage of others:

(black, female, 47, 12 grades plus) That we should have blacks represent us in government — not take over, but represent us.

(black, male, 40, 9 grades plus) Negroes getting the same opportunities as whites when qualified.

(black, male, 24, 12 grades) Negroes should get more power to do the same things which whites do.

(black, female, 52, 12 grades plus) Give us an equal chance.

(black, male, 41, 0 grades) To me it means an open door into integration.

(black, male, 39, 12 grades) Equal rights to any human being.

(black, female, 54, 7 grades) That America is going to have a new power structure so black people can have a share.

(black, male, 23, 10 grades) Getting in possession of something — like jobs and security.

(black, male, 55, 12 grades) It means equal opportunities for both races. What's good for one is good for the other.

About 23 percent of our black respondents gave "black unity" responses.[18] These were more militant in tone than the fair share definitions, sometimes extremely nationalistic, but always (as in the fair share answers) concerned with bettering the situation of the black man and not putting down the white man. In fact, the data suggest to us that blacks who are most favorably disposed towards black power simply do not see the political world as one where blacks can gain something only at the expense of whites and vice versa. As we have seen, however, large numbers of whites do see things this way. For them one group or the other must tend to "take over."

The major difference between the "fair share" and "black unity" groups is that the former places heavy stress on blacks as equal participants in the total society, while the latter emphasizes black togetherness and achievement without the same attention to the traditional symbols of Negro advancement. We know from extended answers to our black power question and others that individuals giving black unity responses want equality and a just share of America's goods, but "thinking black" and speaking militantly and with pride are given primacy when talking about black power.[19] It is not that they are against white people; they are simply *for* black people and deeply committed to the idea of black people working together:

(black, male, 35, 9 grades) People getting together to accomplish things for the group.

(black, male, 36, 12 grades plus) Negroes have never been together on anything. Now with the new movement we gain strength.

(black, male, 24, 12 grades) We people getting together, agreeing on issues and attempting to reach a common goal.

(black, male, 28, 12 grades) Sounds frightening, but really is what whites, Jews, Arabs and people the world over do — divided we fall united we stand.

(black, female, 41, 12 grades plus) Togetherness among Negroes; but it means you can get along with others.

(black, female, 37, 10 grades) It means being true to yourself and recognize yourself as a black American who can accomplish good things in life.

(black, female, 57, 10 grades) The white man separated us when he brought us here and we been that way ever since. We are just trying to do what everybody else has — stick together.

As we have noted, the number of whites giving either the fair share or black unity response is small — just over 10 percent of the white sample. To most whites, even those who think of themselves as liberals, the concept of black power is forbidding. The 1967 riot is certainly one factor that might account for this, but we found little evidence of it. Only 5 whites in the entire sample (one percent) gave answers like the following:

(white, female, 23, college) It's gotten (away) from the original meaning. Means violence to me now.

In addition, as we shall see, even whites who have very sympathetic views about the causes of the disturbances can hardly be described as favorable to black power. The negative presentations of black power in the mass media may be responsible, but Detroit Negroes are also attentive to the same media and their views are quite different. The evidence presented in Table 1 points strongly towards a simple conclusion — the overwhelming majority of whites are frightened and bewildered by the words black power. Some of this seems rooted in abhorrence of stark words like power, but the term *black* power is obviously intolerable. The words conjure up racial stereotypes and suspicions deeply ingrained in the minds of white Americans. The slogan presents an unmistakable challenge to the country's prevailing racial customs and social norms; for precisely this reason it seems exciting and attractive to many blacks.

In summary, the vast majority of white people are hostile to the notion of black power. The most common interpretation is that it symbolizes a black desire to take over the country, or somehow deprive the white man. Blacks, on the other hand, are almost evenly divided in their interpretations with 42.2 percent clearly favorable to black power and 49.6 percent defining it in an unfavorable way. Those blacks who are favorable to black power see it as another call for a fair share for blacks or as a rallying cry for black unity, while those who are negatively inclined tend to see it as empty and meaningless (our "nothing" category, for example). Blacks certainly do not interpret the term the way the whites do. They do not see it as meaning racism, a general black takeover, or violence, and those few blacks who do define the term in this way are negative about such meanings. It is evident that "black power" is a potent slogan which arouses contradictory feelings in large numbers of people. Interpretations of the term may differ, but the slogan clearly stimulates intense feelings and may be exciting enough to move men to purposeful action.

Although these data invite many different forms of analysis, we have decided that an attempt to understand the sources of favorable reactions to the black power slogan is of primary importance. We have, accordingly, conducted a detailed investigation of factors which predispose an individual to give a "fair share" or "black unity" response to our question on the meaning of black power. In the case of blacks, we are confident that all such definitions indicate a favorable attitude and for whites we know that they usually represent a positive attitude and always indicate at least a grudging respect or admiration. Certainly, as indicated above, we will miss a few black people who are favorable to black power if we follow this procedure, but the number is very small. In most cases, in order to keep the tables and text from becoming inordinately complex, we will combine the fair share and black unity categories and speak of individuals favorably interpreting black power, but where differences between respondents giving these two answers are of great importance we will consider them separately.

The Appeal of Black Power:
Social Change, Socialization and Deprivation

Many social scientists in recent years have been struggling to understand the increasing militancy within the black community and the concurrent rise in popularity of slogans like black power. To date, most systematic social science research in this area has centered on the "conventional militancy" of the early 1960's[20] or the backgrounds and attitudes of rioters and those who sympathize with them.[21] The civil disturbances of the mid-1960's were clearly watersheds in American racial history, but most scholars concentrating on the riots would agree that there is more to the current upheaval in the black community — symbolized by the slogan black power — than violence. Recent calls for racial pride, black unity and black self-esteem, and programs to promote these ends, are meant to reach members of the community and help them to become a constructive force in their own behalf.

This section is devoted to a discussion of the factors which predispose an individual to intepret black power favorably. The major emphasis in our analysis will be on our black respondents, but at times we will compare them to whites in order to highlight certain points. The relative lack of support for black power among white respondents prevents a more elaborate analysis of their views in this section stressing favorable versus unfavorable interpretations of the term.

It is probably best to begin by laying to rest the so-called "riffraff" theory, which has been the favorite target of many riot researchers, as a possible explanation for the appeal of the black power slogan. The riffraff theory, drawn from the report of the McCone Commission on the Watts riots of 1964,[22] holds that urban unrest is a product of a deprived underclass of recent unassimilated migrants to the cities. We will discuss the issue of migration below, but neither education (Gamma = $-.02$)[23] nor income (Gamma = $-.06$) nor occupation (Gamma = $.00$) is a very potent predictor of favorable interpretations of black power for blacks. For whites, on the other hand, education (Gamma = $.32$), income (Gamma = $.23$) and occupation (Gamma = $.48$) are associated with positive views of black power, but here it is the upper status elements who interpret the slogan favorably.[24] It is clear that any notion that black power appeals strictly to the less privileged in the black community is without foundation.

Some scholars, and many journalists and politicians, have adopted the clash between generations as a principal explanation of the growing popularity of the black power slogan.[25] The riots in Detroit and Los Angeles are seen as only one manifestation of a worldwide revolt of youth against the established order. The young are said to be more impatient and less willing to accept marginal gains than their elders.

When we divided our respondents according to age, however, we did not find great differences over the interpretation of black power within either racial group, although age was a better predictor for whites (Gamma = −.26) than for blacks (Gamma = −.11). Among blacks, 51 percent of those in their twenties gave the racial unity or fair share interpretations, but almost the same percentage of thirty, forty and fifty-year-olds gave similar responses. Approval of black power drops off among sixty and seventy-year-old blacks, but they constitute a small percentage of our sample. As noted above, age is a better predictor for whites with individuals forty and older somewhat less likely to offer an approving interpretation of black power than those under forty.

Social Change and Socialization: Breaking the Traditional Mold

One might assume after examining this relationship that the much discussed "generation gap" is not very wide, especially in the black community. But that conclusion would be unwarranted. Differences among blacks exist, not between youth and age, but between those who grew up in Michigan and those who were born and grew up in the South. Blacks who were born in Michigan are much more likely to give the racial unity or fair share interpretation of black power than those born in the South (Gamma = .33).[26] When we related age and attitudes toward black power with regional background controlled (Table 2), we found that the

Table 2: Percentages of Black Respondents Favorably Interpreting Black Power* According to Their Ages and Regions of Birth

Present Age (In Ten's)	Southern Born (Arrived in Michigan after Age 21)	Southern Born (Arrived in Michigan before Age 21)	Born in Michigan
10's	**	33%(6)	67%(12)
20's	39%(13)	46%(26)	59%(41)
30's	21%(19)	44%(45)	58%(24)
40's	52%(25)	64%(31)	55%(20)
50's	35%(20)	63%(19)	**
60's	17%(12)	33%(12)	**
70's	33%(12)	**	**
	(Gamma = −.02)	(Gamma =.15)	(Gamma = −.12)

* For economy of presentation and because of the complexity of our black power code, we display only the percentages of respondents favorably interpreting black power, that is, those who gave fair share or black unity interpretations of black power.
** Percentages are not displayed if N is less than 5.

background factors clearly predominated. Those in our sample who were born in Michigan are much younger, on the average, than the rest of our respondents (78 percent are under 40 years old and 98 percent are under 50), but definitions of black power are almost invariable for this group between age categories. There is also very little variance between age categories for those who were born in the South and came to Michigan after they were 21 years old, although, of course, there is much less approval for black power in this group. In both cases, it is regional background and not age which is the most powerful explanatory factor. Further confirmation of this conclusion comes when we examine those respondents who were born in the South, but arrived in Michigan before they were 21.

Within this group we find that the percentage of those voicing approval of black power actually *increases* along with age from the teens to the fifties, and then decreases again for the small number who are in their sixties.

It might be thought that regional differences mask a more fundamental difference between blacks who were born in cities and those raised in rural areas. This is not the case. Thirty-nine percent of Southern-born Negroes who grew up on farms and in small towns favored black power; the percentage giving fair share or black unity interpretations is only 4.3 percent higher (43.3 percent) for respondents raised in the large Southern towns and cities (Gamma = .03).

This evidence leads us to conclude that, for all but the very old, it is primarily the experience of life in Michigan and not the respondent's age which helps determine his reaction to black power.[27] A great migration began during World War II which brought thousands of black workers to the auto plants and foundries of Detroit. Their children are coming of age in the 1960's. It is not their youth, however, which leads them to see black power as a call for racial unity or a fair share for their race; it is their experience with the culture of the urban North. It seems that the further one is from life in the South, and the sooner one experiences life in a city like Detroit, the more likely one is to approve of black power.

Life in the Northern city brings to bear on a black person forces which lead him to reject the traditional, subservient attitudes of Southern Negroes, particularly if these forces represent his major socializing experience. Away from the parochial, oppressive atmosphere of the South, he is born into or slowly appropriates the more cosmopolitan, secularized culture of the North. The new life in the promised lands of Detroit, New York and Chicago is exciting and disillusioning at the same time. It brings new hopes and the promise of a better life, and disappointments when achievements do not live up to expectations.

The Southern migrant arrived in the "promised land" to find bigotry, filth, and a more sophisticated form of degradation. With time, he grasps sufficient information about the urban paradise. Traditional attitudes of deference and political passivity fade as a militant social and political stance gains approval in the community.[28] This is the atmosphere for the emerging popularity of fair share and racial unity interpretations of slogans like black power.

Just as the trip North represented an attempt to find deliverance, so the Negro church was another traditional avenue of entry into the "promised land." Most blacks who break with the church are more likely to define black power in fair share or unity terms.[29] This relationship holds even with region controlled (Table 3). In fact, membership and place of birth exert an independent effect. Michigan-born church members are about mid-way between Southern-born church members and Southern non-members in their approval of black power. Retention of a church affiliation acts as a brake on the effects of being raised in the Northern urban environment. It represents a strong tie to the traditional Negro culture.[30]

Table 3: Percentages of Black Respondents Favorably Interpreting Black Power by Church Affiliation with Birthplace Controlled

Affiliation	Place of Birth	
	South	Michigan
Church Member	33%(143)	39%(58)
Non-member	48%(107)	67%(33)
	(Gamma = −.32)	(Gamma = −.52)

Another aspect of traditional Negro culture is the unique measure of esteem granted the federal government and its personnel. Through the years the federal government, for all its shortcomings, has been the black man's special friend in an otherwise hostile environment. It won him his freedom, gave him the best treatment he received in his worst days in the South, provided relief in the Depression and in the difficult periods which have followed, and has done the most to secure his rights and protect him during his struggle for equality.[31] In addition, it has been the symbol of his intense identification with and "faith in the American Dream."[32] Evalution of local government in the North has been less positive, but still higher than evaluation of local government in the South.

Systematic research on political trust is rather recent, but what does exist indicates that blacks have always had at least the same distribution as whites on answers to political trust questions focused on the federal government.[33] In fact, when one takes into account the extraordinary amount of interpersonal distrust present in the black community,[34] the level of trust in the federal government has always been remarkable. Our data indicate that this pattern is now breaking down, at least in cities like Detroit. Using the Standard University of Michigan Survey Research Center political trust questions, we found blacks less trusting of both the federal and Detroit governments than whites.[35] These differences in levels of political trust are not a function of education, income or other non-racial status discrepancies.

Let us assume that the black power slogan strikes a most responsive chord in the minds of black people who want to break their traditional ties with paternalistic friends and allies. For them, expressing distrust of government, especially the federal government, is in fact a rejection of dependency — an assertion of self-worth and non-utopian thinking about the realities in the United States.[36] As we can see in Table 4, expressions of political trust and approval of black power are indeed inversely related. The higher a person's score on the various trust indices, the less likely he is to favorably interpret black power. This relationship is especially strong for trust in the federal government which has traditionally been granted unique esteem in the black community.

When we consider all three indicators of traditionalism together — place of socialization, church affiliation and level of political trust — we see that each is important in its own right (Table 5). The combined explanatory power of these

Table 4: Gamma Correlations for Blacks between Measures of Political Trust and Favorable Interpretations of Black Power

	Trust Detroit Govern- ment**	Trust Federal Govern- ment***	General (Combined) Measure of Political Trust****
Black power interpretation	—.22	—.52	—.39

* A negative coefficient indicates that the higher a person's score on the various trust indices (high score equals high trust), the less likely he is to favorably interpret black power.
** The Trust Detroit Government measure is a simple additive index of answers to the following questions:
  1. How much do you think we can trust the government in Detroit to do what is right: just about always, most of the time, some of the time, or almost never?
  2. How much do you feel having elections makes the government in Detroit pay attention to what the people think: a good deal, some, or not very much?
*** The Trust Federal Government measure is a simple additive index of answers to the following questions:
  1. How much do you think you can trust the government in Washington to do what is right: just about always, most of the time, some of the time, or almost never?
  2. Would you say that the government in Washington is pretty much run for the benefit of a few big interests or that it is run for the benefit of all the people?
  3. How much do you feel that having elections makes the government in Washington pay attention to what the people think: a good deal, some, or not very much?
**** The General Political Trust Measure runs from 0 to 4 and equally weights the Trust Detroit Government and Trust Washington Government answers.

Table 5: Percentages of Black Respondents Favorably Interpreting Black Power according to Church Affiliation, Place of Birth, and Levels of Trust in Government

Level of Trust in Government*	Born in South		Born in Michigan	
	Church Member	Non-Member	Church Member	Non-Member
High (2–4)	20% (76)	29% (65)	38% (16)	58% (26)
Low (0–1)	55% (40)	66% (73)	44% (16)	77% (31)

* The General Political Trust measure was employed in this table.

variables is substantial. Only 20 percent of the Southern-born church members who exhibit high levels of trust give approving interpretations of black power compared to 77 percent of the Northern-born non-members who are distrustful of government. Michigan-born church members are a particularly interesting group for further study in that church membership significantly depresses the effects of political trust. Our future research will emphasize the impact of socialization into the secular political culture of the Northern black communities, with special attention to the development of more refined indicators which will help us to understand better this acculturation process.

Deprivation: Dissatisfaction and Discrimination

We asked our respondents to tell us about "the life you would most like to lead, the most perfect life as you see it." Once they had described this kind of life they were shown a picture of a ladder with ten rungs and asked to imagine that their ideal lives were at the top of the ladder, on rung number ten. They were then asked to rank, in comparison with their ideal, their present lives, their lives five years ago, and what they expected their lives to be five years in the future.[37] Answers are therefore based on standards meaningful to the individual, with no simple objective indicator of achievement such as education, income or occupation serving as a substitute for his subjectively defined goals.[38]

This question revealed a great deal of current dissatisfaction in the black community, but also substantial optimism about the future. When asked to rank their lives five years ago only 13 percent of our black respondents put themselves in the top four categories (7, 8, 9 and 10); when asked to rank their present lives 23 percent placed themselves within the top four ranks; but 64 percent chose the top four categories to describe their lives as they expected them to be five years in the future.

As Table 6 indicates, both current dissatisfaction and, to a greater extent, pessimism about the future are strongly related to approval of black power in the zero-order case. When we control for level of education, however, the relationship only holds for the lower education group. The same general trend holds true for reports of experiences of discrimination. However, the differences are less pronounced. Experience of discrimination is a more powerful predictor of fair share or racial unity interpretations of black power for the lower than the upper education group, but it still has a noticeable effect for the upper education group.[39]

These data fit a general pattern which we have discussed in detail elsewhere.[40] For lower education blacks, approval of black power is strongly influenced by dissatisfaction with one's current lot and pessimism about the future as well as by reported experiences of discrimination. For blacks with higher levels of educational attainment, however, personal dissatisfaction with present achievements or prospects for the future do not help us to understand favorable interpretations of black

Table 6: Correlations (Gamma) for Blacks between Ladder Positions
on the Self-anchoring Scales, and Approval of Discrimination,
and Approval of Black Power, by Level of Education

Scales	Zero-Order	Low Education*	High Education*
Present Life**	−.27	−.34	.06
Future Life**	−.40	−.47	−.05
Reported Experiences of Discrimination***	.30	.34	.20

* Respondents in the low education group (N = 322) include all those who have completed high school (but had no additional training), while those in the high education group (N = 122) have at minimum gone beyond high school to either specialized training or college. We chose education as a status indicator and dichotomized the sample so as to preserve the maximum number of cases for the analysis.
** The ladders were trichotomized as follows: 1–3 = 0; 4–7 = 1; 8–10 = 2. Therefore, a negative coefficient means that the higher a person's score on the ladder the *less* likely he is to give a fair share or racial unity interpretation of black power.
*** This is a simple additive index of reports of personal experiences of discrimination in Detroit in obtaining housing, in the schools, from a landlord, or in obtaining, holding or advancing on a job.

power. Even reported personal experiences of discrimination are only moderately related to approval of the slogan. The views on black power of this higher education group are more strongly influenced by their identification with others in the community — their feelings for the group.

Upper status blacks who have broken free from traditional moorings become a part of a *black political community* which includes persons from all social classes. The responses of these upper status blacks to questions about the interpretation of significant events and the evaluation of leaders are more strongly affected by their sense of empathy and identification with their racial community than by their feelings of achievement or even their personal expectations about the future. They share a set of beliefs and a mood of protest about racial issues with those lower status segments of the black community who have also assimilated the secular culture typical of the urban North.[41] The major difference between the two groups is that dissatisfaction with one's current lot and prospects for the future interact with church membership, region of socialization and political trust in determining interpretations of black power for the lower education group, but not for the upper education group.

The Black Power Ideology

So far our attention has been concentrated on the demographic and attitudinal correlates of approval of black power. Some scholars have argued that interpretations of this kind of slogan stem from a more comprehensive belief system, a "riot ideology," which is said to be developing within the black community.[42] We found that knowledge of the black power slogan has diffused widely through the black community of Detroit. There are many different interpretations of the slogan, but only about 8 percent of the population were unable to respond when asked about its meaning. The question remains whether an individual's reaction to black power, be it positive or negative, is related in any logical way to his attitudes about other issues of racial policy, his interpretation of significant events, and his choice of leaders or representatives. In order to investigate this question, we turned to our data in search of evidence of a coherent or constrained belief system on racial matters within Detroit's black community; something we might justifiably call a racial ideology.

Anyone acquainted with recent research on public opinion might doubt the existence of a set of ideas resembling a racial ideology among any but a small activist fringe in the black community. Public attitudes about political leaders or questions of public policy are usually fragmentary and contradictory. Citizens readily express opinions about public issues, but these beliefs seldom hang together in a coherent system; knowing an individual's position on one issue does not allow one to predict his positions on other, related issues. The classical liberal or conservative ideologies may often be employed by political activists or leaders as a guide to policy making, but most citizens seem to use as a guide some form of group identification or other considerations of self interest when formulating their attitudes toward political questions.[43]

Converse argues that the degree of constraint in a belief system is determined most directly by the amount of information the individual has acquired about the issues involved. Levels of information, in turn, are usually affected by the relative centrality or importance of the issues to the individual. The more deeply concerned the individual becomes about a subject, the more likely he is to seek information about it, and, as time passes, to form consistent or comprehensive beliefs about the issues involved. Converse, of course, has dealt most often with liberalism and conservatism in their American incarnations. Comprehensive belief systems of this sort generally "rest upon the kinds of broad or abstract contextual information about currents of ideas, people, or society that educated people come to take for granted as initial ingredients of thought."[44] This form of contextual or background information is usually accumulated after extensive, formal education, a factor which seems to be a prerequisite to ideological thinking, in most cases. Since only a small minority of the public possesses this important educational prerequisite, ideological thinking is said to be rare.

Since our respondents share the educational limitations of average Americans, and do not have any special access to political information, we would not expect them to be capable of broadly ideological thinking. As Converse suggests at several points, however, it would be unwarranted to infer from this fact that average citizens are incapable of consistent thinking about all areas of public affairs. Even without a grasp of classical liberalism or conservatism and with a minimum of formal education, respondents might have consistent belief systems concerning subjects which they found to be of inescapable personal importance, and which also involved the social groupings with which they most strongly identify.

Bearing in mind the possibility that considerable structure might be uncovered in the social and political thought of our respondents if the proper issues could be identified, we asked open-ended questions at several points in our interview about topics we thought might be salient for our respondents. Using these methods we discovered clear indications that a coherent belief system dealing with racial matters has developed within Detroit's black community. This belief system seems well organized and serves as a guide for most of our respondents in formulating their answers to our questions about racial problems. The high degree of constraint existing among the elements of this belief system is displayed in Table 7 where we present a matrix of correlations of answers by our black respondents to five questions concerning racial issues.[45] The coefficients appearing below the diagonal are for all those with a high school education, or less, while above the diagonal are findings for those who have, at minimum, progressed beyond high school to either specialized training or college. The relatively high correlations in this table make us feel justified in referring to this set of opinions as a racial ideology.

One of the most significant aspects of Table 7 is the attitudinal consistency existing among those with lower educational achievements. A careful examination of the table shows that the two educational groups display almost the same levels of constraint. Associations among the upper education group are slightly higher, as earlier research on ideology might lead one to expect, but only by .02, on the average. Further, as we shall establish, respondents in our sample are not only capable of consistency, but display, as well, an impressive amount of knowledge about these questions, and demonstrate the capacity to make several subtle distinctions among leaders and political symbols.

The results of Table 7 are even more significant in view of the fact that three of the five items in the matrix were completely open-ended questions. We have already discussed our open question on the meaning of black power and the way in which we constructed our code and identified favorable and unfavorable responses. The question on the word used by the respondents to describe the riot was also open-ended. At the beginning of each interview respondents were asked what word they would use to describe the events "that occurred in Detroit between July 23rd and July 28th" of 1967, and that word was used by the interviewers throughout the interview. Although some responses were quite unorthodox (one young woman called it a "steal-in" and an older woman called it "God's vengeance on man"), we found it possible to code most of the answers into four categories: revolt, riot, disturbance, and lawlessness, which roughly form a dimension from an understanding of the events as an expression of political demands, to a belief that they were an anomic, lawless outburst. We also asked our respondents, without supplying any cues, to name "the single national or local leader who best expresses your views

Table 7: Correlations (Gamma) among Responses to Racial Issues by Black Respondents, by Education*

		High Education (N = 122)				
		1. Approval of Black Power	2. Word to Describe Riot	3. Sympathy for the Rioters	4. Reasons for the Riot	5. Leader Who Represents You
	1. Approval of Black Power**	X	.34	.46	.32	.29
Low Education (N = 322)	2. Word to Describe Riot**	.36	X	.40	.58	.22
	3. Sympathy for the Rioters**	.45	.30	X	.62	.49
	4. Reasons for the Riot**	.64	.37	.48	X	.41
	5. Leader Who Represents You**	.41	.29	.32	.35	X

* Respondents in the low education group include all individuals who have completed high school (but had no additional training), while those in the high education group have, at minimum, gone beyond high school. Correlations for the high education group are recorded above the diagonal, and those for the low education group are below the diagonal.
** The following items make up this table:
1. What do the words "black power" mean to you? For this table only the signs on the black power code are reversed so that all coefficients are positive.
2. What would you call the events that occurred in Detroit between July 23 and July 28? What word would you use? Open-end question coded as follows: 1) Insurrection; 2) Riot; 3) Disturbance; 4) Lawlessness.
3. Do you sympathize with the people who took part in the ((Respondent's term for the event)?: 1) yes; 2) somewhat; 3) no.
4. Which of the following comes closest to explaining why the (Respondent's term for the event) took place?: 1) people were being treated badly; 2) criminals did it; 3) people wanted to take things.
5. What single national or local leader best expresses your views on relations between the races? Open-ended question coded as follows: 1) Militant Black Leaders; 2) Other Black Leaders, excluding Martin Luther King; 3) Martin Luther King; 4) White Leaders, excluding Robert F. Kennedy.
A militant is defined here as someone who unequivocally endorsed black power before the time of our interviewing (September, 1967). Persons identifying Robert F. Kennedy were not considered in the calculation of coefficients for this question because of the special nature of his partisans. See below (footnotes to Table 11) for a discussion of this.

on relations between the races." The list of leaders mentioned were then arranged according to their publicly stated views on black power. This arrangement was made on the basis of our knowledge of these leaders and their public statements.[46]

Open questions require respondents to formulate their own answers, a formidable challenge to those with limited powers of expression. Some error may be introduced by interviewers when recording answers to open questions, and once they have been recorded, they must be coded. It is extremely difficult, both to construct comprehensive codes for responses of this kind, and to complete the coding process without introducing even further error. In view of all these difficulties, the relatively strong associations we have found among the items in Table 7 are strong evidence of the existence of a racial ideology. We believe that the success of these techniques and the high degree of consistency in our respondents' opinions were due to their intense interest and concern with racial issues. It would seem that the relative salience of an issue for an individual, or his interest in a subject, is more important than his educational level or his ability to manipulate abstractions in determining the coherence of his beliefs.[47] Our findings confirm the proposition that where issues of sufficient personal importance are concerned, even the poorly educated are capable of developing relatively sophisticated, inter-related, ideological belief systems.

Black Power Ideology and Integration

Some of our respondents may not have an advanced understanding of the justifications for their views, but we are certain that the questions in our matrix require a choice among legitimate alternatives; they are not being translated by our black respondents into simple tests of racial loyalty. An inspection of our questions will show that we are not asking merely if they are sympathetic or unsympathetic toward the aspirations of blacks in America. Our respondents are being called upon to identify and evaluate political leaders as representatives, interpret the causes of the Detroit riot, and define the meaning of a controversial political slogan. One can be closely identified with his racial group and greatly concerned for its welfare, and yet be either *positive* or passionately *negative* about black power, the riot, or many black political leaders. Our black respondents are prevented from employing some simple form of racial chauvinism as a guide for answering our questions because of the necessity of choosing sides in fundamental disputes over the role of blacks in American society which have traditionally divided their racial community.

Some symbols and ideas, of course, seem to be accepted by virtually all members of the black community. Had questions concerning these topics been included in our matrix we would not have such strong evidence of a racial ideology, because our responses could then be interpreted as mere expressions of support for the black community. This would have been true, for example, of any questions dealing directly with racial integration. In order to find how both racial groups felt about this issue, each of our respondents was asked whether he favored "racial integration, total separation of the races, or something in between." In response to this question, 27 percent of our white respondents endorsed integration, 17 percent favored total separation, and 54 percent chose "something in between." Even the most sympathetic whites overwhelmingly disapprove of black power, but as we can see in Table 8, approving interpretations of black power came most often from those whites who endorsed integration. The relationship was matched by a separate finding that whites who reported having friends among blacks were somewhat more approving of black power, although blacks who reported having white friends did not differ appreciably from others in their interpretation of the slogan. All of the aversion of whites toward black power cannot be attributed to an aversion toward blacks; some of it grows out of a fear and dislike of the general use of power to achieve social ends, and an unease and resentment of all forms of protest. Nevertheless, it is our impression that when most whites are asked about symbols like black power

Table 8: Percentages of Respondents Favorably
Interpreting Black Power, by Race, According
to Attitudes toward Integration

Form of Race Relations Preferred	Percent Favorably Interpreting Black Power	
	Whites	Blacks
Integration	25%(96)	46%(364)
Something in Between	8%(197)	46%(54)
Separation	5%(65)	*
	Gamma	Gamma
	= −.57	=.01

* N is less than 5.

and integration, they are less likely to respond directly to the complicated issues being raised, but are tempted to translate the questions into the much simpler issue of whether they are favorable or unfavorable toward black people.[48]

When our black respondents were asked the same question about racial integration, 86 percent endorsed integration, while only 1 percent chose separation. Years of struggle against institutionalized segregation and great efforts by opinion leaders in both racial communities for almost a century have made integration a potent, positive symbol for blacks. Asking for an endorsement of this idea is almost akin to asking for an expression of loyalty to the black community. Since we recognized the emotional connotation of these terms we substituted the word "separation" for "segregation" in our questions, but even in this form the positive attraction of integration proved overwhelming. The consensus on the desirability of integration includes most black writers and intellectual leaders as well as the average citizens. Debate over the idea has remained sharp and vigorous, but it has primarily concerned the question of whether integration ultimately should result in virtual assimilation, or in some form of social pluralism.[49]

In view of the special status of integration as a symbol within the black community, it is not surprising that we should find conclusive evidence that approval for black power among blacks *does not* imply approval of racial separation. In Table 8 there are no appreciable differences in approval for black power between black respondents who endorse integration and those who do not.

The racial ideology we have identified, even though not merely an expression of racial loyalty, may still have social rather than purely intellectual origins. An individual's status or the role he plays in the economy may prompt him to adopt the beliefs of the leaders of his social group because he is convinced that this is a way to advance his own interests. This form of intellectual emulation would be most likely among those, like many of our respondents, who have little education or experience with abstract thinking, and also have a strong sense of group identification. Several beliefs may be appropriated by an individual under these circumstances which may appear to him as natural collections of interdependent ideas, even if he does not have the intellectual capacity to make a similar synthesis of his own. In other words, he may know that several different elements of his belief system naturally go together, and he may also know that certain kinds of responses are considered appropriate for certain kinds of questions, without having any notion of why.[50]

Our respondent's racial ideologies may have originated through this process of social diffusion and group mobilization, but we find enough subtlety in the responses to conclude that many individuals have developed a surprisingly elaborate understanding of the applicability and meaning of the beliefs they hold. For example, although virtual unanimity exists within the black community about the desirability of integration as an ultimate goal, there is considerable disagreement over how soon it might occur. As we can see in Table 9, those who believe that realization

Table 9: Percentages of Black Respondents Favorably Interpreting Black Power According to When They Believe Integration Will Occur

Time for Integration	Favorable Interpretations of Black Power		
	Fair Share	+ Black Unity	= Total
Near Future	18%	16%	34% (140)
Distant Future	22%	33%	55% (206)

of the goal is in the distant future are more likely to approve of black power than those who believe it will soon appear. In analyzing our data we have found that the perception of obstacles to racial progress, or the actual experience of some form of discrimination, is related to approval of black power. Table 9 demonstrates that the more pessimistic respondents are also more likely to interpret black power as an appeal for racial unity rather than a call for a fair share or an equal opportunity. There is evidence in this table, and in others we shall present, that the capacity for subtle shifts of emphasis and interpretation is not merely confined to the community's activist minority, but instead is widely diffused among a large segment of Detroit's black population.

Black Power Ideology and the Detroit Riot

The Detroit riot of July, 1967 caused fear and anxiety among almost all the citizens of the city, both black and white. Immediate reactions to the event ranged from those who believed it was a sign that the Negro citizens of the city were rising up in revolt against discrimination and injustice to those who saw it as an uncivilized expression of lawlessness and hooliganism. If, as we have suggested, responses to black power are a part of an individual's basic orientation toward race relations, there should be a strong relationship between his response to this slogan and his evaluation of the causes and consequences of the riot.

In Table 10a we can see that in both races those who use the word "revolt" to describe the events were much more likely to express approval for black power. In Table 10b where the black respondents are divided according to whether they

Table 10: Percentages of Respondents Favorably Interpreting Black Power, by Race, According to Word They Use to Describe the Riot

a. Total Sample

Word Used to Describe Riot	Percent Favorably Interpreting Black Power	
	Whites	Blacks
Revolt	32%(28)	62%(51)
Riot	10%(212)	50%(194)
Disturbance	0%(19)	33%(42)
Lawlessness	8%(25)	27%(33)

b. Black Respondents Only

Word Used to Describe Riot	Interpretation of Black Power		
	Fair Share	+ Racial Unity	= Total
Revolt	25%	37%	62%(51)
Riot	23%	27%	50%(194)
Disturbance	19%	14%	33%(42)
Lawlessness	21%	6%	27%(33)

gave racial unity or fair share responses we find that racial unity interpretations clearly predominate among those who see the riot as a protest against injustice. This is another demonstration of the shift in emphasis that occurs among those who are most aware and resentful of discrimination and inequality. The more convinced our black respondents are of the existence of injustice, the more they begin to interpret black power as a call for racial solidarity.

Black Power Ideology and the Choice of Leaders

Our respondents were asked to name "the single national or local leader who best expresses your views on relations between the races." This question, like the one on black power, was completely open ended. Table 11 displays the relationship for Negroes between the selection of various leaders and fair share or black unity interpretations of black power.

The list of leaders is arranged so that the percentage totals of respondents

Table 11: Percentage of Black Respondents Favorably Interpreting Black Power According to Their Selection of a Leader Best Representing Their Views on Race Relations

Leader Best Representing Respondent*	Black Power Interpretation		
	Fair Share	+ Racial Unity	= Total
Militant Black Leaders (N = 59)	26%	50%	76%
Robert F. Kennedy (N = 17)	12%	47%	59%
Other Black Leaders, excluding Martin Luther King (N = 107)	17%	34%	51%
"No One" (N = 20)	10%	30%	40%
Martin Luther King (N = 150)	28%	10%	38%
White leaders, excluding Robert F. Kennedy (N = 30)	11%	13%	24%

* Question: What single national or local leader best expresses your views on relations between the races?

N's in parentheses are the bases for the calculation of percentages, i.e., persons giving don't know or no answer responses to the black power question were not used in the table.

Total N's for the categories on leadership are given in the explanations of the leader classifications below:

A militant black leader (N = 61) is defined here as someone who unequivocally endorsed black power before the time of our interviewing (September, 1967). They include: Muhammed Ali (N = 3); H. Rap Brown (N = 9); Stokely Carmichael (N = 13); State Senator James Del Rio (N = 13); Dick Gregory (N = 6); Floyd McKissick (N = 3); Adam Clayton Powell (N = 8); and Rev. Albert Cleage (N = 4). Del Rio and Cleage are local figures.

Robert F. Kennedy (N = 21).

Other black leaders, excluding Martin Luther King (N = 111) mentioned were: Senator Edward Brooke (N = 16); Ralph Bunche (N = 3); U.S. Representative John Conyers (N = 31); U.S. Representative Charles Diggs (N = 17); Detroit Common Councilman Nicholas Hood (N = 10); Detroit Urban League Head Francis Kornegay (N = 1); Judge Thurgood Marshall (N = 4); Carl Rowan (N = 1); Roy Wilkins (N = 17); State Senator Coleman Young (N = 1); Whitney Young (N = 5). Hood, Kornegay and C. Young are local figures.

"No One" (N = 21).

Martin Luther King (N = 165).

White Leaders, excluding Robert F. Kennedy (N = 33), mentioned were: Senator Dirksen (N = 1); President Eisenhower (N = 1); TV Commentator Lou Gordon (N = 1); Vice President Humphrey (N = 1); President Johnson (N = 14); President Kennedy (N = 9); Walter Reuther (N = 3); Governor Romney (N = 3). Gordon is a local figure.

The total N = 412. Of the remaining 49 individuals in our black sample, 26 could not answer the question and 22 mentioned their minister (no name given), coach or assorted persons (including themselves). We could not categorize with confidence on a leadership spectrum.

favoring black power are in descending order. The table seems to us to indicate the validity of our measure since respondents identifying with militant black leaders are the most favorably disposed towards black power while those choosing white leaders are least positive. In addition, the assumptions we made earlier about the meaning of the "black take-over" and "nothing" responses also seem warranted as individuals who identify with the least militant leaders most often give responses of this kind.

There are some more subtle differences revealed in this table. Negroes who felt best represented by black leaders other than the late Martin Luther King favored racial unity over fair share definitions of black power by a ratio of two to one. Dr. King's partisans, however, heavily emphasized fair share definitions. In addition, the likelihood of a favorable definition of black power is a direct function of the type of black leader selected. As a general rule, the more militant the leader who represents the respondent, the greater the chance of a positive orientation toward black power.

Over seventy-five percent of our Negro respondents chose a black leader who best represented their views, but there were white leaders selected as well and instances where the interviewee could make no selection. The number of respondents who could not name a leader is small and we have divided them into two groups. "No one" is a category for individuals who decisively stated that they had no representative. This tiny group was often cynical about black power (and everything else) with over one-third saying that black power meant "nothing" to them. When they did define the slogan, however, black unity was the dominant theme. Another small group (N = 25) simply could not think of any person who represented them and they were also unlikely to answer the question about black power (i.e., they were coded in the don't know or no answer category on black power). These individuals were not visibly cynical about racial leaders or approaches; they were simply uninformed.

Thirty-one respondents identified with white leaders other than the late Senator Robert F. Kennedy. They were generally negative about black power, showing no meaningful preference for either positive interpretation. Over fifty percent of the black respondents who selected Senator Kennedy, however, gave favorable definitions of black power and they were disposed towards racial unity definitions of the term by a ratio of four to one. While the number of people who named Senator Kennedy is small, his importance as a link with the more militant elements in the black community should not be underestimated. The severing of this connection between the white and black worlds is a major tragedy. In the next phase of our research we will explore the impact of the deaths of both Kennedy and King on the beliefs of their followers.

Black Power Ideology: An Overview

Black power has no direct, generally accepted meaning, but the slogan still provokes strong responses from both blacks and whites. The power of all effective political slogans lies in "the emotional charges or valences they carry, the very elements that make cognitions dissonant or consonant," and in "their associative meanings, the very ambiguities that permit them, like Rorschach ink blots, to suggest to each person just what he wants to see in them."[51] In their efforts to shape a meaning for black power, our black respondents have fallen back upon fundamental sets of beliefs which have spread throughout all sectors of their racial community. Many of those who share these beliefs may be unaware of their most profound implications, but the beliefs are consistently organized in the minds of our respondents primarily because they are securely focused on the issue of racial injustice in America, a problem faced by most blacks in one form or another virtually every day of their lives.

When Converse speaks of ideological thinking, of course, he usually refers to "belief systems that have relatively wide ranges and that allow some centrality to political objects."[52] The racial ideology we have identified has a much narrower range. Given the limitations of our data, we cannot be sure that individuals holding a consistent racial ideology would also have consistent opinions about federal aid to education, or governmental measures designed to ensure full employment. Those with a racial ideology might be able to think in coherent ways only about questions of public policy which bear some relationship to the status of blacks in American society, but not about the general relationship between government and private business, or about America's relations with foreign countries.

The ideology of black power is not a wide ranging, highly elaborated, political world view. Nevertheless, the tone and quality of American political life in the latter 1960's was profoundly altered by the development of this belief system and its exceptionally wide diffusion among black Americans. In its radical form, as it is developing among our more disillusioned black respondents, the belief system includes doubts about the possibilities of realizing the goal of integration in the near future, sympathetic explanations of the July, 1967 disturbances in Detroit and a revolutionary label for them, selection of a militant leader as a spokesman, skepticism about improvements in the quality of life in the future, and a definition of black power which stresses the need for greater racial solidarity. This system of beliefs does not arm many of our respondents with concrete programs of social and economic reform, but in spite of its limited scope, its existence is of great potential significance. Its impressively wide diffusion is a striking indication of the growing mobilization and increasing sense of group identification within the black community.

Summary and Conclusions

Black power is a potent, meaningful slogan for most of our respondents. Some react with fear, others with cynicism, many with warm approval or strong disapproval, but in most cases reactions are intense and interpretations of the idea's meaning are related to an individual's basic orientation toward social and political problems. Whites have an overwhelmingly negative reaction to black power. The slogan is seen by most whites as an illegitimate, revengeful challenge. Among blacks, however, about forty-two percent of our sample see the term either as a call for equal treatment and a fair share for Negroes, or as an appeal for racial solidarity in the struggle against discrimination.

The partisans of black power among Negroes are somewhat younger than the rest of the black community, but neither their age nor other standard demographic factors, such as income, occupation, and education, are very helpful in explaining the distributions we have found. Sharp divisions exist within the Detroit black community, but they are not merely the result of a clash between young and old;

instead, they represent a clash between those who have appropriated the cosmopolitan, secularized culture typical of the North and those whose social outlook and political attitudes are rooted in the paternalistic culture of the South. Approval for black power, as our analysis has shown, comes most often from those who were born or grew up in Detroit, are not members of churches, and have begun to doubt the trustworthiness of government in both Detroit and Washington.

Black power is the rallying cry of a generation of blacks whose fathers fled from the South to seek a new life in the "promised lands" of Detroit, New York, or Chicago. The move from the grinding poverty and overt oppression of the South to the cities of the North was seen as a great step forward by the original pioneers, but most of their children cannot be satisfied by these changes. In the words of Claude Brown:

> The children of these disillusioned colored pioneers inherited the total lot of their parents — the disappointments, the anger. To add to their misery, they had little hope of deliverance. For where does one run to when he's already in the promised land?[53]

This modern generation finds little compensation or hope in the evangelical, "old time religion" of their parents, nor do they share the traditional faith of Southern Negroes in the ultimate benevolence of white men. Many are distrustful of government, unimpressed with most of the civic notables and established political leaders of both the black and white communities, and increasingly pessimistic about their chances to achieve a satisfactory life in this country. They have not surrendered the ultimate aim of social equality and racial integration, but they have begun to doubt that the goal will be reached in the foreseeable future.

We encountered few racist, anti-white interpretations of black power among our black respondents and most of those came from respondents who were *not* sympathetic to black power. There were chauvinism and some glorification of blackness, especially among those who interpret black power as a call for racial unity or solidarity, but most were pro-black rather than anti-white. Black unity definitions of black power are not disguised appeals for separation from American society; at least, not at the present moment. If insufficient progress toward racial accommodation is made in the future and tensions continue to mount, separationist sentiments might begin to spread within the black community. Today, we find, instead, a deep concern with the rights of and desires for respect within the American black community. These feelings are most eloquently expressed in the interpretation of black power given by one of our young respondents:

> (black, male, 19, 12 grades) It means mostly equality. You know, to have power to go up to a person, you know, no matter what his skin color is and be accepted on the same level, you know, and it doesn't necessarily have to mean that you gotta take over everything and be a revolutionary and all this; just as long as people are

going to respect you, you know, for what you are as a person and not, you know, what your skin color has to do with the thing.

Restraining ties with the traditional culture of the South are being steadily eroded as the percentage of blacks who were born and grew up in the North increases, the influence of the church wanes, and faith in the benevolence of paternalistic friends and allies weakens. The children born in Detroit since World War Two are coming of age politically in the midst of a social revolution. Events as diverse as the Detroit riot, the dominance of black athletes in every major American spectator sport, the collapse of colonial empires in Asia and Africa, the total integration of the American armed forces, and the murders of Martin Luther King and Robert Kennedy are all accelerating the break with traditional modes of thought and accommodation. The reservoir of potential supporters for black power is bound to grow.

The social revolution now in progress has resulted in a more unified, more highly mobilized black political community. Franklin Frazier's accommodating, apolitical "black bourgeoisie"[54] is rapidly disappearing as the sense of empathy and racial identification among the black middle class grows stronger. This developing racial community is profoundly restless and is searching for new forms of political expression and participation. The result of this search is likely to be increased activity of all kinds, both conventional and unconventional. Our data indicate a willingness to participate in political campaigns and elections on the part of even the most militant advocates of black power. Their involvement in this activity, however, would not preclude their taking part in other, more flamboyant, forms of protest.

No single, dominant tactical stance is likely to evolve among blacks; questions about the feasibility and utility of tactics are major sources of disagreement within the black community. Most of our black respondents, for example, believe the Detroit riots of 1967 were an understandable reaction to social injustice, and there is some sympathy for the individuals who actually did the rioting, but there is almost no approval of the sniping and fire bombing that took place. Extreme violence of this kind is presently thought of as a legitimate or useful expression of grievances by only a tiny minority of blacks in Detroit, but many others express considerable ambivalence about the utility of violent protests. For example, when we asked our black respondents, "Can you imagine any situation in which you would take part in a ———— (respondent's term for the events of July, 1967)?" a majority said no, but, as we can see in Table 12, respondents who expressed ambivalence were even more supportive of black power than those who said they definitely would participate. This undecided group is a substantial proportion of our sample, they have made the sharpest break with traditional forms of social thought, they are the most sympathetic toward the black power ideology, and they are wavering.

The outcome of this search by blacks for acceptable modes of political expression will depend primarily on the behavior of whites, both those who control all

Table 12: Percentages of Black Respondents
Favorably Interpreting Black Power According
to Their Willingness to Take Part in a Riot

Would You Riot*	Percent Favorably Interpreting Black Power
No:	35%(262)
Yes:	57%(60)
Maybe:	69%(93)

* Question: Can you imagine any situation in which you would take part in a ———— (respondent's term for the events of July, 1967)?

the public and private institutions that matter, and the average citizens who must adjust to changes in prevailing customs. If Detroit's future is to be peaceful, ways must be found to pull down the barriers to equal opportunity which now exist, and there must be radical improvement in the prospects for personal advancement of the city's black population. Although success in these efforts depends, in large measure, on the flexibility and compassion of the whites, it also depends on the capacity of many public and private governmental institutions to mobilize the resources necessary to create a decent, livable, urban environment.

Some of the most important decisions about Detroit's future will not be made in the city, but in Washington, in suburban city halls, or in the state capitol in Lansing; the policies adopted by labor unions, businesses and manufacturers in the city will probably be more important than anything done by the officials of city government. This complex, decentralized system of social choice, with its elaborate checks and balances and its many barriers to radical change, will be faced during the next decade with an insistent challenge from a new generation of black Americans. To successfully meet their demands large efforts will have to be made toward the creation of a truly inter-racial society. Depending on the extent and success of these efforts, this new black generation could either become a persuasive and creative new influence within the democratic system, or a force bent on the violent disruption of American urban life.

Notes

[1] William J. Brink and Louis Harris, *Black and White* (New York: Simon and Schuster, 1966), p. 50.

[2] *New York Times,* July 6, 1966, p. 14.

[3] *Ibid.,* July 6, 1966, p. 15, and July 9, 1966, p. 8.

[4] James Baldwin, *Notes of a Native Son* (Boston: Little, Brown, 1955), p. 122.

[5] Cruse, for example, in his provocative series of essays, *The Crisis of the Negro Intellec-*

tual (New York: William Morrow, 1967), p. 557, says that "the radical wing of the Negro movement in America sorely needs a social theory based on the living ingredients of Afro-American history. Without such a theory all talk of Black Power is meaningless."

⁶ *Ibid.*, p. 545.

·⁷ Charles Hamilton, "An Advocate of Black Power Defines It," *New York Times Magazine*, April 14, 1968, pp. 22–23, 79–83, reprinted in full in Robert L. Scott and Wayne Brockriede, eds., *The Rhetoric of Black Power* (New York: Harper and Row, 1969), pp. 178–194. This statement is found on p. 179.

⁸ Stokely Carmichael and Charles V. Hamilton, *Black Power: The Politics of Liberation in America* (New York: Vintage Books, 1967), p. 44.

⁹ Hamilton, *op. cit.*, p. 179. For a view of the concept from a broader perspective see, Locksley Edmondson, "The Internationalization of Black Power: Historical and Contemporary Perspectives," *Mawaso* (December, 1968), pp. 16–30.

¹⁰ Riot areas were defined by a location map of fires considered riot-related by the Detroit Fire Department.

¹¹ See our discussion below of "nothing" as a response.

¹² The correlation between interpretations of black power on the open-ended question in 1967 and interpretations in 1968 is (Gamma) .54 for blacks and .78 for whites. We will be gathering data from the same respondents once again in September, 1970, and will report our findings in detail after the third round is completed.

¹³ We will present our codings below. A more conservative coefficient for demonstrating the relationship between interpretations of black power on the open-ended question and approval or disapproval on the close-ended question would be Kendall's tau-beta. See Leo A. Goodman and William H. Kruskal, "Measures of Association for Cross Classification," *Journal of the American Statistical Association* (December, 1954). The tau-beta correlations are .86 for blacks and .60 for whites. The lower coefficient in the white case reflects the relatively large percentage of whites who give favorable interpretations of black power but disapprove of the slogan. This will be discussed in more detail in the text.

¹⁴ For the blacks, the riot area respondents gave a greater emphasis to black unity as opposed to fair share interpretations of black power, but the differences are not great. Non-riot area respondents actually were slightly more favorable to black power if we consider unity and fair share responses as indicators of positive feelings.

¹⁵ The quotes presented here are typical examples of black power definitions coded in each category. Respondents are identified by race, sex, age and educational attainment for the benefit of the reader. In cases where the respondent has some specialized training, he is coded with a "plus" after his grade level.

¹⁶ All of the few whites who interpreted black power as "nothing" in 1968 were negative about the slogan.

¹⁷ In a few cases (N = 20) respondents stressed black unity in order to achieve a fair share. We are considering first mentions here and in our analysis, but will prove this in detail when we have more time.

¹⁸ We will combine black unity definitions with the few racial pride references for purposes of analysis.

¹⁹ See footnote 17. About 20 percent of the black respondents mentioning racial unity saw it as a means of achieving equality. For example:

(black, male, 42, 12 grades) Negroes getting together and forcing whites to realize our importance — our worth to the United States. Gaining respect and equality.

The more articulate members of the black unity group are concerned with ends as well as means. See Carmichael and Hamilton, *op. cit.*, pp. 46–47.

²⁰ The best example of work in this area is Gary T. Marx, *Protest and Prejudice: A Study of Belief in the Black Community* (New York: Harper and Row, 1967). Marx defined "conventional militancy" by the standards of civil rights activists and organizations at the time of his

study (1964). All were (pp. 40–41) "urgently aware of the extensiveness of discrimination faced by the American black man. All called for an end to discrimination and segregation and demanded the admission of the Negro to the economic and political mainstream of American life. And they wanted these changes quickly — 'Freedom Now.' In pursuit of this end, participation in peaceful demonstrations was encouarged."

[21] Riot research is widespread. See, especially, David O. Sears and John B. McConahay, "Riot Participation," and Raymond J. Murphy and James M. Watson, "The Structure of Discontent: Grievance and Support for the Los Angeles Riot," *Los Angeles Riot Study* (Los Angeles: Institute of Government and Public Affairs, University of California, 1967); Nathan S. Caplan and Jefferey M. Paige, "A Study of Ghetto Rioters," *Scientific American* (August, 1968), pp. 15–21, also reported in the *Report of the National Advisory Commission on Civil Disorders (The U.S. Riot Commission Report)*, Washington: United States Government Printing Office, 1968); *Supplemental Studies for the National Advisory Commission on Civil Disorders* (Washington: U.S. Government Printing Office, 1968), especially Angus Campbell and Howard Schuman, *Racial Attitudes in Fifteen American Cities*, Chapters 5–6 and Robert M. Fogelson and Robert B. Hill, *Who Riots: A Study of Participation in the 1967 Riots;* and Louis H. Masotti and Don R. Bowen, eds., *Riots and Rebellion: Civil Violence in the Urban Community* (Beverly Hills: Sage Publications, 1968). Studies which emphasize aggregate data can be found in Ted R. Gurr and Hugh D. Davis, eds., *The History of Violence in America* (New York: Bantam Press, 1969).

[22] *Violence in the City — An End or a Beginning? A Report by the Governor's Commission on the Los Angeles Riots* (Los Angeles: McCone Commission Report, 1965).

[23] In the calculations which follow, unless otherwise noted, the black power variable is dichotomized with a favorable interpretation ("fair share" or "racial unity") scored *one* and unfavorable interpretations scored *zero*. Respondents with "don't know" or "no answer" responses were not used in the analysis. In this association, for example, those with low educational achievement were slightly less likely to approve of black power (give the "fair share" or "racial unity" interpretations) than those with substantial educational achievement.

[24] We do not think that this is simply because their higher level of education makes them more aware of the content of the actual debate over black power. Relative youth, education, and support of integration are all intertwined and each of these factors is related to a favorable interpretation of black power.

[25] See Jerome H. Skolnick, *The Politics of Protest* (New York: Simon and Schuster, 1969), p. 162, and *The U.S. Riot Commission Report, op. cit.,* especially p. 93 where "a new mood among Negroes, particularly among the young" is described. "Self-esteem and enhanced racial pride are replacing apathy and submission to 'the system.' Moreover, Negro youth, who make up over half of the ghetto population, share the growing sense of alienation felt by many white youth in our country. Thus, their role in recent civil disorders reflects not only a shared sense of deprivation and victimization by white society but also the rising incidence of disruptive conduct by a segment of American youth throughout the society."

[26] We have defined the South as the 11 states of the Confederacy (N = 255) and the border states of Kentucky, Maryland, Oklahoma, and West Virgina (N = 49). Blacks born in border states were actually less likely to interpret black power in fair share or black unity terms than those born in the former states of the Confederacy, although the differences are small. One hundred and seven of our black respondents were born in Michigan (coded *one*). This accounts for only 412 respondents. Of those remaining, 43 were born in the United States, but outside of Michigan and the South, 1 in Canada, 1 in the West Indies and 1 in Puerto Rico. We lack information on 3 individuals. The 43 respondents born in the U.S., but not in Michigan or in the South, come from a wide variety of places. They are more favorably disposed toward black power than the Southerners but less so than the Michigan-born.

[27] Other bodies of data and our own show that almost all riot participants are young and that age does have an impact on favorable attitudes toward violence, especially for young men. This is not surprising in light of the physical attributes helpful to a participant in a disturbance and the bravado of the young. However, age is unrelated to more general notions of whether riots helped or hurt the black cause (Murphy and Watson, *op. cit.,* p. 82) as well as to attitudes

toward black power. It is clear that age is an important variable in the study of our recent strife, but by itself it does not explain contemporary militancy or even sympathy for those who participate in civil disturbances.

[28] See Samuel P. Huntington, *Political Order in Changing Societies* ((New Haven: Yale University Press, 1968), pp. 280–283 for a discussion of the potential for "political radicalism" of second generation slumdwellers. Claude Brown makes the same points in the graphic Foreword to his autobiography, *Manchild in the Promised Land* (New York: Macmillan, 1965). We will make some distinctions between the effects of dissatisfaction on lower and upper status groups in the section on deprivation below.

[29] The sample was divided into church (coded *one*), non-members (coded *zero*) and members of groups, usually action groups, connected with a church (not included in the analysis). People in the latter category ($N = 25$) chose to emphasize their group above their church affiliation in answering our open-ended question on membership in "church or church-connected groups." They were about as likely as the non-members to approve of black power and should be the subject of intensive study because of their pivotal position in the black community.

For a detailed discussion of the similar influence of religion on conventional militancy among blacks, including consideration of denomination and religiosity, see: Gary T. Marx, "Religion: Opiate or Inspiration of Civil Rights Militancy Among Negroes," *American Sociological Review* (1967), pp. 64–72.

[30] The impact of region as a variable will surely diminish over time as the effects of national black leadership and the messages of the media and relatives are diffused throughout the nation. However, church affiliation is likely to remain important.

[31] For example, see William Brink and Louis Harris, *The Negro Revolution in America* (New york: Simon and Schuster, 1964), pp. 131 and 232–233 on black attitudes towards various political institutions and figures.

[32] See Louis E. Lomax, *The Negro Revolt* (New York: Harper and Row, 1962), p. 250, and also Gunnar Myrdal, *An American Dilemma* (New York: Harper and Row, 1944), pp. 3–5, 880 and 1007 on blacks as "exaggerated Americans."

[33] Donald E. Stokes, "Popular Evaluations of Government: An Empirical Assessment," in Harlan Cleveland and Harold D. Lasswell (eds.), *Ethics and Bigness* (New York: Harper and Brothers, 1962), pp. 61–73 and Joel D. Aberbach, *Alienation and Race* (unpublished Ph.D. Dissertation, Yale University, 1967), pp. 119–126.

[34] Lee Rainwater's "Crucible of Identity — The Negro Lower-Class Family" in *DAEDALUS* (1966), especially pp. 204–205 and 215 is very insightful on this point, but this distrust is not confined to lower class ghetto dwellers. See Aberbach, *op. cit.,* pp. 104–114 for a detailed discussion.

[35] For a detailed discussion of our findings and a critique of the existing literature on Political Trust see Joel D. Aberbach and Jack L. Walker, "Political Trust and Racial Ideology," a paper delivered at the 1969 Annual Meetings of the American Political Science Association, especially pp. 2–7. A revised version will appear in this *Review,* (December, 1970).

[36] Political trust has complex roots. See *ibid.,* pp. 7–13 for an analysis of its origins.

[37] This is the famous Cantril Self-Anchoring Scale which indicates the discrepancy between an individual's definition of the "best possible life" for him and his past, present, or future situation. See Hadley C. Cantril, *The Pattern of Human Concerns* (New Brunswick: Rutgers University Press, 1965). Our respondents were given the following set of questions:

Now could you briefly tell me what would be the best possible life for you? In other words, how would you describe the life you would most like to lead, the most perfect life as you see it? (Show R card with a Ladder)

Now suppose that the top of the ladder represents the best possible life for you, the one you just described, and the bottom represents the worst possible life for you.

"Present Life" A. Where on the ladder do you feel you personally stand at the present time?

"Past Life" B. Where on the ladder would you say you stood five years ago? "Future Life" C. Where on the ladder do you think you will be five years from now?

[38] In the black community sample, for example, level of education is correlated (Gamma) .06 with scores on the past life ladder, .09 with the present life ladder and .29 with the future life ladder. Education is, therefore, only important as a predictor of assessments of future prospects and even here other factors are obviously at work. Income and occupation work much the same way. It is clear that people's evaluations of their achievements vary more within than between objectively defined status groupings.

[39] Reported experiences of discrimination are unrelated to education (Gamma = .01).

[40] Aberbach and Walker, op. cit., (1969), especially pp. 11–16.

[41] The correlations (Gamma) between church membership, place of birth and approval of black power are actually slightly higher in the upper education than in the lower education group:

Black Power by	Low Education	High Education
Church Membership	—.38	—.42
Place of Birth	.31	.34
Political Trust	—.39	—.37

[42] T. M. Tomlinson, "The Development of a Riot Ideology Among Urban Negroes," *American Behavioral Scientist* (1968), pp. 27–31.

[43] The best single statement is Philip E. Converse, "The Nature of Belief Systems in Mass Publics," in David E. Apter (ed.), *Ideology and Discontent* (New York: Free Press, 1964), pp. 206–262. For a brief review of this literature see: Lester W. Mibrath, *Political Participation* (Chicago: Rand McNally, 1965); and Herbert McClosky, "Consensus and Ideology in American Politics," this Review (1964), 361–382. For some recent work see: Robert Axelrod, "The Structure of Public Opinion on Policy Issues," *Public Opinion Quarterly* (1967), 49–60; and Norman R. Luttbeg, "The Structure of Beliefs Among Leaders and the Public," *Public Opinion Quarterly* (1968), 398–410.

[44] Converse, op. cit., p. 255.

[45] To judge the relative strength of these relationships, see a similar matrix for a national cross-section sample in Converse, op. cit., p. 228.

[46] The two remaining questions in the matrix were close-ended and provided respondents with a set of alternative answers from which to choose. See the footnotes of Table 7 for their exact wording.

[47] See Converse, op. cit.; and Roy T. Bowles and James T. Richardson, "Sources of Consistency of Political Opinion," *American Journal of Sociology* (1969), who argue on p. 683, that "interest in politics is a more powerful predictor of both ideological conceptualization and consistency of opinion than is ability to use abstract ideas."

[48] The issue of the nature of racial ideology among whites will be explored in Joel D. Aberbach and Jack L. Walker, *Race and the Urban Political Community* (Boston: Little, Brown, forthcoming).

[49] Strong advocates of black power are almost uniformly in favor of social pluralism and reject cultural assimilation as resting on the demeaning "assumption that there is nothing of value in the black community" (Carmichael and Hamilton, op. cit., p. 53). However, they do not endorse separatism holding that black power is "ultimately not separatist or isolationist" (Hamilton, op. cit., p. 193). The basic idea is that after the black man develops "a sense of pride and self-respect . . . if integration comes, it will deal with people who are psychologically and mentally healthy, with people who have a sense of their history and of themselves as whole human beings" (Hamilton, op. cit., p. 182). Detailed discussion on the meanings of assimilation

can be found in Milton M. Gordon, *Assimilation in American Life* (New York: Oxford University Press, 1964).

[50] Converse discusses this possibility in a section called "Social Sources of Constraint." Converse, *op. cit.*, pp. 211–213. For other treatments of the origins of ideology, see William H. Form and Joan Rytina, "Ideological Beliefs on the Distribution of Power in the United States," *American Sociological Review* (1969), pp. 19–30; Samuel H. Barnes, "Ideology and the Organization of Conflict," *Journal of Politics* (1966), 513–530; Richard M. Merelman, "The Development of Political Ideology: A Framework for the Analysis of Political Socialization," this REVIEW (1969), 750–767; Everett C. Ladd, Jr., *Ideology in America* (Ithaca: Cornell University Press, 1969), pp. 341–350; and Robert E. Lane, *Political Ideology* (New York: Free Press, 1962), pp. 213–439.

[51] Robert E. Lane, *Political Thinking and Consciousness* (Chicago: Markham, 1969), p. 316.

[52] Converse, *op. cit.*, pp. 208–209.

[53] Claude Brown, *op. cit.*, p. 8.

[54] E. Franklin Frazier, *Black Bourgeoisie* (New York: Free Press, 1957).

Riot Ideology in Los Angeles: A Study of Negro Attitudes[1]

David O. Sears
T. M. Tomlinson

Each summer from 1964 through 1967 saw urban Negroes in America involved in a series of violent riots. Among the most critical consequences of the riots were the decisions made by the white population about the social changes required to prevent further rioting. These decisions rested in part on the whites' assumptions about the nature and extent of the Negro community's involvement in the riots. Matters of simple fact such as how many people took part in the riots, whether the rest of the Negro community repudiated the rioters, and whether it viewed the riots as representing some form of collective protest against injustice and poverty, were initially quite unclear. Yet whites quickly made their own assumptions about such matters, and these strongly influenced their stance toward the riots and the entire racial problem.

There appear to be three widely held myths about the Negro community's response to riots. The first is that the riots are participated in and viewed favorably by only a tiny segment of the Negro community. The figure often cited by news media and political spokesmen (both black and white) is between 2 and 5 per cent of the Negro population. Since riot supporters are thought to be so few in number, a further assumption is that they come from such commonly condemned fringe groups as Communists, hoodlums, and Black Muslims.[2]

The second myth is that most Negroes see the riots as purposeless, meaningless, senseless outbursts of criminality. Many white public officials certainly professed to see nothing in the riots but blind hostility and malicious mischief, drunkenness, and material greed. Perhaps because they held this view so strongly themselves, they tended to assume that Negroes shared it as well.

The third myth is that Negroes generally believe that no benefit will result from the riots. Negroes are supposed to view them with horror, seeing the physical destruction wrought in black ghettos, as well as the destruction of the good will patiently accumulated during early days of campaigning for civil rights. According

Reprinted with permission from the *Social Science Quarterly*, 49, December 1968, pp. 485–503.

to this myth, Negroes foresee "white backlash" and cities laid waste, rather than betterment in their life situations, as the main effect of the riots.

The response of the Negro community to the riots is a crucial consideration in determining how the society as a whole should respond to them. If these three myths are correct, perhaps the customary mechanisms for dealing with individual criminal behavior are not only morally justified but also the most practicable means for handling riots. If these myths are incorrect, if Negroes support the riots, see them as expressing meaningful goals, and expect them to better the conditions of their lives, then the responses traditionally used for dealing with criminals would be inappropriate. They would be impractical, ineffective, and likely to exacerbate an already difficult situation. Instead it would be essential to devise policies which took into account the fact that the riot highlighted a problem pervading the whole Negro community, rather than one limited to a few deviant individuals.

It is apparent that many Americans, black and white alike, have already rejected these myths. Others, however, retain them — those in positions of authority as well as those in the broader white community. Moreover, systematic data on them have not been widely available. Since these myths have had and will continue to have great influence in determining the white population's response to urban problems, it is vital that their validity be subjected to close empirical test. The primary purpose of this article is to present some convincing evidence of their inaccuracy, at least in the important case of the Los Angeles Negro community's response to the Watts riots.

Method[3]

The data on which this article is based were obtained from interviews conducted with three samples of respondents in Los Angeles County in late 1965 and early 1966. The most important was a representative sample of Negroes living in the large area (46.5 square miles) of South-Central Los Angeles sealed off by a curfew imposed during the rioting. This sample, numbering 586 respondents, will be referred to below as the "Negro curfew zone" sample. The curfew zone contains about three-fourths of the more than 450,000 Negroes living in Los Angeles County, and is over 80 per cent Negro.[4] Hence it represents the major concentration of Negroes in the Los Angeles area. The sampling was done by randomly choosing names from the 1960 census lists, then over-sampling poverty-level census tracts by a cluster-sampling procedure to compensate for the underrepresentation of low-income respondents due to residential transience. Another 124 Negro respondents, all arrested in the riot, were contacted principally through lawyers providing free legal aid. This "arrestee" sample was not representative but provided a useful reference point. Both Negro samples were interviewed by black interviewers living in the curfew zone. Though the interviews were long (averaging about two hours), interest was high and the refusal rate low. Checks were run on the possible biases introduced by the interviewers' own views and these do not give unusual reason for concern. The same interview schedule was used for all Negro respondents; it was structured, and included both open-ended and closed-ended items.

The third sample included 586 white respondents from six communities in Los Angeles County, half of which were racially integrated and half nonintegrated, with high, medium, and low socioeconomic levels. This sample is thus not wholly representative of the county, overrepresenting racial hostilities. Some, but not all, of the items on the Negro interview schedule were also used with white respondents. The main emphasis in this article is upon Negro opinion, so the white sample is not referred to except when explicitly indicated.

The Three Myths

Data relevant to the first myth — that only a small fraction of the Negro community participated in the riot of August, 1965, and that nearly everyone else was antagonistic to it — show that it was clearly erroneous on both counts.

The authors' best estimate is that approximately 15 per cent of the Negroes in the area participated in the riot. This was the proportion of curfew zone respondents who stated that they had been "very" or "somewhat" active in the riot and that they had seen crowds of people, and stores being burned and looted. The self-report of active participation, whether wholly accurate or not, indicates, at least, that numerous Los Angeles Negroes (22 per cent of the sample) were willing to identify themselves with the riot.[5]

Furthermore, the Negro community as a whole was not overwhelmingly antagonistic to the riot. This point may be demonstrated in two ways. First, respondents were asked to estimate the proportion of "people in the area" (referring generally to the curfew zone) who had supported or opposed the riot. The mean estimate was that 34 per cent had "supported" the riot, and that 56 per cent had been "against it."

Second, each respondent was asked his own feeling about the riot in a series of open-ended questions. He was asked directly how he felt about the riot, how he felt about the events of the riot, and how he felt about the people who were involved. Answers to these questions yielded three measures of feeling or affect toward the riot.[6] A little under one-third of the Negro curfew zone sample expressed approval of the riot on each of these three measures, and about half disapproved of the riot, as shown in Table 1. This finding closely resembled the respondents' own estimates of public opinion in the area, as cited above.

Clearly, then, support for the riot was far more extensive than the public has

Table 1: Evaluation of Riot and Rioters[a]

	Overall Feeling about Riot	Feeling about Events	Feeling about Participants
Negro curfew zone (N = 586)			
Very or somewhat favorable	27%	29%	30%
Ambivalent or neutral	16	1	19
Strongly or moderately unfavorable	50	67	42
Don't know, no answer	7	3	8
Total	100%	100%	99%
Arrestee sample (N = 124)			
Very or somewhat favorable	52%	50%	57%
Ambivalent or neutral	10	4	12
Strongly or moderately unfavorable	32	45	23
Don't know, no answer	6	1	7
Total	100%	100%	99%

[a] The specific questions were as follows:
For column 1, "Now that it is over, how do you feel about what happened?"
For column 2, "What did you like about what was going on?" and "What did you dislike about what was going on?"
For column 3, "What kinds of people supported it?" and "What kinds of people were against it?"
These questions were not asked of the white sample.

been led to believe, numbering about a third of the area's adult residents, though a majority did disapprove of it. Even while disapproving, however, Negro respondents were markedly more lenient toward the riot's supporters than they were toward the destruction of life and property that occurred. Table 1 shows that 42 per cent disapproved of the participants, while 67 per cent disapproved of the events of the riot.

The riot as a protest   The second myth — that the riot was a meaningless, haphazard expression of disregard for law and order — was not commonly held among Negroes in Los Angeles. Many viewed the riot in revolutionary or insurrectional terms; most thought it had a purpose and that the purpose was, in part at least, a Negro protest.

Official utterances and the mass media, almost without exception, had described the events as being a "riot." Each respondent was asked what term he would use to describe the events. Table 2 shows that, given this free choice, over a third of the Negro sample selected "revolt," "insurrection," "rebellion," "uprising," "revenge," or other revolutionary term, thus flying in the face of the conventional definition. Other items given in Table 2 posed the question of a meaningful protest more directly, and show that a majority of the Negro community did indeed see the riot in these terms. Substantial majorities felt that it did have a purpose, that it was a Negro protest, and that those outsiders attacked in the riot deserved what they got.

Table 2: The Riot as Protest

	Whites	Negroes (Curfew Zone)	Arrestees
What word or term would you use in talking about it?			
Riot	58%	46%	44%
Revolt, revolution, insurrection	13	38	45
Other (disaster, tragedy, mess, disgrace, etc.)	27	8	10
Don't know, no answer	2	8	2
Total	100%	100%	101%
Why were targets attacked?[a]			
Deserved attack	—	64%	75%
Ambivalent, don't know	—	17	21
Did not deserve attack	—	14	0
No answer	—	5	4
Total		100%	100%
Did it have a purpose or goal?			
Yes	33%	56%	56%
Don't know, other	4	11	13
No	62	28	29
No answer	—	5	2
Total	99%	100%	100%
Was it a Negro protest?			
Yes	54%	62%	66%
Don't know, other	3	12	15
No	42	23	16
No answer	—	2	3
Total	99%	99%	100%

[a] This question was not asked of white respondents.

Anticipating favorable effects   The third myth — that Negroes viewed the riot with alarm for the future — also was not subscribed to in Los Angeles. Most (58 per cent) foresaw predominantly beneficial effects, and only a minority (26 per cent) anticipated predominantly unfavorable effects. Similarly, more thought it would "help" the Negro cause than thought it would "hurt" it. These data are given in Table 3.

Thus, a large minority of the Negroes in the curfew zone, about one-third, were favorable to the rioting, and the others' disapproval focused more upon the events than upon the participants. Over half saw the riot as a purposeful protest, many even speaking of it in revolutionary terms. Favorable effects were much more widely anticipated than unfavorable effects. This evidence indicates that the three myths cited above were invalid for the Los Angeles Negro community. It did not whole-heartedly reject and condemn its 1965 riot.

Participants' attitudes   Negroes clearly had more sympathy for the partici-pants than for the events of the riot. In fact, the participants and the community as a whole had rather similar attitudes about the riot. The arrestees were considera-

Table 3: Expected Effects of the Riot

	Whites	Negroes (Curfew Zone)	Arrestees
What will the main effects be?[a]			
Very or somewhat favorable	—	58%	57%
Neutral, ambivalent, don't know	—	12	14
Very or somewhat unfavorable	—	26	27
No answer	—	3	2
Total		99%	100%
Do you think it helped or hurt the Negro's cause?			
Helped	19%	38%	54%
No difference, don't know	5	30	33
Hurt	75	24	9
No answers, other	1	8	4
Total	100%	100%	100%

[a] This question was not asked of white respondents.

bly more favorable toward the riot than was the community as a whole (see Table 1), but the community was equally optimistic about the effects of the riot, and as willing to interpret it as a purposeful protest (see Tables 2 and 3). Data presented elsewhere compare participants and nonparticipants within the Negro curfew zone sample, and yield almost exactly the same picture. Most participants tended to approve of the riot, while more nonparticipants disapproved than approved of it. However, in both groups a majority expressed optimism about the effects of the riot, and interpreted it as a meaningful protest. In fact participants and nonparticipants hardly differed at all in the latter two respects.[7] This similarity of feeling between the participants (whether arrested or not) and the Negro community as a whole suggests both that the participants were not particularly unusual or deviant in their thinking, and that members of the community were not wholly willing to condemn nor to symbolically ostracize the rioters.

White attitudes   The picture is quite different with respect to whites. As might now be expected, their attitudes toward the riot were considerably less favorable. Table 2 shows that whites thought it was nothing more meaningful than a "riot." Though most did feel it was a Negro protest, the consensus of opinion was that it was a purposeless, meaningless outburst. Table 3 shows that whites felt it definitely had "hurt" the Negro cause. Thus the cleavage in opinion that developed in Los Angeles after the riot was not so much between rioters and the law-abiding people of both races as between whites and blacks.

Other riots, other communities   This is not the place to attempt a complete review of Negro opinion in other communities, or about other riots, but a brief discussion will indicate that results obtained here were similar to those obtained elsewhere in this nation.

Items directly analogous to those here evaluating riots and rioters have not been widely used. A *Fortune Magazine* national survey in 1967 did find that only 14 per cent felt the "violence and rioting that has already occurred" was "essentially good," while 58 per cent felt it was "essentially bad."[8] Similarly, a 1967 Harris national survey found that 10 per cent felt "most Negroes support riots" and 75 per cent felt that "only a minority" supports them.[9] These results indicate disapproval of riots by a substantial majority of Negroes. yet the same Harris poll reveals that 62 per cent felt looters should not be shot, and 27 per cent felt they should be (in contrast to the 62 per cent of whites who felt shooting was appropriate for looters).[10] Clearly there are substantial limits on the strength of Negro disapproval and condemnation of Negro rioters.

Optimism about the effects of riots has also been characteristic. In several studies, Negroes have been asked whether riots "help" or "hurt" their cause, and the preferred answer has generally been that they "help." This was the result of a 1966 Harris national survey, a 1966 Harris survey of Negro leadership, and surveys of the Negro populations of Los Angeles (1966) and Oakland (1967).[11] The two exceptions have been a 1966 survey in Houston, a Southern city, where a slight plurality felt that riots "hurt," and the 1967 Harris survey (presumably national), which reported that only 12 per cent felt they would help — a result that is grossly out of line with all other surveys and thus difficult to interpret.

The Riot Ideology of the Negro Community

Ambivalent evaluations of the riot, the feeling that it was meaningful, and optimism about its effects represent the simple elements around which a more complex belief system about the riot developed within the Negro community. This centered on a view of the riot as an instrument of Negro protest against real grievances. The substance of this view may be examined through the content of the protest and the grievances. First, let us consider in more detail the question of general community sympathy for the rioters.

Riot events and participants: the community's sympathetic defense   Evaluations of the riot events and riot participants, shown in Table 1, gave the impression that the events of the riot were condemned more heartily than the rioters. Does the content of the respondents' attitudes support this impression?

The actual events of the riot were almost universally condemned. When asked "What did you like about what was going on?" 63 per cent of the Negroes sampled replied, "Nothing." The others gave widely dispersed responses. Crimes against property (such as burning and looting) and crimes against persons (such as killing and shooting) were cited about equally often as disliked aspects of the riot, as shown in Table 4. However, while the events of the riot were generally disliked and

Table 4: What Did You Dislike about the Riot?[a]

	Negroes (Curfew Zone)	Arrestees
Crimes against property (burning, destruction, looting)	47%	26%
Crimes against persons	43	70
Negro attacks on white	(1)	(0)
Police shooting, killing, brutality	(14)	(32)
Killing, bloodshed, violence, shooting in general	(28)	(38)
Practical inconveniences	9	5
Negroes breaking law	1	0
Total	100%	100%

[a] Not asked of white respondents.

disapproved, they were not flatly repudiated. About 75 per cent couched their disapproval in terms suggesting sorrow and remorse (e.g., "regretful," "a sad thing," "a shame," "glad it's over") while only 25 per cent responded in a fashion suggesting repudiation of the riot (e.g., "disgusted," "disgrace," "unnecessary," "senseless"). Since disapproval of the riot did not necessarily include total dissociation from and repudiation of it, it is perhaps not surprising that the rioters and riot supporters were less harshly criticized than the event they created.

Indeed, the Negro community's description of the riot supporters, on the one hand, and the authorities on the other, reveal considerably more sympathy for those fomenting the riot than for those who tried to stop it. The descriptions of who had supported the riot, shown in Table 5, indicate that such sympathetic and understanding descriptions as "people who suffer" or "people wanting freedom" outnumbered such unsympathetic and repudiating responses as "hoodlums" or "Communists." The predominant conception of a riot supporter was not of a criminal, or

Table 5: What Kinds of People Supported the Riot?[a]

	Negroes (Curfew Zone)	Arrestees
Sympathetic descriptions	45%	59%
Everyone	(10)	(15)
Good people (people wanting freedom, sympathetic people, etc.)	(5)	(8)
Deprived, mistreated (unemployed people who suffer, have-nots, poor people)	(30)	(36)
Unsympathetic descriptions	34	16
Anti-social (hoodlums, corrupt)	(12)	(10)
Political (Communists, Muslims)	(2)	(0)
Irresponsible (teenagers, fools, uneducated, thrill seekers)	(20)	(6)
Other	21	25
Estranged people (hopeless people, old people)	(5)	(9)
Middle class (business people)	(1)	(1)
Don't know, no answer	(15)	(15)
Total	100%	100%

[a] Not asked of white respondents.

of a disreputable or despicable person, but evidently of a person not so very dissimi-
lar from the respondent himself, though perhaps somewhat down on his luck.

In contrast, much antagonism was expressed toward the authorities' role in
the riot. Only 28 per cent thought the authorities had handled the riot "well," and
65 per cent felt they had handled it "badly." The further breakdown of these
responses is shown in Table 6; Negroes who thought the authorities had done badly

Table 6: Did the Authorities Handle It Well or Badly?

	Whites	Negroes (Curfew Zone)	Arrestees
Well	66%	28%	15%
Badly	32	65	77
Should have stopped it sooner	(26)	(27)	(14)
They made it worse, were intransigent	(6)	(33)	(56)
Other	(0)	(5)	(7)
Don't know, no answer, other	2	8	9
Total	100%	101%	101%

were split between those who felt they should have put an end to the riot earlier,
and those who felt the authorities had exacerbated the situation. Many Negro
respondents did not like what had happened then, but their disposition was to
defend and justify the actions of Negro rioters, and to criticize the actions of the
white authorities.

Explanations of the causes of the riot also demonstrated a sympathetic defense
of the rioters, as shown in Table 7. The dominant tendency was to blame the riot

Table 7: What Caused the Riot?

	Whites	Negroes (Curfew Zone)	Arrestees
Specific grievances	20%	38%	51%
Discrimination, mistreatment by whites	(5)	(7)	(4)
Poverty, economic deprivation, inadequate services	(11)	(10)	(5)
Police mistreatment	(4)	(21)	(42)
Pent-up hostility, desire for revenge, fed-up	14	26	34
Frye incident	18	11	8
Undesirable groups	29	9	2
Communists, Muslims, civil rights groups, organized groups, KKK, agitators	(16)	(3)	(0)
Criminals, looters	(8)	(2)	(0)
Foolish people, teenagers, Southerners	(5)	(4)	(2)
Spontaneous explosion, accident, weather	10	0	0
Don't know, no answer	10	17	6
Total	101%	101%	101%

on legitimate grievances, such as discrimination, poverty, or police mistreatment (38 per cent), or on long-standing hostility and other pent-up emotions (26 per cent). Relatively few attributed the riot mainly to the incident that precipitated it, the fracas with the Frye family, or blamed any of the obvious candidates for a scapegoat, such as the Communists or gang members.

The contrast with opinions expressed by white residents of Los Angeles was a vivid one. By attributing the riot to grievances and to years of frustration, the Negro respondents suggested that the people who supported the riot had legitimate reasons for doing so. Whites, on the other hand, praised the work of the authorities, or even criticized them for not being more punitive with the rioters (Table 6). Whites were much more inclined to attribute the riot to agitators, Communists, criminals, the weather, or simply to write it off as arising from the Frye incident (Table 7). The Negro community as a whole was much closer to the explicit sympathy for the rioters expressed by the arrestees. Both gave relatively sympathetic descriptions of the rioters (Table 5), harshly criticized the authorities (Table 6), and attributed the riot to legitimate grievances rather than to chance or whimsical or illegal and un-American factors (Table 7).

This contrast between black sympathy for the rioters and white condemnation of them, as reflected in explanations for the riot, has also been obtained in several more recent surveys made in other areas. For example, in Harris's 1967 survey, Negroes were about twice as likely as whites to attribute recent riots to grievances over jobs, education, housing, police, and inequality. Whites were more likely than Negroes to blame outside agitation, lack of firmness by government authorities, the desire to loot, or a desire for violence.[12] Negroes thought the riots were spontaneous; a vast majority of the whites thought they had been organized.[13] Negroes thought the looted stores had been charging exorbitant prices; whites thought they had not.[14] Among whites, 62 per cent felt looters should be shot; among Negroes, only 27 per cent felt that action was justifiable.[15] In other post-riot surveys, Negroes in Detroit and in Watts have generally explained the rioting in terms of a response to grievances about housing, jobs, the police, and poverty.[16] The most impressive difference of opinion about the rioters, then, is not between the law-abiders and the law-breakers in the Negro community, but between blacks and whites.

The purpose of the riot: to call attention.   Looking back on the riot, Los Angeles Negroes were largely agreed that it had been a purposeful, directed protest. But if Negroes saw the riot as a meaningful event, what was the meaning? What was the purpose of the riot; what was it supposed to accomplish? Negroes' perceptions on these matters may illuminate in what respects their hopes have subsequently been frustrated or fulfilled.

The dominant "purpose" of the riot, according to retrospective Negro perceptions, was to call the attention of whites to Negro problems. Fifty-six per cent of the Negro curfew zone sample had felt the riot had a purpose (see Table 2); of these,

41 per cent identified it as an attempt to call attention to Negro problems, and most of these saw the call directed specifically at white people. Smaller numbers saw it as an expression of accumulated hostility and resentment (33 per cent) or thought it was intended to implement some specific social or economic changes (26 per cent), e.g., to get more jobs, improve conditions, or get equal rights. The "message" from the Negro citizenry to the broader, predominantly white community is thus a two-edged one: a request for attention to their problems, and at the same time, an expression of accumulated angers and resentments from past grievances.

The specific problems being protested follow a line now familiar. The main targets of attack were seen as being merchants (38 per cent), white people in general (28 per cent), and the police (17 per cent). As already indicated (Table 2), most respondents felt these targets deserved the attacks they received. The predominant reasons given for the attacks had to do with justifiable grievances. Mistreatment of Negroes, in terms of discrimination or brutality, was the most common (31 per cent). Economic exploitation or disadvantage (e.g., overcharging, or unemployment) was next most frequent (19 per cent). These two categories accounted for the reasons given by half the Negro curfew zone respondents. "Chance" (10 per cent) and mere "criminal intent" (1 per cent) were relatively rare responses. However, 17 per cent explained the attacks in terms of the rioters' longstanding frustration, anger, and resentment.

So, Los Angeles Negroes tended to interpret the riot as a purposeful protest. In retrospect, they saw its aims as twofold: a call for attention to their problems, and an expression of hostility and resentment over genuine grievances. Much of this interpretation must represent a rationale constructed after the fact for a violent and confusing series of events that almost certainly had no single cause and was not deliberately planned.[17] Nevertheless, the riot was a widely based outburst of Negro hostility, fed upon reservoirs of resentment and hatred that had not been perceived earlier or understood well by white people. It had a clear focus on racial antagonisms: the objects of hostility were not other Negroes, but white people, primarily merchants, and almost any symbol of constituted authority. Even if the "purposeful" quality of the riot was a rationalization, it described a moderately "rational" series of events.

Expected outcomes of the riot: help for the ghetto   In seeing the riot as a protest, a majority of the Negro population thought of it as a social-change action the principal aims of which were change in living conditions and aggression against the oppressor. Expectations about outcomes should thus serve as critical considerations in Negroes' thinking about the value of riots as instruments of social change. In the most general terms, these expectations were mostly optimistic, as seen earlier (Table 3). A further question is how Negroes expected the riot to affect the conditions of their lives, and, particularly, how they expected constituted authority and the broader white community to react.

By all odds the most salient expectation was that whites would begin to redress Negro grievances. The effect of the riot mentioned first by 43 per cent of the Negro respondents was from outside the Negro community. An additional 13 per cent cited the effect of greater white awareness of Negro problems, and more comfortable relations between whites and Negroes. Thus, a majority thought first of favorable change among whites. These data are shown in Table 8. Similar thoughts were expressed by those who thought the riot would affect the Negro's cause, or affect the gap between the races. Table 9 shows that the most common reasons Negroes gave for why the riot might help or hurt the Negro's cause had to do with white reactions to it. Similarly, of those who thought it would increase or decrease the gap between the races, 54 per cent expected some change in whites, 28 per cent expected change in both races, and only 12 per cent expected change among Negroes themselves. Hence the clearest expectation among Negro respondents was that the riot would effect favorable change among white people.

While Negroes expected a favorable response from whites, they did not expect a massive one. Table 10 shows that greater white awareness of Negro problems was almost universally expected, and most Negroes expected more sympathetic treatment. However, opinion was much more divided with respect to changes in the

Table 8: What Will the Main Effects of the Riot Be?

	Negroes (Curfew Zone)
Negroes will be helped or rewarded by others	43%
Negro-white relations will be changed for the better	13
Whites will be more aware of Negroes	(11)
Negroes and whites will get along together	(2)
Negro-white relations will change for the worse	13
Negroes will gain self-respect, get new leadership	2
Hope for something good	3
Nothing, no change	11
Don't know, no answer	14
Total	99%

Table 9: Why Will It Help or Hurt Negroes?[a]

	Negroes (Curfew Zone)
Change whites for the better	42%
Greater attention to Negroes	(29)
More positive toward Negroes	(13)
Change whites for the worse, more prejudice, etc.	8
Change Negroes	15
For worse (give bad name, make worse off)	(12)
For better (greater self-confidence, morale)	(3)
Economic effects (fewer jobs, stores)	30
Other	5
Total	100%

[a] Asked of the 62 per cent of the sample who said the riot would help or hurt the Negro cause.

Table 10: Perceived Effects of Riot on Negro-White Relations

	Whites	Negroes (Curfew Zone)	Arrestees
Are whites more aware of Negro problems?			
More aware	79%	84%	80%
No change	18	13	17
Less aware	2	2	1
Other	1	2	2
Total	100%	101%	100%
Are whites more sympathetic to Negro problems?			
More sympathetic	32%	51%	49%
No change	27	31	38
Less sympathetic	37	12	9
Other	4	6	4
Total	100%	100%	100%
Did the riot increase or decrease the gap between the races?			
Increase	71%	23%	15%
No change	11	38	37
Decrease	13	24	22
Other	4	16	27
Total	99%	101%	100%

social distance between the races.[18] About the same number of Negroes felt "more at ease" (10 per cent) than felt "less at ease" (8 per cent) in the contacts with white people after the riot, and no change was reported in the frequency of contact with whites. So most Negroes seem to have expected more sympathetic attention to their problems, but relatively few expected more commitment from whites at the level of personal relationships.

Two possibilities Negroes rarely mentioned, curiously enough, were "white backlash" and greater Negro solidarity. Anticipation of greater white hostility or greater racial prejudice was mentioned by only 13 per cent as the most likely effect of the riot (Table 8) and by 8 per cent as the main reason why the riot might help or hurt the Negro cause (Table 9). Effects upon Negroes aside from effects upon whites were also rarely mentioned. Two per cent saw new self-respect or leadership among Negroes as a main effect of the riot, and 15 per cent and 12 per cent, respectively, cited change among Negroes as the main reasons why the riot might help or hurt the Negro's cause and increase or decrease the gap between the races.

In retrospect this seems surprising because these two effects seem to have materialized to a far greater degree than the generally predicted white sympathetic attention. At the time, whites indeed felt more aware of Negro problems, but scarcely more sympathetic, as shown in Table 10. And whites predicted a considerable widening of the gap between the races. The rise in Negro solidarity is more difficult to determine directly from these data, but it seems evident that the riot drew more support from Negroes than anyone could have expected, and that in many respects the community as a whole rallied behind the rioters.

Thus the changes described by both races follow a well-worn path in American race relations. The white population is mainly willing to adjust when it is easy and convenient to do so. Both races expected the riot to increase the awareness of Negro problems among the dominant majority whites, and it seems to have done just that. However, a misjudgment occurred on the more difficult issue of white sympathy with Negro problems. Here Negroes hoped for change, while whites frankly expected a deterioration of race relations. More helpful, perhaps, are the social distance data. Here Negroes' expectations may have been more accurate than those of whites. The white population's racial nightmares have traditionally been filled with the horrors of intimate social contact with Negroes, rather than the more ritualized contacts of occupational or political interdependence. So more pessimism on the social distance dimension than on the awareness or sympathy dimensions could reasonably have been expected. But these data (and Negroes' expectations) do not reveal an actual widening of the gap between the races, contrary to whites' expectations.[19] The "backlash" may mean a slowdown rather than an actual deterioration in race relations.

Preferred Mechanisms of Grievance Redress

A riot ideology appears to have developed among Negroes in the curfew zone, in part justifying the Los Angeles riot as an instrument of protest. To what extent did rioting thus become thought of as a legitimate and effective mechansim of grievance redress for the future? Not widely, apparently. Answers to the open-ended question "What must Negroes do to get what they want?" reveal a preponderantly conventional approach to equal rights, as shown in Table 11. Over half of the Negro respondents see some form of conventional middle-class behavior as the road to

Table 11: What Must Negroes Do to Get What They Want?

	Negroes (Curfew Zone)	Arrestees
Conventional approaches	56%	51%
Get more education	(27)	(15)
Work hard, strive and succeed	(23)	(32)
Get jobs, acquire wealth	(2)	(2)
Change stereotyped qualities	(4)	(2)
Political action	19	15
Vote more, follow their leaders, etc.	(6)	(6)
Protest, make needs known	(13)	(9)
Violent action	3	10
Increase morale	7	12
Remove self-hatred	(1)	(0)
Increase racial solidarity	(6)	(12)
Change whites, change both races	1	0
Other	5	7
Don't know, no answer	9	5
Total	100%	100%

success (e.g., more education and hard work). Another 19 per cent see more efficient and active political participation as the answer, while only 3 per cent contend that violence is necessary for equal rights. So the majority of Negroes in Los Angeles, even after a riot they perceived as likely to have beneficial effects, still opted for moderate grievance redress procedures and for traditional methods of personal advancement.

The question still remains how strong this preference for conventional mechanisms actually is, and whether or not the riot affected it. A sizable number of respondents expressed interest in demonstrations and nonviolent protest. Only a few (6 per cent) had participated in pre-riot civil rights activity, but 37 per cent said after the riot that they were willing to participate in demonstrations. Thirteen per cent said the riot had made them more willing to do so; so perhaps the riot made some Negroes more militant and unified.

It is hard to determine from the data whether it also increased their attraction to violence. However, when asked the most effective method to use in protest, given the alternatives of negotiation and nonviolent protest, 12 per cent selected violent protest (of the arrestees, 22 per cent did so). And 34 per cent thought there would be a recurrence of rioting in Los Angeles. Another 37 per cent felt they could not predict whether or not there would be another riot, thereby reflecting a lack of confidence in the durability of civic peace. While these data do not suggest that a majority of Negroes in Los Angeles advocate violence, the minority that does is rather sizable, and the expectation of further violence on the part of many others is an ominous sign; prophecies of that kind have a way of becoming self-fulfilling.[20]

Conclusions

This paper has been primarily concerned with the reaction of the Los Angeles Negro population to the Watts Riots of 1965. The principal findings follow:

1. It is not correct that all but a small minority strongly disapproved of the riots, felt they were a meaningless and random outburst of violence, and felt deeply pessimistic about the probable effects of the riots on the welfare of Negroes. Actually, a large minority (about one-third) approved of the rioting, most Negro residents of the riot area felt it had been a meaningful protest, and most were optimistic about its effects on their life situation.

2. A widespread "riot ideology" appears to have developed in the Negro community following the riot, with the following elements. The events of the riot were deplored, and the wish was expressed that the authorities had stopped it earlier. Yet the authorities tended to be criticized and the rioters defended. The causes of the riot were described in terms of genuine grievances with those who were attacked; e.g., a history of friction, discrimina-

tion, and economic exploitation with local merchants and police. The purpose of the riot was seen as being, on the one hand, to call the attention of whites to Negro problems, and on the other, to express resentment against malefactors. The riot was expected to bring help to the Negro population from whites, though major improvement in interracial personal relationships was not expected. This "riot ideology" seemed to justify and defend the riot, but violence was not often advocated for the future.[21]

3. The major cleavage that developed after the riot was between the white and black populations of Los Angeles, not between lawbreakers and lawabiders within the black population. Whites were much readier to condemn the riot, to see only purposeless violence in it, and to foresee a gloomy future for race relations. Whites were likely to ascribe the riot to agitators and criminal impulse, and less likely to attribute it to genuine grievances. These divisions of opinion along racial lines seem to be characteristic of the ways in which the two racial groups have responded across the country to recent race riots.[22]

Perhaps the most important fact of all is that so many Negroes felt disposed to justify and ennoble the riot after it was all over. It was not viewed as an alien disruption of their peaceful lives, but as an expression of protest by the Negro community as a whole, against an oppressive majority. Here perhaps lies one of the tragedies of the riot. While it was, in the eyes of many Negroes, an outburst against an oppressive social system, the response of whites to the call for attention and help was hoped to be favorable. Perhaps this was an analogy taken from the white response to the Southern civil rights battles of the preceding decade. However, relatively little help has in fact been forthcoming, and it is not clear that whites expect to give very much. Awareness of the problem seems obviously to have increased, but the retaliatory aspect of the "message" of the riot seems as salient to whites as the plea for help.

Notes

[1] This study was conducted under a contract between the Office of Economic Opportunity and the Institute for Government and Public Affairs at UCLA, while both authors were members of the Department of Psychology, UCLA. The Coordinator of the research was Nathan E. Cohen. We owe a profound debt of gratitude to the many persons who worked on the Los Angeles Riot Study, with special thanks to Diana TenHouten and John B. McConahay. We also wish to express our appreciation to Esther Spachner for editorial help and to Peter Orleans for his comments on an earlier draft of this paper.

[2] See the attributions of the Watts riot to "young hoodlums," "the criminal element," and black nationalists by the mayor and police chief of Los Angeles, in the *New York Times,* Aug. 13, 1965, p. 26; Aug. 14, 1965, p. 8; Sept. 14, 1965, p. 22.

[3] For more complete accounts of the method, see T. M. Tomlinson and Diana L. Ten-Houten, "Method: Negro Reaction Survey," and Richard T. Morris and Vincent Jeffries, "The

White Reaction Study," *Los Angeles Riot Study* (Los Angeles: Institute of Government and Public Affairs, University of California, 1967). See also R. T. Morris and V. Jeffries, "Violence Next Door," *Social Forces,* 46 (March, 1968), pp. 352–358.

⁴ See U.S., Bureau of the Census, *U.S. Census of Population: 1960,* Vol. 1: *Characteristics of the Population,* Part 6: California (Washington, D.C.: U.S. Government Printing Office, 1963). Also David O. Sears and John B. McConahay, "Riot Participation," *Los Angeles Riot Study.*

⁵ For a detailed consideration of these data, see Sears and McConahay, *ibid.* Rates of participation in the Newark and Detroit riots of 1967 appear to have been similarly high, according to data published in *The Report of the National Advisory Commission on Civil Disorders* (New York: Bantam Books, 1968), p. 172.

⁶ For a detailed description of the coding procedure, see Tomlinson and TenHouten, "Method: Negro Reaction Survey." The coding reliabilities were all over .95.

⁷ See David O. Sears and John B. McConahay, "The Politics of Discontent: Blocked Mechanisms of Grievance Redress and the Psychology of the New Urban Black Man," *Los Angeles Riot Study.*

⁸ Roger Beardwood, "The New Negro Mood," *Fortune,* 77 (Jan., 1968), p. 146.

⁹ See Hazel Erskine, "The Polls: Demonstrations and Race Riots," *Public Opinion Quarterly,* 31 (Winter, 1967), pp. 655–677, for many of the results of these polls. This finding is given on p. 671.

¹⁰ *Ibid.,* p. 674.

¹¹ See W. Brink and Louis Harris, *Black and White* (New York: Simon and Schuster, 1966), pp. 264–265; *Federal Role in Urban Affairs,* Hearings before the Subcommittee on Executive Reorganization of the Committee on Government Operations, U.S. 89th Congress, 2nd Session, Senate, Part 6, p. 1387; William McCord and John Howard, "Negro Opinions in Three Riot Cities," *American Behavioral Scientist,* 11 (March–April, 1968), p. 26.

¹² McCord and Howard, *Ibid.;* Erskine, "The Polls," p. 662.

¹³ Erskine, "The Polls," p. 666.

¹⁴ *Ibid.,* p. 665.

¹⁵ *Ibid.,* p. 674.

¹⁶ Detroit Urban League, "A Survey of Attitudes of Detroit Negroes after the Riot of 1967," Detroit, 1967. See also *Federal Role in Urban Affairs,* p. 1387. The vivid contrast between whites and Negroes also appears in a Brandeis University survey: Lemberg Center for the Study of Violence, "A Survey of Racial Attitudes in Six Northern Cities: Preliminary Findings," Waltham, Mass., 1967, pp. 15–16. (Mimeographed.)

¹⁷ Some surveys may elicit a grander ideological structure than actually exists by utilizing a carefully designed Socratic progression of questions. However the section of the present schedule dealing with the riot began with only the simplest open-ended items; i.e., those listed in Tables 1, 4, 5, 6, 7, the first two items of Table 2, and the first item of Table 3. Only later were more leading structured questions raised (e.g., the remaining items in Tables 2 and 3). Hence most of the discussion of "riot ideology" rests on spontaneously reported responses, not on interviews "leading" the respondent on.

¹⁸ An additional coding of the "increased gap" responses indicated that few Negroes thought increased separation a good thing, despite the popularity of separatist ideology among many activists.

¹⁹ See also Morris and Jeffries, "The White Reaction Study."

²⁰ Particularly ominous, as might be expected, were the attitudes of the more militant respondents. Subdividing the curfew zone sample in terms of relative militance reveals considerably greater support for riots and higher endorsement of violence among the militants than among the more conservative respondents. For a detailed account of these data, see T. M. Tomlinson, "Ideological Foundations for Negro Action: A Comparative Analysis of Militant and Non-Militant Views of the Los Angeles Riot," *Los Angeles Riot Study.* See also T. M.

Tomlinson, "The Development of a Riot Ideology Among Urban Negroes," *American Behavioral Scientist,* 11 (March–April, 1968), pp. 27–31.

Findings from other surveys on the level of endorsement of violence are not strictly comparable, because of different question wording. The range of estimates is substantial. In 1964, Kraft surveys in Harlem, Chicago, and Baltimore found 5 per cent saying violence was necessary, but one in Watts after the riot found that 14 per cent thought it was. See *Federal Role in Urban Affairs,* p. 1399. A complex question used by Harris in national surveys in 1963 and 1966 found 22 per cent and 21 per cent, respectively, thinking violence was needed. See Brink and Harris, *Black and White,* p. 260. After the Detroit riot of 1967, an Urban League survey found 24 per cent feeling there was more to gain than lose with violence (see Detroit Urban League, "A Survey of Attitudes"). And the 1967 *Fortune* survey found 35 per cent saying that riots and violence are necessary (see Beardwood, "The New Negro Mood," p. 148). Whether these represent secular changes or merely differently worded questions is unclear.

[21] There is considerable justification for speaking of this pattern of beliefs in terms of an "ideology," based on the pattern of interrelationships between various of them. Approval of the riot, optimism about its effects, and perceiving the riot as a meaningful protest were all strongly correlated with one another.

[22] This observation of racial differences might seem to set a new record for banality in social science. The impressive finding here is not that whites and Negroes disagree, but that disagreement penetrates so deeply into each group, well beyond those that normally concern themselves with public affairs. It could be, for example, that relatively few people care very much about riots, and that most people of both races reject them as they reject criminal behavior in general. That is not the case, however.

Internal Colonialism and Ghetto Revolt[1]

Robert Blauner

It is becoming almost fashionable to analyze American racial conflict today in terms of the colonial analogy. I shall argue in this paper that the utility of this perspective depends upon a distinction between colonization as a process and colonialism as a social, economic, and political system. It is the experience of colonization that Afro-Americans share with many of the nonwhite people of the world. But this subjugation has taken place in a societal context that differs in important respects from the situation of "classical colonialism." In the body of this essay I shall look at some major developments in Black protest — the urban riots, cultural nationalism, and the movement for ghetto control — as collective responses to colonized status. Viewing our domestic situation as a special form of colonization outside a context of a colonial system will help explain some of the dilemmas and ambiguities within these movements.

The present crisis in American life has brought about changes in social perspectives and the questioning of long accepted frameworks. Intellectuals and social scientists have been forced by the pressure of events to look at old definitions of the character of our society, the role of racism, and the workings of basic institutions. The depth and volatility of contemporary racial conflict challenge sociologists in particular to question the adequacy of theoretical models by which we have explained American race relations in the past.

For a long time the distinctiveness of the Negro situation among the ethnic minorities was placed in terms of color, and the systematic discrimination that follows from our deep-seated racial prejudices. This was sometimes called the caste theory, and while provocative, it missed essential and dynamic features of American race relations. In the past ten years there has been a tendency to view Afro-Americans as another ethnic group not basically different in experience from previous ethnics and whose "immigration" condition in the North would in time follow their upward course. The inadequacy of this model is now clear — even the Kerner Report devotes a chapter to criticizing this analogy. A more recent (though hardly

Robert Blauner, "Internal Colonialism and Ghetto Revolt," *Social Problems,* Vol. 12, Spring 1969, pp. 393–408. Reprinted by permission of The Society for the Study of Social Problems and the author.

new) approach views the essence of racial subordination in economic class terms: Black people as an underclass are to a degree specially exploited and to a degree economically dispensable in an automating society. Important as are economic factors, the power of race and racism in America cannot be sufficiently explained through class analysis. Into this theory vacuum steps the model of internal colonialism. Problematic and imprecise as it is, it gives hope of becoming a framework that can integrate the insights of caste and racism, ethnicity, culture, and economic exploitation into an overall conceptual scheme. At the same time, the danger of the colonial model is the imposition of an artificial analogy which might keep us from facing up to the fact (to quote Harold Cruse) that "the American black and white social phenomenon is a uniquely new world thing."[2]

During the late 1950's, identification with African nations and other colonial or formerly colonized peoples grew in importance among Black militants.[3] As a result the U.S. was increasingly seen as a colonial power and the concept of domestic colonialism was introduced into the political analysis and rhetoric of militant nationalists. During the same period Black social theorists began developing this frame of reference for explaining American realities. As early as 1962, Cruse characterized race relations in this country as "domestic colonialism."[4] Three years later in *Dark Ghetto,* Kenneth Clark demonstrated how the political, economic, and social structure of Harlem was essentially that of a colony.[5] Finally in 1967, a full-blown elaboration of "internal colonialism" provided the theoretical framework for Carmichael and Hamilton's widely read *Black Power.*[6] The following year the colonial analogy gained currency and new "respectability" when Senator McCarthy habitually referred to Black Americans as a colonized people during his campaign. While the rhetoric of internal colonialism was catching on, other social scientists began to raise questions about its appropriateness as a scheme of analysis.

The colonial analysis has been rejected as obscurantist and misleading by scholars who point to the signifcant differences in history and social-political conditions between our domestic patterns and what took place in Africa and India. Colonialism traditionally refers to the establishment of domination over a geographically external political unit, most often inhabited by people of a different race and culture, where this domination is political and economic, and the colony exists subordinated to and dependent upon the mother country. Typically the colonizers exploit the land, the raw materials, the labor, and other resources of the colonized nation; in addition a formal recognition is given to the difference in power, autonomy, and political status, and various agencies are set up to maintain this subordination. Seemingly the analogy must be stretched beyond usefulness if the American version is to be forced into this model. For here we are talking abut group relations within a society; the mother country–colony separation in geography is absent. Though whites certainly colonized the territory of the original Americans, internal colonization of Afro-Americans did not involve the settlement of whites in any land that was unequivocably Black. And unlike the colonial situation, there has been no formal recognition of differing power since slavery was abolished outside the

South. Classic colonialism involved the control and exploitation of the majority of a nation by a minority of outsiders. Whereas in America the people who are oppressed were themselves originally outsiders and are a numerical minority.

This conventional critique of "internal colonialism" is useful in pointing to the differences between our domestic patterns and the overseas situation. But in its bold attack it tends to lose sight of common experiences that have been historically shared by the most subjugated racial minorities in America and non-white peoples in some other parts of the world. For understanding the most dramatic recent developments on the race scene, this common core element — which I shall call colonization — may be more important than the undeniable divergences between the two contexts.

The common features ultimately relate to the fact that the classical colonialism of the imperialist era and American racism developed out of the same historical situation and reflected a common world economic and power stratification. The slave trade for the most part preceded the imperialist partition and economic exploitation of Africa, and in fact may have been a necessary prerequisite for colonial conquest — since it helped deplete and pacify Africa, undermining the resistance to direct occupation. Slavery contributed one of the basic raw materials for the textile industry which provided much of the capital for the West's industrial development and need for economic expansionism. The essential condition for both American slavery and European colonialism was the power domination and the technological superiority of the Western world in its relation to peoples of non-Western and non-white origins. This objective supremacy in technology and military power buttressed the West's sense of cultural superiority, laying the basis for racist ideologies that were elaborated to justify control and exploitation of non-white people. Thus because classical colonialism and America's internal version developed out of a similar balance of technological, cultural, and power relations, a common *process* of social oppression characterized the racial patterns in the two contexts — despite the variation in political and social structure.

There appear to be four basic components of the colonization complex. The first refers to how the racial group enters into the dominant society (whether colonial power or not). Colonization begins with a forced, involuntary entry. Second, there is an impact on the culture and social organization of the colonized people which is more than just a result of such "natural" processes as contact and acculturation. The colonizing power carries out a policy which constrains, transforms, or destroys indigenous values, orientations, and ways of life. Third, colonization involves a relationship by which members of the colonized group tend to be administered by representatives of the dominant power. There is an experience of being managed and manipulated by outsiders in terms of ethnic status.

A final fundament of colonization is racism. Racism is a principle of social domination by which a group seen as inferior or different in terms of alleged biological characteristics is exploited, controlled, and oppressed socially and psychically by a superordinate group. Except for the marginal case of Japanese imperialism, the major examples of colonialism have involved the subjugation of non-white Asian, African, and Latin American peoples by white European powers. Thus racism has generally accompanied colonialism. Race prejudice can exist without colonization — the experience of Asian-American minorities is a case in point — but racism as a system of domination is part of the complex of colonization.

The concept of colonization stresses the enormous fatefulness of the historical factor, namely the manner in which a minority group becomes a part of the dominant society.[7] The crucial difference between the colonized Americans and the ethnic immigrant minorities is that the latter have always been able to operate fairly competitively within that relatively open section of the social and economic order because these groups came voluntarily in search of a better life, because their movements in society were not administratively controlled, and because they transformed their culture at their own pace — giving up ethnic values and institutions when it was seen as a desirable exchange for improvements in social position.

In present-day America, a major device of Black colonization is the powerless ghetto. As Kenneth Clark describes the situation:

Ghettoes are the consequence of the imposition of external power and the institutionalization of powerlessness. In this respect, they are in fact social, political, educational, and above all — economic colonies. Those confined within the ghetto walls are subject peoples. They are victims of the greed, cruelty, insensitivity, guilt and fear of their masters. . . .

The community can best be described in terms of the analogy of a powerless colony. Its political leadership is divided, and all but one or two of its political leaders are shortsighted and dependent upon the larger political power structure. Its social agencies are financially precarious and dependent upon sources of support outside the community. Its churches are isolated or dependent. Its economy is dominated by small businesses which are largely owned by absentee owners, and its tenements and other real property are also owned by absentee landlords.

Under a system of centralization, Harlem's schools are controlled by forces outside of the community. Programs and policies are supervised and determined by individuals who do not live in the community . . . .[8]

Of course many ethnic groups in America have lived in ghettoes. What make the Black ghettoes an expression of colonized status are three special features. First, the ethnic ghettoes arose more from voluntary choice, both in the sense of the choice to immigrate to America and the decision to live among one's fellow ethnics. Second, the immigrant ghettoes tended to be a one and two generation phenomenon; they were actually way-stations in the process of acculturation and assimilation. When they continue to persist as in the case of San Francisco's Chinatown, it is because they are big business for the ethnics themselves and there is a new stream of immigrants. The Black ghetto on the other hand has been a more permanent phenomenon, although some individuals do escape it. But most relevant is the third point. European ethnic groups like the Poles, Italians, and Jews generally only experienced a brief period, often less than a generation, during which their residential buildings, commercial stores, and other enterprises were owned by outsiders.

The Chinese and Japanese faced handicaps of color prejudice that were almost as strong as the Blacks faced, but very soon gained control of their internal communities, because their traditional ethnic culture and social organization had not been destroyed by slavery and internal colonization. But Afro-Americans are distinct in the extent to which their segregated communities have remained controlled economically, politically, and administratively from the outside. One indicator of this difference is the estimate that the "income of Chinese-Americans from Chinese-owned businesses is in proportion to their numbers 45 times as great as the income of Negroes from Negro-owned businesses."[9] But what is true of business is also true for the other social institutions that operate within the ghetto. The educators, policemen, social workers, politicians, and others who administer the affairs of ghetto residents are typically whites who live outside the Black community. Thus the ghetto plays a strategic role as the focus for the administration by outsiders which is also essential to the structure of overseas colonialism.[10]

The colonial status of the Negro community goes beyond the issue of ownership and decison-making within Black neighborhoods. The Afro-American population in most cities has very little influence on the power structure and institutions of the larger metropolis, despite the fact that in numerical terms, Blacks tend to be the most sizeable of the various interest groups. A recent analysis of policy-making in Chicago estimates that "Negroes really hold less than 1 percent of the effective power in the Chicago metropolitan area. [Negroes are 20 percent of Cook County's population.] Realistically the power structure of Chicago is hardly less white than that of Mississippi."[11]

Colonization outside of a traditional colonial structure has its own special conditions. The group culture and social structure of the colonized in America is less developed; it is also less autonomous. In addition, the colonized are a numerical minority, and furthermore they are ghettoized more totally and are more dispersed than people under classic colonialism. Though these realities affect the magnitude and direction of response, it is my basic thesis that the most important expressions of protest in the Black community during the recent years reflect the colonized status of Afro-America. Riots, programs of separation, politics of community control, the Black revolutionary movements, and cultural nationalism each represent a different strategy of attack on domestic colonialism in America. Let us now examine some of these movements.

Riot or Revolt?

The so-called riots are being increasingly recognized as a preliminary if primitive form of mass rebellion against a colonial status. There is still a tendency to absorb their meaning within the conventional scope of assimilation-integration politics: some commentators stress the material motives involved in looting as a sign that the rioters want to join America's middle-class affluence just like everyone else. That motives are mixed and often unconscious, that Black people want good furniture and television sets like whites is beside the point. The guiding impulse in most major outbreaks has not been integration with American society, but an attempt to stake out a sphere of control by moving against that society and destroying the symbols of its oppression.

In my critique of the McCone Report I observed that the rioters were asserting a claim to territoriality, an unorganized and rather inchoate attempt to gain control over their community or "turf."[12] In succeeding disorders also the thrust of the action has been the attempt to clear out an alien presence, white men and officials, rather than a drive to kill whites as in a conventional race riot. The main attacks have been directed at the property of white business men and at the police who operate in the Black community "like an army of occupation" protecting the interests ·of outside exploiters and maintaining the domination over the ghetto by the central metropolitan power structure.[13] The Kerner Report misleads when it attempts to explain riots in terms of integration: "What the rioters appear to be seeking was fuller participation in the social order and the material benefits enjoyed by the majority of American citizens. Rather than rejecting the American system, they were anxious to obtain a place for themselves in it."[14] More accurately, the revolts pointed to alienation from this system on the part of many poor and also not-so-poor Blacks. The sacredness of private property, that unconsciously accepted bulwark of our social arrangements, was rejected; people who looted apparently without guilt generally remarked that they were taking things that "really belonged" to them anyway.[15] Obviously the society's bases of legitimacy and authority have been attacked. Law and order has long been viewed as the white man's law and order by Afro-Americans; but now this perspective characteristic of a colonized people is out in the open. And the Kerner Report's own data question how well ghetto rebels are buying the system: In Newark only 33 percent of self-reported rioters said they thought this country was worth fighting for in the event of a major war; in the Detroit sample the figure was 55 percent.[16]

One of the most significant consequences of the process of colonization is a weakening of the colonized's individual and collective will to resist his oppression. It has been easier to contain and control Black ghettoes because communal bonds and group solidarity have been weakened through divisions among leadership, failures of organization, and a general disspiritment that accompanies social oppression. The riots are a signal that the will to resist has broken the mold of accommodation. In some cities as in Watts they also represented nascent movements toward community identity. In several riot-torn ghettoes the outbursts have stimulated new organizations and movements. If it is true that the riot phenomenon of 1964–68 has passed its peak, its historical import may be more for the "internal" organizing momentum generated than for any profound "external" response of the larger society facing up to underlying causes.

Despite the appeal of Frantz Fanon to young Black revolutionaries, America is not Algeria. It is difficult to foresee how riots in our cities can play a role equivalent to rioting in the colonial situation as an integral phase in a movement for national liberation. In 1968 some militant groups (for example, the Black Panther Party in Oakland) had concluded that ghetto riots were self-defeating of the lives and interests of Black people in the present balance of organization and gunpower, though they had served a role to stimulate both Black consciousness and white awareness of the depths of racial crisis. Such militants have been influential in "cooling" their communities during periods of high riot potential. Theoretically oriented Black radicals see riots as spontaneous mass behavior which must be replaced by a revolutionary organization and consciousness. But despite the differences in objective conditions, the violence of the 1960's seems to serve the same psychic function, assertions of dignity and manhood for young Blacks in urban ghettoes, as it did for the colonized of North Africa described by Fanon and Memmi.[17]

Cultural Nationalism

Cultural conflict is generic to the colonial relation because colonization involves the domination of Western technological values over the more communal cultures of non-Western peoples. Colonialism played havoc with the national integrity of the peoples it brought under its sway. Of course, all traditional cultures are threatened by industrialism, the city, and modernization in communication, transportation, health, and education. What is special are the political and administrative decisions of colonizers in managing and controlling colonized peoples. The boundaries of African colonies, for example, were drawn to suit the political conveniences of the European nations without regard to the social organization and cultures of African tribes and kingdoms. Thus Nigeria as blocked out by the British included the Yorubas and the Ibos, whose civil war today is a residuum of the colonialist's disrespect for the integrity of indigenous cultures.

The most total destruction of culture in the colonization process took place not in traditional colonialism but in America. As Frazier stressed, the integral cultures of the diverse African peoples who furnished the slave trade were destroyed because slaves from different tribes, kingdoms, and linguistic groups were purposely separated to maximize domination and control. Thus language, religion, and national loyalties were lost in North America much more completely than in the Caribbean and Brazil where slavery developed somewhat differently. Thus on this key point America's internal colonization has been more total and extreme than situations of classic colonialism. For the British in India and the European powers in Africa were not able — as outnumbered minorities — to destroy the national and tribal cultures of the colonized. Recall that American slavery lasted 250 years and its racist aftermath another 100. Colonial dependency in the case of British Kenya and French Algeria lasted only 77 and 125 years respectively. In the wake of this more drastic uprooting and destruction of culture and social organization, much more powerful agencies of social, political, and psychological domination developed in the American case.

Colonial control of many peoples inhabiting the colonies was more a goal than a fact, and at Independence there were undoubtedly fairly large numbers of Africans who had never seen a colonial administrator. The gradual process of extension of control from the administrative center on the African coast contrasts sharply with the total uprooting involved in the slave trade and the totalitarian aspects of slavery in the United States. Whether or not Elkins is correct in treating slavery as a total institution, it undoubtedly had a far more radical and pervasive impact on American slaves than did colonialism on the vast majority of Africans.[18]

Yet a similar cultural process unfolds in both contexts of colonialism. To the extent that they are involved in the larger society and economy, the colonized are caught up in a conflict between two cultures. Fanon has described how the assimilation-oriented schools of Martinique taught him to reject his own culture and Blackness in favor of Westernized, French, and white values.[19] Both the colonized elites under traditional colonialism and perhaps the majority of Afro-Americans today experience a parallel split in identity, cultural loyalty, and political orientation.[20]

The colonizers use their culture to socialize the colonized elites (intellectuals, politicians, and middle class) into an identification with the colonial system. Because Western culture has the prestige, the power, and the key to open the limited opportunity that a minority of the colonized may achieve, the first reaction seems to be an acceptance of the dominant values. Call it brainwashing as the Black Muslims put it; call it identifying with the aggressor if you prefer Freudian terminology; call it a natural response to the hope and belief that integration and democratization can really take place if you favor a more commonsense explanation, this initial acceptance in time crumbles on the realities of racism and colonialism. The colonized, seeing that his success within colonialism is at the expense of his group and his own inner identity, moves radically toward a rejection of the Western culture and develops a nationalist outlook that celebrates his people and their traditions. As Memmi describes it:

Assimilation being abandoned, the colonized's liberation must be carried out through a recovery of self and of autonomous dignity. Attempts at imitating the colonizer required self-denial; the colonizer's rejection is the indispensible prelude to self-discovery. That accusing and annihilating image must be shaken off; oppression must be attacked boldly since it is impossible to go around it. After having been rejected for so long by the colonizer, the day has come when it is the colonized who must refuse the colonizer.[21]

Memmi's book, *The Colonizer and the Colonized,* is based on his experience as a Tunisian Jew in a marginal position between the French and the colonized Arab majority. The uncanny parallels between the North African situation he describes and the course of Black-white relations in our society is the best impressionist argument I know for the thesis that we have a colonized group and a colonizing system in America. His discussion of why even the most radical French anti-colonialist cannot participate in the struggle of the colonized is directly applicable to the situation of the white liberal and radical vis-à-vis the Black movement. His portrait of the colonized is as good an analysis of the psychology behind Black Power and Black nationalism as anything that has been written in the U.S. Consider for example:

Considered *en bloc* as *them, they,* or *those,* different from every point of view, homogeneous in a radical heterogeneity, the colonized reacts by rejecting all the colonizers *en bloc.* The distinction between deed and intent has no great significance in the colonial situation. In the eyes of the colonized, all Europeans in the colonies are de facto colonizers, and whether they want to be or not, they are colonizers in some ways. By their privileged economic position, by belonging to the political system of oppression, or by participating in an effectively negative complex toward the colonized, they are colonizers. . . . They are supporters or at least unconscious accomplices of that great collective aggression of Europe.[22]

The same passion which made him admire and absorb Europe shall make him assert his differences; since those differences, after all, are within him and correctly constitute his true self.[23]

The important thing now is to rebuild his people, whatever be their authentic nature; to reforge their unity, communicate with it, and to feel that they belong.[24]

Cultural revitalization movements play a key role in anti-colonial movements. They follow an inner necessity and logic of their own that comes from the consequences of colonialism on groups and personal identities; they are also essential to provide the solidarity which the political or military phase of the anti-colonial revolution requires. In the U.S. an Afro-American culture has been developing since slavery out of the ingredients of African world-views, the experience of bondage, Southern values and customs, migration and the Northern lower-class ghettoes, and most importantly, the political history of the Black population in its struggle against racism.[25] That Afro-Americans are moving toward cultural nationalism in a period when ethnic loyalties tend to be weak (and perhaps on the decline) in this country is another confirmation of the unique colonized positon of the Black group. (A similar nationalism seems to be growing among American Indians and Mexican-Americans.)

The Movement for Ghetto Control

The call for Black Power unites a number of varied movements and tendencies.[26] Though no clear-cut program has yet emerged, the most important emphasis seems to be the movement for control of the ghetto. Black leaders and organizations are increasingly concerned with owning and controlling those institutions that exist within or impinge upon their community. The colonial model provides a key to the understanding of this movement, and indeed ghetto control advocates have increasingly invoked the language of colonialism in pressing for local home rule. The framework of anti-colonialism explains why the struggle for poor people's or community control of poverty programs has been more central in many cities than the content of these programs and why it has been crucial to exclude whites from leadership positions in Black organizations.

The key institutions that anti-colonialists want to take over or control are business, social services, schools, and the police. Though many spokesmen have advocated the exclusion of white landlords and small businessmen from the ghetto, this program has evidently not struck fire with the Black population and little concrete movement toward economic expropriation has yet developed. Welfare recipients have organized in many cities to protect their rights and gain a greater voice in the decisons that affect them, but whole communities have not yet been able to mount direct action against welfare colonialism. Thus schools and the police seem now to be the burning issues of ghetto control politics.

During the past few years there has been a dramatic shift from educational integration as the primary goal to that of community control of the schools. Afro-Americans are demanding their own school boards, with the power to hire and fire principals and teachers and to construct a curriculum which would be relevant to the special needs and culture style of ghetto youth. Especially active in high schools and colleges have been Black students, whose protests have centered on the incorporation of Black Power and Black culture into the educational system. Consider how similar is the spirit behind these developments to the attitude of the colonized North African toward European education:

He will prefer a long period of educational mistakes to the continuance of the colonizer's school organization. He will choose institutional disorder in order to destroy the institutions built by the colonizer as soon as possible. There we will see, indeed a reactive drive of profound protest. He will no longer owe anything to the colonizer and will have definitely broken with him.[27]

Protest and institutional disorder over the issue of school control came to a head in 1968 in New York City. The procrastination in the Albany State legislature, the several crippling strikes called by the teachers union, and the almost frenzied response of Jewish organizations makes it clear that decolonization of education faces the resistance of powerful vested interests.[28] The situation is too dynamic at present to assess probable future results. However, it can be safely predicted that some form of school decentralization will be institutionalized in New York, and the movement for community control of education will spread to more cities.

This movement reflects some of the problems and ambiguities that stem from the situation of colonization outside an immediate colonial context. The Afro-American community is not parallel in structure to the communities of colonized nations under traditional colonialism. The significant difference here is the lack of fully developed indigenous institutions besides the church. Outside of some area of the South there is really no black economy, and most Afro-Americans are inevitably caught up in the larger society's structure of occupations, education, and mass communication. Thus the ethnic nationalist orientation which reflects the reality of colonization exists alongside an integrationist orientation which corresponds to the reality that the institutions of the larger society are much more developed than those of the incipient nation.[29] As would be expected the movement for school control reflects both tendencies. The militant leaders who spearhead such local movements may be primarily motivated by the desire to gain control over the community's institutions — they are anti-colonialists first and foremost. Many parents who support them may share this goal also, but the majority are probably more concerned about creating a new education that will enable their children to "make it" in the society and the economy as a whole — they know that the present school system fails ghetto children and does not prepare them for participation in American life.

There is a growing recognition that the police are the most crucial institution maintaining the colonized status of Black Americans. And of all establishment institutions, police departments probably include the highest proportion of individual racists. This in no accident since central to the workings of racism (an essential component of colonization) are attacks on the humanity and dignity of the subject group. Through their normal routines the police constrict Afro-Americans to Black neighborhoods by harassing and questioning them when found outside the ghetto; they break up groups of youth congregating on corners or in cars without any provocation; and they continue to use offensive and racist language no matter how many intergroup understanding seminars have been built into the police academy. They also shoot to kill ghetto residents for alleged crimes such as car thefts and running from police officers.[30]

Police are key agents in the power equation as well as the drama of dehumanization. In the final analysis they do the dirty work for the larger system by restricting the striking back of Black rebels to skirmishes inside the ghetto, thus deflecting energies and attacks from the communities and institutions of the larger power structure. In a historical review, Gary Marx notes that since the French revolution, police and other authorities have killed large numbers of demonstrators and rioters; the rebellious "rabble" rarely destroys human life. The same pattern has been repeated in America's recent revolts.[31] Journalistic accounts appearing in the press recently suggest that police see themselves as defending the interests of white people against a tide of Black insurgence; furthermore the majority of whites appear to view "blue power" in this light. There is probably no other opinion on which the races are as far apart today as they are on the question of attitudes toward the police.

In many cases set off by a confrontation between a policeman and a Black citizen, the ghetto uprisings have dramatized the role of law enforcement and the issue of police brutality. In their aftermath, movements have arisen to contain police activity. One of the first was the community alert Patrol in Los Angeles, a method of policing the police in order to keep them honest and constrain their violations of personal dignity. This was the first tactic of the Black Panther Party which originated in Oakland, perhaps the most significant group to challenge the police role in maintaining the ghetto as a colony. The Panther's later policy of openly carrying guns (a legally protected right) and their intention of defending themselves against police aggression has brought on a series of confrontations with the Oakland police department. All indications are that the authorities intend to destroy the Panthers by shooting, framing up, or legally harassing their leadership — diverting the group's energies away from its primary purpose of self-defense and organization of the Black community to that of legal defense and gaining support in the white community.

There are three major approaches to "police colonialism" that correspond to reformist and revolutionary readings of the situation. The most elementary and also superficial sees colonialism in the fact that ghettoes are overwhelmingly patrolled by white rather than by Black officers. The proposal — supported today by many police departments — to increase the number of Blacks on local forces to something like their distribution in the city would then make it possible to reduce the use of white cops in the ghetto. This reform should be supported, for a variety of obvious reasons, but it does not get to the heart of the police role as agents of colonization.

The Kerner Report documents the fact that in some cases Black policemen can be as brutal as their white counterparts. The Report does not tell us who polices the ghetto, but they have compiled the proportion of Negroes on the forces of the major cities. In some cities the disparity is so striking that white police inevitably dominate ghetto patrols. (In Oakland 31 percent of the population and only 4 percent of the police are Black; in Detroit the figures are 39 percent and 5 percent; and in New Orleans 41 and 4.) In other cities, however, the proportion of Black cops is approaching the distribution in the city: Philadelphia 29 percent and 20 percent; Chicago 27 percent and 17 percent.[32] These figures also suggest that both the extent and the pattern of colonization may vary from one city to another. It would be useful to study how Black communities differ in degree of control over internal institutions as well as in economic and political power in the metropolitan area.

A second demand which gets more to the issue is that police should live in the communities they patrol. The idea here is that Black cops who lived in the ghetto would have to be accountable to the community; if they came on like white cops then "the brothers would take care of business" and make their lives miserable. The third or maximalist position is based on the premise that the police play no positive role in the ghettoes. It calls for the withdrawal of metropolitan officers from Black communities and the substitution of an autonomous indigenous force that would maintain order without oppressing the population. The precise relationship between such an independent police, the city and county law enforcement agencies, a ghetto governing body that would supervise and finance it, and especially the law itself is yet unclear. It is unlikely that we will soon face these problems directly as they have arisen in the case of New York's schools. Of all the programs of decolonization, police autonomy will be most resisted. It gets to the heart of how the state functions to control and contain the Black community through delegating the legitimate use of violence to police authority.

The various "Black Power" programs that are aimed at gaining control of individual ghettoes — buying up property and businesses, running the schools through community boards, taking over anti-poverty programs and other social agencies, diminishing the arbitrary power of the police — can serve to revitalize the institutions of the ghetto and build up an economic, professional, and political power base. These programs seem limited; we do not know at present if they are enough in themselves to end colonized status.[33] But they are certainly a necessary first step.

The Role of Whites

What makes the Kerner Report a less-than-radical document is its superficial treatment of racism and its reluctance to confront the colonized relationship between Black people and the larger society. The Report emphasizes the attitudes and feelings that make up white racism, rather than the system of privilege and control which is the heart of the matter.[34] With all its discussion of the ghetto and its problems, it never faces the question of the stake that white Americans have in racism and ghettoization.

This is not a simple question, but this paper should not end with the impression that police are the major villains. All white Americans gain some privileges and advantage from the colonization of Black communities.[35] The majority of whites also lose something from this oppression and division in society. Serious research should be directed to the ways in which white individuals and institutions are tied into the ghetto. In closing let me suggest some possible parameters.

1. It is my guess that only a small minority of whites make a direct economic profit from ghetto colonization. This is hopeful in that the ouster of white business-men may become politically feasible. Much more significant, however, are the private and corporate interests in the land and residential property of the Black community; their holdings and influence on urban decision-making must be exposed and combated.

2. A much larger minority have occupational and professional interests in the present arrangements. The Kerner Commission reports that 1.3 million non-white men would have to be up-graded occupationally in order to make the Black job distribution roughly similar to the white. They advocate this without mentioning that 1.3 million specially privileged white workers would lose in the bargain.[36] In addition there are those professionals who carry out what Lee Rainwater has called the "dirty work" of administering the lives of the ghetto poor: the social workers, the school teachers, the urban development people, and of course the police.[37] The social problems of the Black community will ultimately be solved only by people and organizations from that community; thus the emphasis within these professions must shift toward training such a cadre of minority personnel. Social scientists who teach and study problems of race and poverty likewise have an obligation to replace themselves by bringing into the graduate schools and college faculties men of color who will become the future experts in these areas. For cultural and intellectual imperialism is as real as welfare colonialism, though it is currently screened behind such unassailable shibboleths as universalism and the objectivity of scientific in-quiry.

3. Without downgrading the vested interests of profit and profession, the real nitty-gritty elements of the white stake are political power and bureaucratic security. Whereas few whites have much understanding of the realities of race relations and ghetto life, I think most give tacit or at least subconscious support for the contain-ment and control of the Black population. Whereas most whites have extremely distorted images of Black Power, many — if not most — would still be frightened by actual Black political power. Racial groups and identities are real in American life; white Americans sense they are on top, and they fear possible reprisals or disruptions were power to be more equalized. There seems to be a paranoid fear in the white psyche of Black dominance; the belief that Black autonomy would mean unbridled license is so ingrained that such reasonable outcomes as Black political majorities and independent Black police forces will be bitterly resisted.

On this level the major mass bulwark of colonization is the administrative need for bureaucratic security so that the middle classes can go about their life and business in peace and quiet. The Black militant movement is a threat to the orderly procedures by which bureaucracies and suburbs manage their existence, and I think today there are more people who feel a stake in conventional procedures than there are those who gain directly from racism. For in their fight for institutional control, the colonized will not play by the white rules of the game. These administrative rules have kept them down and out of the system; therefore they have no necessary intention of running institutions in the image of the white middle class.

The liberal, humanist value that violence is the worst sin cannot be defended today if one is committed squarely against racism and for self-determination. For some violence is almost inevitable in the decolonization process; unfortunately racism in America has been so effective that the greatest power Afro-Americans (and perhaps also Mexican-Americans) wield today is the power to disrupt. If we are going to swing with these revolutionary times and at least respond positively to the anti-colonial movement, we will have to learn to live with conflict, confrontation, constant change, and what may be real or apparent chaos and disorder.

A positive response from the white majority needs to be in two major directions at the same time. First, community liberation movements should be supported in every way by pulling out white instruments of direct control and exploitation and substituting technical assistance to the community when this is asked for. But it is not enough to relate affirmatively to the nationalist movement for ghetto control without at the same time radically opening doors for full participation in the institutions of the mainstream. Otherwise the liberal and radical position is little different than the traditional segregationist. Freedom in the special conditions of American colonization means that the colonized must have the choice between participation in the larger society and in their own independent structures.

Notes

[1] This is a revised version of a paper delivered at the University of California Centennial Program, "Studies in Violence," Los Angeles, June 1, 1968. For criticisms and ideas that have improved an earlier draft, I am indebted to Robert Wood, Lincoln Bergman, and Gary Marx. As a good colonialist I have probably restated (read: stolen) more ideas from the writings of Kenneth Clark, Stokely Carmichael, Frantz Fanon, and especially such contributors to the Black Panther Party (Oakland) newspaper as Huey Newton, Bobby Seale, Eldridge Cleaver, and Kathleen Cleaver than I have appropriately credited or generated myself. In self-defense I should state that I began working somewhat independently on a colonial analysis of American race relations in the fall of 1965; see my "Whitewash Over Watts: The Failure of the McCone Report," *Trans-action*, 3 (March-April, 1966), pp. 3–9, 54.

[2] Harold Cruse, *Rebellion or Revolution*, New York: 1968, p. 214.

[3] Nationalism, including an orientation toward Africa, is no new development. It has been a constant tendency within Afro-American politics. See Cruse, *ibid*, esp. chaps. 5–7.

[4] This was six years before the publication of *The Crisis of the Negro Intellectual*, New York: Morrow, 1968, which brought Cruse into prominence. Thus the 1962 article was not widely read until its reprinting in Cruse's essays, *Rebellion or Revolution, op. cit.*

[5] Kenneth Clark, *Dark Ghetto*, New York: Harper and Row, 1965. Clark's analysis first appeared a year earlier in *Youth in the Ghetto*, New York: Haryou Associates, 1964.

[6] Stokely Carmichael and Charles Hamilton, *Black Power*, New York: Random, 1967.

[7] As Eldridge Cleaver reminds us "Black people are a stolen people held in a colonial

status on stolen land, and any analysis which does not acknowledge the colonial status of black people cannot hope to deal with the real problem." "The Land Question," *Ramparts*, 6 (May, 1968), p. 51.

[8] *Youth in the Ghetto, op. cit.*, pp. 10–11; 79–80.

[9] N. Glazer and D. P. Moynihan, *Beyond the Melting Pot*, Cambridge, Mass.: M.I.T., 1963, p. 37.

[10] "When we speak of Negro social disabilities under capitalism, . . . we refer to the fact that he does not own anything — *even what is ownable in his own community*. Thus to fight for black liberation *is to fight for his right to own*. The Negro is politically compromised today because he owns nothing. He has little voice in the affairs of state because he owns nothing. The fundamental reason why the Negro bourgeois-democratic revolution has been aborted is because American capitalism has prevented the development of a black class of capitalist owners of institutions and economic tools. To take one crucial example, Negro radicals today are severely hampered in their tasks of educating the black masses on political issues because Negroes do not own any of the necessary means of propaganda and communication. The Negro owns no printing presses, he has no stake in the networks of the means of communication. Inside his own communities he does not own the house he lives in, the property he lives on, nor the wholesale and retail sources from which he buys his commodities. He does not own the edifices in which he enjoys culture and entertainment or in which he socializes. In capitalist society, an individual or group that does not own anything is powerless." H. Cruse, "Behind the Black Power Slogan," in Cruse, *Rebellion or Revolution, op. cit.*, pp. 238–39.

[11] Harold M. Baron, "Black Powerlessness in Chicago," *Trans-action*, 6 (Nov., 1968), pp. 27–33.

[12] R. Blauner, "Whitewash Over Watts," *op. cit.*

[13] "The police function to support and enforce the interests of the dominant political, social, and economic interests of the town" is a statement made by a former police scholar and official, according to A. Neiderhoffer, *Behind the Shield*, New York: Doubleday, 1967 as cited by Gary T. Marx, "Civil Disorder and the Agents of Control," *Journal of Social Issues*, forthcoming.

[14] Report of the National Advisory Commission on Civil Disorders, New York: Bantam, March, 1968, p. 7.

[15] This kind of attitude has a long history among American Negroes. During slavery, Blacks used the same rationalization to justify stealing from their masters. Appropriating things from the master was viewed as "*taking* part of his property for the benefit of another part; whereas, *stealing* referred to appropriating something from another slave, an offense that was not condoned," Kenneth Stampp, *The Peculiar Institution*, Vintage, 1956, p. 127.

[16] Report of the National Advisory Commission on Civil disorders, *op. cit.*, p. 178.

[17] Frantz Fanon, *Wretched of the Earth*, New York: Grove, 1963; Albert Memmi, *The Colonizer and the Colonized*, Boston: Beacon, 1967.

[18] Robert Wood, "Colonialism in Africa and America: Some Conceptual Considerations," December, 1967, unpublished paper.

[19] F. Fanon, *Black Skins, White Masks*, New York: Grove, 1967.

[20] Harold Cruse has described how these two themes of integration with the larger society and identification with ethnic nationality have struggled within the political and cultural movements of Negro Americans. *The Crisis of the Negro Intellectual, op. cit.*

[21] Memmi, *op. cit.*, p. 128.

[22] *Ibid.*, p. 130.

[23] *Ibid.*, p. 132.

[24] *Ibid.*, p. 134.

[25] In another essay, I argue against the standard sociological position that denies the existence of an ethnic Afro-American culture and I expand on the above themes. The concept of "Soul" is astonishingly parallel in content to the mystique of "Negritude" in Africa; the Pan-African culture movement has its parallel in the burgeoning Black culture mood in

Afro-American communities. See "Black Culture: Myth or Reality" in Peter Rose, editor, *Americans From Africa,* Atherton, 1969.

[26] Scholars and social commentators, Black and white alike, disagree in interpreting the contemporary Black Power movement. The issues concern whether this is a new development in Black protest or an old tendency revised; whether the movement is radical, revolutionary, reformist, or conservative; and whether this orientation is unique to Afro-Americans or essentially a Black parallel to other ethnic group strategies for collective mobility. For an interesting discussion of Black Power as a modernized version of Booker T. Washington's separatism and economism, see Harold Cruse, *Rebellion or Revolution, op. cit.,* pp. 193–258.

[27] Memmi, *op. cit.,* pp. 137–138.

[28] For the New York school conflict see Jason Epstein, "The Politics of School Decentralization," *New York Review of Books,* June 6, 1968, pp. 26–32; and "The New York City School Revolt," *ibid.,* 11, no. 6, pp. 37–41.

[29] This dual split in the politics and psyche of the Black America was poetically described by Du Bois in his *Souls of Black Folk,* and more recently has been insightfully analyzed by Harold Cruse in *The Crisis of the Negro Intellectual, op. cit.* Cruse has also characterized the problem of the Black community as that of underdevelopment.

[30] A recent survey of police finds "that in the predominantly Negro areas of several large cities, many of the police perceive the residents as basically hostile, especially the youth and adolescents. A lack of public support — from citizens, from courts, and from laws — is the policeman's major complaint. But some of the public criticism can be traced to the activities in which he engages day by day, and perhaps to the tone in which he enforces the "law" in the Negro neighborhoods. Most frequently he is 'called upon' to intervene in domestic quarrels and break up loitering groups. He stops and frisks two or three times as many people as are carrying dangerous weapons or are actual criminals, and almost half of these don't wish to cooperate with the policeman's efforts." Peter Rossi *et al.,* "Between Black and White — The Faces of American Institutions and the Ghetto," in Supplemental Studies for The National Advisory Commission on Civil Disorders, July 1968, p. 114.

[31] "In the Gordon Riots of 1780 demonstrators destroyed property and freed prisoners, but did not seem to kill anyone, while authorities killed several hundred rioters and hung an additional 25. In the Rebellion Riots of the French Revolution, though several hundred rioters were killed, they killed no one. Up to the end of the Summer of 1967, this pattern had clearly been repeated, as police, not rioters, were responsible for most of the more than 100 deaths that have occurred. Similarly, in a related context, the more than 100 civil rights murders of recent years have been matched by almost no murders of racist whites." G. Marx, "Civil Disorders and the Agents of Social Control," *op. cit.*

[32] Report of the National Advisory Commission on Civil Disorders, *op. cit.,* p. 321. That Black officers nevertheless would make a difference is suggested by data from one of the supplemental studies to the Kerner Report. They found Negro policemen working in the ghettoes considerably more sympathetic to the community and its social problems than their white counterparts. Peter Rossi *et al.,* "Between Black and White — The Faces of American Institutions in the Ghetto," *op. cit.,* chap. 6.

[33] Eldridge Cleaver has called this first stage of the anti-colonial movement *community* liberation in contrast to a more long-range goal of *national* liberation. E. Cleaver, "Community Imperialism," Black Panther Party newspaper, 2 (May 18, 1968).

[34] For a discussion of this failure to deal with racism, see Gary T. Marx, "Report of the National Commission: The Analysis of Disorder or Disorderly Analysis," 1968, unpublished paper.

[35] Such a statement is easier to assert than to document but I am attempting the latter in a forthcoming book tentatively titled *White Racism, Black Culture,* to be published by Little Brown, 1970.

[36] Report of the National Advisory Commission on Civil Disorders, *op. cit.,* pp. 253–256.

[37] Lee Rainwater, "The Revolt of the Dirty-Workers," *Trans-action,* 5 (Nov., 1967), pp. 2, 64.

Conflict, Race, and System-Transformation in the United States

Charles V. Hamilton

Traditional discussion of racial problems in the United States has usually centered around efforts to change the laws of race relations in this country, with the assumption that the basic institutions of official decision-making were valid and viable. What was required, it was felt, was to make the existing structures conform in practice to a particular conception of the "American Creed." In speaking of the "Negro revolution," one had in mind the intense legal and pressure-group activity aimed at this goal. Little thought was given to the notion that before many of the problems of race could be resolved, there would have to be a substantial transformation of the political system itself.

This article suggests a different analysis: that one has to understand racial conflict in the United States as reflecting the need to change substantially the way decisions are made in this society — not the mere decisions themselves. The United States is, in fact, undergoing a social revolution. It is not the type usually associated with the American or French revolutions, but rather, it constitutes a form unique to the modern, industrialized twentieth-century United States. At times it is not less violent than some traditional kinds of revolutions, but clearly it has repercussions and sustaining forms quite different from the Russian, Cuban or Chinese models. At the same time, many things happening in this country have parallels in other parts of the world, particularly in new, developing nations. One hears today the statement that the black ghettos of America are colonies struggling for their freedom and development in many ways similar to Asian and African societies. The term "modernizing" is applied to those societies, and this article will attempt to indicate that many of the processes of modernization can be observed in the United States. Hence, while there are many aspects of social change which are quite peculiar to this country, it is still possible to identify phenomena of growth common to other societies.

The United States is undergoing a process of political modernization which

Charles V. Hamilton, "Conflict, Race and System-Transformation in the United States," *Journal of International Affairs*, XXIII, No. 1, 1969, pp. 106–118. Reprinted by permission of the *Journal of International Affairs*.

should be viewed as revolutionary in this time and place. The racial conflicts provide a useful focal point for studying this process. Indeed, the demands coming out of the racial protest must be seen as challenging more than the *effectiveness* of the existing institutions. Those demands are calling into question the *legitimacy* of those institutions.[1] In a sense, then, our concern must be with political legitimacy; David Apter has suggested: "Politics is peculiar insofar as principles of legitimacy are normative first and structural second."[2] We must examine certain normative values in order to make the discussion of certain structural arrangements comprehensible.

Principles of Legitimacy and Political Modernization

Apter suggests two principles of legitimacy: one is embodied in the egalitarian-libertarian tradition; the second is a "fulfillment of potentiality." Before we can proceed to talk about what constitutes a legitimate political society, we should examine the particular normative values of the groups in the society. In Western, democratic societies there is an assumption, stemming as much from John Locke as from anyone, that man is basically rational, capable of knowing his self-interest and capable (if not always willing) of effecting a political compromise based on that self-interest. People in the society act within a consensual framework which assumes that political conflicts have their limits. Indeed, there are certain issues that are not introduced into the political system — such as essentially moral issues[3] — because such issues are not readily susceptible to the political compromise which is seen as essential. Politics is viewed as a protracted process, slow, but ultimately rewarding. Power is dispersed, and objectives are limited. One does not get all he bargains for today, but lives to fight another day.[4]

This first principle strongly emphasizes the processes of debate and dialogue. It implies, "Come, let us reason together," precisely because it assumes (or at least hopes for) a consensus and a shared view of political reality. With such notions it is understandable why violence, as a mechanism for effecting change, is eschewed. Violence represents the breakdown of the political process, the failure of the political system.

The egalitarian principle advocates public policy which is basically color-blind. ("We hire on the basis of merit, not race.") Position is obtained through achievement, not ascription; and leadership and authority are rational-legal, not traditional or charismatic. Emphasis is on individual freedom.

This principle operates best in those societies of relatively high industrial, economic, capitalistic development. This level of development is important because it means that the political system is not the only — or perhaps even the primary — focal point of societal demands. It guards against stressing and straining the political system with an overload of demands. Societies of abundance are better suited for the operation of the first principle of legitimacy. ". . . the emphasis is on a framework that will prevent coercion and provide limited government. The usual realization of this need is a system of representative government with checks and balances designed to prevent tyranny."[5] Apter further describes the first model:

In such a system it is implied that the values of the community are already enshrined in law and custom and that they will maintain the political conditions we have already suggested. Hence, just as in the pure theory of competition there should be no monopoly, so in the secular-libertarian polity there should be no monopoly of power. Power needs to be dispersed. . . .

Such, briefly, is the ideal of Western libertarian government. It has a high commitment to rules and laws. When the discrepancy between theory and practice is great, individuals become lonely and divorced from the system. If too many withdraw from the political marketplace, a general condition of alienation from the society results. . . . The theme of alienation runs through the history of secular-libertarian models.[6]

The second principle of legitimacy, fulfillment of potentiality, is more closely associated with underdeveloped societies, with people emerging from colonial rule, moving into a new day of freedom and independence. Emphasis is not on the individual, but on the group, the collectivity. The primary goal is group development: solidarity, not fragmentation, is sought. More frequently than not a consensus cannot be assumed, but as Apter suggests, it must be imposed. This principle is very group conscious. It cannot afford the color-blind stance of egalitarianism. (Thus, in the United States, some black people are heard to say: "We insist on black principals and black teachers for those predominantly or all-black schools.")

Debate, discussion, and dialogue are considered luxuries these people cannot afford. Protracted politics is a process of delay, and these are people in a hurry, rushing out of oppression into the promise of a new beginning. In some African countries, they find it necessary to reject a two-party or multi-party system as dysfunctional to development; therefore, they opt for the less competitive mass, single-party. It is irrelevant to tell them that this latter approach is taking them toward dictatorship and totalitarianism. Either they (1) are operating from a different vantage point of political reality, and thus do not agree; or (2) have weighed the alternatives and settled on that approach which they think best; or (3) must find out for themselves.

Leaders of some new nations, or of social movements within developing societies, see the first principle of legitimacy as dysfunctional to rapid growth. It is an ideology that holds them back. Leonard Binder makes the following observation:

The United States has not really argued that the developing nations ought to accept our laws and institutions, nor have we argued against change. Instead we have pressed for peaceful and gradual change. We have argued for the importance of stability and have decried attempts at violent revolution. There is no doubt that this American preference is deeply rooted in American thought, but the implication of our view in the context of the developing nations is quite different. Our emphasis on the rational and peaceful pursuit of self-interest, for evolutionary change and for gradualism, has been based on the argument that change thus achieved will be more firmly rooted. But to the leaders of revolutionary movements, the ideological content of our argument appears to be opposition to change and indirect support of the status quo.[7]

The second principle seems to be anti-democratic, but Apter prefers to call it pre-democratic, with the supposition that in time it will develop democratic regimes.

It is important to bear in mind that the second principle of legitimacy is operative in a society where the political system is the primary agency for mobilization. The economic and social systems are not adequately developed to siphon off and satisfy the many demands certain to be made. Thus, new rising elites in under-developed countries turn more to careers in government than to the private sector, and a strong, centralized government, rather than a fragmented, pluralist polity is conceived as best. "Seen as a modernizing force, the sacred-collectivity model[8] stresses the unity of the people, not their diversity . . . . Social life is directed toward the benefit of the collectivity rather than that of the self. . . . The objective is moral discipline, consensus, and similarity of outlook. Planning, rationality, and progress become associates with the sacred-collectivity model; individualism, private gain, and the market become little more than other names for egotism and opportunism, and are seen as parochialism and a narrowness of outlook."[9]

These are two principles of *legitimacy*. One is not legitimate and the other illegitimate. Rather, the second is seen as more effective than the first for the goals of (usually rapid) development and consensus. Of the sacred-collectivity model, Apter says:

With the emphasis on highly centralized authority, any dispersal of it is seen as dangerous to the whole. Such a system can be based on equality — but equality does not have the same significance it has in the first model, since it does not lead to the realization of individual wants. The secular-libertarian model assumes that equilibrium is produced by means of a policy representing a summation of the wants of its members, carried out within the framework of given values of rationality, freedom, and competition. The sacred-collectivity model assumes that any such policy would be inadequate because of deficiencies of knowledge among the people. Instead, the system must express values of unity, growth, and development. The collectivity type creates authority and carefully allocates it within a community. It can be seen as a community-creating process.[10]

Without question, assuming one is concerned about the creation of a free, just and open society, the dangers of the second principle of legitimacy achieving precisely the opposite are numerous. This is true whether one refers to a new nation of Africa, where established leadership can become entrenched and dictatorial or to the development of black people in the United States, where race relations can result in permanently polarized groups. We shall return to this problem later.

These principles of legitimacy should be seen as related to the overall process of political modernization. By this phrase, three processes are described.[11] First, it means that political authority constantly is being centralized. This involves the accumulation of power in national government, as opposed to local units of authority.[12] One sees this in the break-up of feudalism and the movement to monarchical government in Europe and to parliamentary government in England. Second, political modernization is the continuing examination of old values and the search for and implementation of new forms of decision-making. As Samuel Huntington points out, this means "the differentiation of new political functions and the development of specialized structures to perform those functions. . . . Administrative hierarchies become more elaborate, more complex, more disciplined."[13] Third, those societies undergoing modernization are constantly broadening the base of political participation. More and more groups are becoming involved in the political process.

The problems of race provide a good focal point for studying political modernization in the United States. One of the most crucial times in the history of the country, when it had to test its ability to maintain central authority over the states — the Civil War — centered around the issue of slavery and its extension. Clearly, the gains black people have made in the past one hundred years have been the result, largely, of authority and programs exercised at the level of the central government. Mayor Ivan Allen, Jr. of Atlanta, Georgia, a city frequently noted for having racial policies more enlightened than most southern cities, states: "The only reason Atlanta has been able to keep from being swallowed up by the great forces of social change has been . . . a positive and expeditious program of Federal assistance by the United States Government. And what is called 'Federal encroachment' has been the 'Federal salvation' of Atlanta."[14]

One understands the significance of the racial struggle to the extent that one views it as requiring this country to re-examine its present values, and to search for new ones. There has been an assumption that all that was required was to bring practice into conformity with a particular libertarian creed. Few social scientists bothered to raise the question of the possibility that the American society might, in fact, be an institutionally racist society, and hence, to ask what implications this had for public policy and subsequent significant change.

Finally, the political history of black Americans is a history of becoming increasingly involved in the political process. The story of the successes and failures is a story of the weaknesses and strengths of the various institutions of the society at given moments in history.

Leadership and Transformation: Four Analytical Types

The political history of black Americans is in many ways the story of the struggle of their leaders. However, the current descriptions of black leaders and groups serve largely to oversimplify a complex situation. One hears the dichotomies of moderate-militant; responsible-agitator; integrationist-separatist. These characterizations must be examined more closely. We suggest here that it is preferable to think in terms of four distinct leadership styles.

Political bargainer   This type is not alienated from the existing political processes, but rather believes that substantial progress in race relations can be made by operating within the two-party system and with existing structures such as the Congress, courts and administrative agencies. The Bargainer adheres to the first principle of legitimacy — egalitarianism-liberarianism — and his primary goal is the equitable distribution of goods and services (more jobs, more and better housing, integrated schools). Emphasis is placed on bringing lower-class black people into the American "mainstream." This type receives considerable "active" support from the middle-class (black and white). Very committed to the sanctity of "the law," the Bargainer is careful not to engage in those forms of protest actions which violate the law. It is better to bring a law suit than to engage in "civil disobedience."

Moral crusader   This type thinks and acts not only in terms of equitable distribution of goods and services, but also in terms of changing the moral nature of the society — of creating, ultimately, a "beloved community." Unlike the Bargainer, this second type is very willing to introduce morality into the political arena, not only as a tool or strategy, but as a goal. Because of this, the Moral Crusader is frequently criticized by the Bargainer as politically naïve. The Crusader talks and acts in terms of "dramatizing" grievances and is prone to engage in mass protest action. This type is committed to the philosophy and tactic of nonviolence as a way to transform the "soul" of the society. Frequently, the Moral Crusader is caught between rhetoric and reality, inasmuch as moral exhortations are used to mobilize and sustain a mass following, and issues are articulated in all-or-nothing terms. Once negotiations begin, compromise is inevitable, and this leaves the Moral Crusader open to charges from his followers of "sell-out" and "Uncle Tom." The constituency of this type stems essentially from church-going black people and middle-class whites.

Alienated reformer   This third type of leadership does not have the faith in the existing political structures characteristic of the Political Bargainer. The Alienated Reformer, in fact, is distrustful, suspicious and willing to talk and act in terms of creating new institutions of decision-making. This type pursues the second principle of legitimacy, is very group-conscious, and with him we begin to find intense emphasis on Black Power, Black Consciousness, Black Pride. The Reformer emphasizes local control of black communities by local black people — in much the same way that we heard Nkrumah admonish his people to "Seek ye first the political kingdom," and in similar ways that we see the process of "Africanization" taking place in some African countries. This type speaks not only of equitable distribution of goods and services, but of equitable distribution of decision-making power, especially at the local, grass-roots level. While the Reformer is not sanguine about the ability of the established political process to bring about substantial change, he is nonetheless amenable to electoral politics from the base of an independent black constituency. This obviously creates problems because the moment the Alienated Reformer gains elective office, the traditional processes of bargaining, negotiating and compromising must be pursued. The Reformer is forced to use one particular rhetoric with his constituents (language of alienation) and to pursue another particular approach (conciliation) with those with whom he must deal. In this regard, the Reformer is somewhat (not entirely) akin to the traditional ethnic politician. More frequently than not, however, the Reformer is not part of the official representative system. This is similar to a period in development described by Apter in new, developing societies:

Probably the most exciting period in the transition from dependence to independence is the representative stage because, although there are legislative bodies, the responsibility for government remains outside the colony. It becomes an outrageous political condition for many potential politicians, stimulating them to organize followers and to capitalize on grievances. This is the period in which what we call "Robin Hood" roles are formed — and played by semi-charismatic figures who can rally around them the disadvantaged and confused.[15]

So in the period in which personal politics and conciliar forms coincide, a period in which there are widespread unrest and political irresponsibility, the conditions are ripe for nationalist movements, which have as their object the achievement of some new and higher synthesis of modern life, free of the enslavement of race, of subservience, and of inferiority. It is in this context that nationalism emerges with particular sharpness in the colonial societies and attacks government, an alien fortress.[16]

The Alienated Reformer draws support mostly from younger (college-age and below) groups and individuals. In addition, this type is found among new groups such as teachers (National Association of Afro-American Educators), social workers (National Association of Black Social Workers), policemen (Afro-American Patrolmen's League), student groups, lawyers, and black caucuses in white religious denominations.[17]

Alienated revolutionary   This fourth type of leadership feels that no substantial change can take place in this society without calculated acts of instrumental violence. The Alienated Revolutionary clearly is distrustful of the existing order and is prone to think and talk of attempting to establish a separate black nation. The greatest support for this type is found among the younger people — those under twenty-five. Basically, the Revolutionary is not unhappy with acts of expressive violence (riots) and uses these acts to forecast coming acts of instrumental violence (urban guerrilla warfare). His heroes are Mao Tse-tung, Che Guevara, and Robert Williams among others, although it is questionable whether more than a mere commitment to violence as a political weapon attracts the Alienated Revolutionary: the substance of any theories of nation-building is rarely absorbed.

Linkage   All these leadership types function simultaneously in the black community, each competing with the other not so much for the same following — they appeal largely to different kinds of constituencies — but for attention from the mass media and for access to certain levels of official decision-making. At times there is intense rivalry to be considered "the" legitimate spokesman for "the black community." Hence, there are charges and countercharges of being "out of touch with the masses."

In such times linkage roles are important. It is important that roles be developed that can link the old with the new, the white with the black, the "ins" with the "outs." Such functions are attempted by different types in different circumstances. As already noted, when the Alienated Reformer assumes official office, he must straddle two positions. At times the Moral Crusader sees his views on nonviolence losing respect among the community and then decides to escalate his nonviolent protest, even to the extent of possibly engaging in the massive disruptive tactics of civil disobedience. In this way, the Moral Crusader tries to serve as a linkage between contentious positions: he offers nonviolent but vigorous protest for the Bargainer; continued insistence on working with whites, which appeals to poor whites as well as to liberal white groups; and militant, disruptive tactics for the Reformer and Revolutionary.

The Political Bargainer consciously attempts to maintain connection between the black community at large and white society. The Bargainer is aware of a growing polarization between the races and, through rhetoric and action, attempts to blunt the impact of confrontation. These efforts at linkage are difficult and precarious precisely because some of the groups are, in fact, pursuing entirely different principles of legitimacy. The various groups are operating from different vantage points of political reality. The conflicts are not of the nature that will likely lead to resolution after the fashion of African and Asian societies gaining political autonomy from the Metropolitan government. Black Americans will remain political, legal citizens of the United States and, at the same time, one will observe the tension resulting from the clash of the two principles of legitimacy.

The serious political task becomes how to cope with these inevitable tensions in a viable way. In the political modernization process, what are the prospects for

system-transformation in the United States? What new set of political relationships — what new system of political legitimacy — might one envision?

System-Transformation: A Paradigm

It is possible to talk about a new model of decision-making which attempts
to reconcile the various imperatives involved. Clearly, the Federal government will
continue to accumulate power unto itself. Increasingly the central government will
become the locus of policy, funds and, to an extent, initiative. We can perceive this
occurring in education, welfare, and various programs to alleviate poverty and to
renew the cities. This is a trend that will accelerate at given moments and slow down
at others, but the precedent for permanent, intense central involvement is established.

At the same time we can observe greater attention being given to the necessity
to "decentralize" certain functions of government. Too often, not enough time is
spent specifying precisely what functions should be lodged in what particular social
units. Here it is necessary to make such distinctions. We can talk about the necessity
to move toward metropolitan or regional government for the purpose of conducting
some functions of society. These functions we can list as relating to the "hygiene"
of the community: air pollution, water pollution, mass transportation, higher education, advanced medical care. It is crucial that broader advantages be reaped from
an expanded tax base. In this category it is neither wise nor necessary to emphasize
"community control" (broadened participation, but not small, local control units)
because that would not be a feasible way to develop public policy. Forms of representation could be developed depending on the functions involved, and the size and
nature (rural, urban) of the area concerned.

Another set of problems, it would seem, comes under the category of the
"health" of the community. In this regard we are talking about intimate, active
involvement of large numbers of people in the processes of decision-making. This
category would be most susceptible to community, or even neighborhood, control:
lower education, job-training, law enforcement, community mental health, recreation, urban renewal. It would be important to distinguish between a form of decentralization and community control. Bearing in mind that in a *national* body politic
ultimate authority will be vested in the central government, it is still possible to
construct a policy where vast numbers of functions could be administered (with
varying degrees of authority) at the community level. These community organizations should have direct access to the central authority. Admittedly, this schema
is seemingly more complex and hierarchical than those that now exist, but such
is the nature of the modernization process.

It is important to understand the demands of an increasingly politicized mass to become involved and to have control. Thus, it is necessary to begin devising ways to effect that involvement without the ultimate fracturing demands for a separate state or absolute autonomy.

Grant McConnell describes correctly the usefulness of small, local groups, but he misreads the times when he concludes that American society has not reached the point of requiring such transformation.

It can be readily agreed that if explosive mass movements are a genuine threat to America, a politics of narrow constituencies might be desirable to counter the danger. Small associations probably do provide order and stability for any society. . . . Nevertheless, it should be clear that a substantial price is paid for any guarantee against mass movements provided by a pattern of small constituencies. That price is paid in freedom and equality. Although the price would be worth paying if the danger were grave, it can hardly be argued that such an extremity is present.[18]

The evidence would indicate that the danger *is* grave and that the extremity *is* present.

Such system-transformation would require serious reordering of the constitutional structure and this would require a thoroughly sincere commitment to the value of political inclusion of people. Given the ferment of the times, it is no reasonable response to admonish that the more the society introduces new groupings into the decision-making process, the fewer decisions are made. The fact is that the society *is* confronted with such demands. Once large numbers of people become alienated from the existing order, the chance is probably lost to effect change by old, established processes. Those in power must understand this, and they must come to see that once legitimate demands for inclusion have been initiated by "outsiders," the "insiders" might well have lost the upper hand in staying on top of the direction and pace of change.

It would seem that this would apply as much to the ferment and turmoil sweeping American college campuses today as to the strictly racial demands. If one sees the seeming chaos as a fad soon to pass away, then this analysis will not be relevant. But I suggest that the problem is deeper. The Vietnam war finally alerted millions of people to a realization of the extent to which greatly important areas of decision-making were simply beyond their control. People subsequently objected. Black people have become increasingly impatient with the insensitive assumptions of a white-dominated society. All of these forces coincide with world-wide developments of people pushing for their political independence and economic growth.

If political modernization involved only centralization and the revision of structures, there would not be conflict. But it also involves broadening the base of political participation. This is not a factor to condemn, necessarily, or to lament; it is something to understand and work with. The United States probably has faced no greater challenge as a national body politic since the Civil War. If it would survive as a viable society, it would respond and proceed with the function of system-transformation.

Notes

[1] For a good discussion of the distinction between effectiveness and legitimacy, see Seymour Martin Lipset, *Political Man: The Social Bases of Politics* (New York: Doubleday, 1963), p. 64.

[2] David E. Apter, *The Politics of Modernization* (Chicago: University of Chicago Press, 1965), p. 16.

[3] See Herbert Agar, *The Price of Union* (Boston: Houghton Mifflin Company, 1950).

[4] The literature on American pluralist politics is prolific on the point. See for example, V. O. Key, Jr., *Politics, Parties and Pressure Groups* (New York: Thomas Y. Crowell Company, 1964); David B. Truman, *The Governmental Process* (New York: Alfred A. Knopf, 1951); James Q. Wilson, *Negro Politics* (Glencoe: Free Press, 1960).

[5] Apter, *op. cit.,* p. 28.

[6] *Ibid.,* pp. 30–31.

[7] Leonard Binder, "Ideology and Political Development," in *Modernization: The Dynamics of Growth,* Myron Weiner, editor (New York: Basic Books, Inc., 1966).

[8] This model is identified with the second principle of legitimacy. The secular-libertarian model is related to the first principle.

[9] Apter, *op. cit.,* pp. 32–33.

[10] *Ibid.,* p. 33.

[11] I have borrowed Samuel P. Huntington's three criteria as set forth in his excellent article, "Political Modernization: America vs. Europe," *World Politics,* Volume XVIII, Number 3, April 1966, pp. 378–414.

[12] S. N. Eisenstadt writes: "In the political sphere, modernization has been characterized, first, by growing extension of the territorial scope and especially by the intensification of the power of the central, legal, administrative, and political agencies of the society. Second, it has been characterized by the continual spread of potential power to wider groups in the society — ultimately to all adult citizens and their incorporation into a consensual moral order. Third, modern societies are in some sense democratic or at least populistic societies." *Modernization: Protest and Change* (Englewood Cliffs: Prentice-Hall, Inc., 1966), p. 4.

[13] Huntington, *op. cit.,* p. 378.

[14] Quoted in "Allen of Atlanta Collides with Black Power and White Racism," by Reese Cleghorn. *The New York Times Magazine,* October 16, 1966, p. 139.

[15] Apter, *op. cit.,* p. 55.

[16] Apter, *ibid.,* p. 56.

[17] See, for example, Charles V. Hamilton, "Race and Education: A Search for Legitimacy," *Harvard Educational Review,* Volume 38, Number 4, Fall, 1968; Alex Poinsett, "Black Revolt in White Churches," *Ebony,* Volume XXIII, Number 11, September 1968, pp. 63–68.

[18] Grant McConnell, *Private Power and American Democracy* (New York: Alfred A. Knopf, 1966), pp. 355–356.

Suggestions for Further Reading

There exist few scholarly studies on the black protest movement of our times. We list below some of the more significant books which will be helpful to the interested student.

Floyd Barbour, ed., *The Black Power Revolt* (Boston, Porter Sargent, Inc., 1968)

Inge Powell Bell, *CORE and the Strategy of Nonviolence* (New York, Random House, 1968)

John H. Bracey, Jr., August Meier, and Elliott Rudwick, eds., *Black Nationalism in America* (Indianapolis, Bobbs-Merrill, 1970)

Stokely Carmichael and Charles V. Hamilton, *Black Power: The Politics of Liberation* (New York, Random House, 1967)

Eldridge Cleaver, *Soul on Ice* (New York, McGraw-Hill, 1968)

William Corson, *Promise or Peril* (New York, Norton, 1970)

E. U. Essien-Udom, *Black Nationalism: A Search for an Identity in America* (Chicago, University of Chicago Press, 1962)

James Farmer, *Freedom — When?* (New York, Random House, 1965)

Lewis Killian, *The Impossible Revolution: Black Power and the American Dream* (New York, Random House, 1968)

Lewis Killian and Charles Grigg, *Racial Crisis in America: Leadership in Conflict* (Englewood Cliffs, N.J., Prentice-Hall, 1964)

Julius Lester, *Look Out Whitey! Black Power's Gon' Get Your Mama!* (New York, Dial Press, 1968)

David Lewis, *King: A Critical Biography* (New York, Praeger, 1970)

C. Eric Lincoln, *The Black Muslims in America* (Boston, Beacon Press, 1961)

Louis Lomax, *The Negro Revolt* (New York, Harper, 1962)

Malcolm X, *The Autobiography of Malcolm X* (New York, Grove, 1965)

Gary T. Marx, *Protest and Prejudice: A Study of Belief in the Black Community,* revised ed. (New York, Harper & Row, 1969)

Louis H. Masotti and Don R. Bowen, eds., *Riots and Rebellion: Civil Violence in the Urban Community* (Beverly Hills, Sage Publications, 1968)

August Meier, Elliott Rudwick, and Francis Broderick, eds., *Black Protest Thought in the Twentieth Century,* revised ed. (Indianapolis, Bobbs-Merrill, 1971)

Martin Oppenheimer, *The Urban Guerrilla* (Chicago, Quadrangle Books, 1969)

Thomas F. Pettigrew, *A Profile of the Negro American* (New York, Van Nostrand, 1964)

Report of the National Advisory Committee on Civil Disorders (New York, Bantam Books, 1968)

Pat Watters and Reese Cleghorn, *Climbing Jacob's Ladder: The Arrival of Negroes in Southern Politics* (New York, Harcourt Brace Jovanovich, 1967)

Howard Zinn, *SNCC: The New Abolitionists* (Boston, Beacon Press, 1964)

A Wadsworth Series:
Explorations in the Black Experience

General Editors

John H. Bracey, Jr.
Northern Illinois University

August Meier
Kent State University

Elliott Rudwick
Kent State University

American Slavery: The Question of Resistance

Introduction

1 The Classic Debate: Accommodation vs. Resistance

Ulrich B. Phillips, "Racial Problems, Adjustments and Disturbances"; Harvey Wish, "American Slave Insurrections before 1861;" Raymond A. Bauer and Alice H. Bauer, "Day of Resistance to Slavery"; Kenneth M. Stampp, "A Troublesome Property"

2 Elkins and His Critics

Stanley Elkins, "Slave Personality and the Concentration Camp Analogy"; Earle E. Thorpe, "Chattel Slavery and Concentration Camps"; Eugene D. Genovese, "Rebelliousness and Docility in the Negro Slave: A Critique of the Elkins Thesis"

3 The Vesey Plot: Conflicting Interpretations

Herbert Aptheker, "On Denmark Vesey"; Richard C. Wade, "The Vesey Plot: A Reconsideration"; Robert S. Starobin, "Denmark Vesey's Slave Conspiracy of 1882: A Study in Rebellion and Repression"

4 New Approaches

Gerry Mullin, "Religion, Acculturation, and American Negro Slave Rebellions: Gabriel's Insurrection"; George M. Fredrickson and Christopher Lasch, "Resistance to Slavery"; H. Orlando Patterson, "The General Causes of Jamaican Slave Revolts"

Suggestions for Further Reading

Free Blacks in America, 1800–1860

Introduction

1 Free Blacks in the South

Charles S. Sydnor, "The Free Negro in Mississippi before the Civil War"; E. Horace Fitchett, "The Traditions of the Free Negro in Charleston, South Carolina"; Roger A. Fischer, "Racial Segregation in Ante-Bellum New Orleans"; John Hope Franklin, "The Free Negro in the Economic Life of Ante-Bellum North Carolina"; Robert Brent Toplin, "Peter Still versus the Peculiar Institution"

2   Free Blacks in the North and West

Carter G. Woodson, "The Negroes of Cincinnati Prior to the Civil War"; Julian Rammelkamp, "The Providence Negro Community, 1820–1842"; Dixon Ryan Fox, "The Negro Vote in Old New York"; Rudolph M. Lapp, "The Negro in Gold Rush California"; Robert Austin Warner, "The Rise of Negro Society"

3   Free Blacks and the Federal Government

Leon Litwack, "The Federal Government and the Free Negro"

Suggestions for Further Reading

Blacks in the Abolitionist Movement

Introduction

1   Four Black Abolitionists

Ray Allen Billington, "James Forten: Forgotten Abolitionist"; Benjamin Quarles, "Abolition's Different Drummer: Frederick Douglass"; William F. Cheek, "John Mercer Langston: Black Protest Leader and Abolitionist"; Larry Gara, "William Still and the Underground Railroad"

2   The Abolitionist Movement: The Negro's Role

Charles H. Wesley, "The Negro in the Organization of Abolition"; Leon F. Litwack, "The Emancipation of the Negro Abolitionist"; James McPherson, "The Negro: Innately Inferior or Equal?"; William H. Pease and Jane H. Pease, "Antislavery Ambivalence: Immediatism, Expediency, Race"; August Meier and Elliott Rudwick, "The Role of Blacks in the Abolitionist Movement"; Howard H. Bell, "National Negro Conventions of the Middle 1840's: Moral Suasion vs. Political Action"

3   The Blacks and John Brown

W. E. B. Du Bois, "The Black Phalanx"; David Potter, "John Brown and the Paradox of Leadership among American Negroes"; Philip Foner, "Douglass and John Brown"

Suggestions for Further Reading

The Rise of the Ghetto

Introduction

1   Nineteenth-Century Roots

Richard C. Wade, "Residential Segregation in the Ante-bellum South"; Robert A. Warner, "Residential Segregation in Ante-bellum New Haven"; John Daniels, "Origins of the Boston Ghetto"; Paul J. Lammermeier, "Cincinnati's Black Community: The Origins of a Ghetto, 1870–1880"; W. E. B. Du Bois, "Philadelphia's Seventh Ward, 1896"; Mary White Ovington, "Before Harlem: The Black Ghetto in New York City"

2   The Emerging Ghetto

Philip M. Hauser, "Demographic Factors in the Integration of the Negro"; Chicago Commission on Race Relations, "The Migration of Negroes from the South, 1916–1918"; Allan H. Spear, "The Rise of the Chicago Black Belt"; E. Franklin Frazier, "Chicago Black Belt: Residential Patterns and Social Class"; E. Franklin Frazier, "Housing in Harlem, 1935"; Karl E. Taeuber and Alma F. Taeuber, "Residential Segregation in the Twentieth-Century South"

3   The Process of Ghettoization: External Pressures

Chicago Commission on Race Relations, "White Violence versus Black Expansion"; David E. Lilienthal, "The Ossin–Sweet Case";

Robert C. Weaver, "The Villain—Racial Covenants"; Robert C. Weaver, "The Role of the Federal Government"; Herman H. Long and Charles S. Johnson, "The Role of Real Estate Organizations"; Loren Miller, "Supreme Court Covenant Decision—An Analysis"; Herbert Hill, "Demographic Change and Racial Ghettos: The Crisis of American Cities"; Roy Reed, "Resegregation: A Problem in the Urban South"

4   The Process of Ghettoization: Internal Pressures

Arnold Rose and Caroline Rose, "The Significance of Group Identification"; W. E. B. Du Bois, "The Social Evolution of the Black South"; Allan H. Spear, "The Institutional Ghetto"; Chicago Commission on Race Relations, "The Matrix of the Black Community"; E. Franklin Frazier, "The Negro's Vested Interest in Segregation"; George A. Nesbitt, "Break Up the Black Ghetto?"; Lewis G. Watts, Howard E. Freeman, Helen M. Hughes, Robert Morris, and Thomas F. Pettigrew, "Social Attractions of the Ghetto"

5   Future Prospects

Karl E. Taeuber and Alma F. Taeuber, "Is the Negro an Immigrant Group?"; H. Paul Friesema, "Black Control of Central Cities: The Hollow Prize"

Suggestions for Further Reading

Black Matriarchy: Myth or Reality?

Introduction

1   The Frazier Thesis

E. Franklin Frazier, "The Negro Family in America"; E. Franklin Frazier, "The Matriarchate"

2   The Question of African Survivals

Melville J. Herskovits, "On West African Influences"

3   The Frazier Thesis Applied

Charles S. Johnson, "The Family in the Plantation South"; Lee Rainwater, "Crucible of Identity: The Negro Lower-Class Family"; Elliot Liebow, "Fathers without Children"

4   The Moynihan Report

Daniel P. Moynihan, "The Negro Family: The Case for National Action"; Hylan Lewis and Elizabeth Herzog, "The Family: Resources for Change"

5   New Approaches

Herbert H. Hyman and John Shelton Reed, " 'Black Matriarchy' Reconsidered: Evidence from Secondary Analysis of Sample Surveys"; Virginia Heyer Young, "Family and Childhood in a Southern Negro Community"

Suggestions for Further Reading

Black Workers and Organized Labor

Introduction

Sidney H. Kessler, "The Organization of Negroes in the Knights of Labor"; Bernard Mandel, "Samuel Gompers and the Negro Workers, 1886–1914"; Paul B. Worthman, "Black Workers and Labor Unions in Birmingham, Alabama, 1897–1904"; William M. Tuttle, Jr., "Labor Conflict and Racial Violence: The Black Worker in Chicago, 1894–1919"; Sterling D. Spero and Abram L. Harris, "The Negro Longshoreman, 1870–1930"; Sterling D. Spero and Abram L. Harris, "The Negro and the IWW"; Brailsford R. Brazeal, "The Brotherhood of Sleeping Car Porters"; Horace R. Cayton and George S. Mitchell, "Blacks and Organized Labor in the Iron and Steel Industry, 1880–1939"; Herbert R. Northrup, "Blacks in the United Automobile Workers Union"; Sumner M. Rosen, "The CIO Era, 1935–1955"; William Kornhauser, "The Negro Union Official: A Study of Sponsorship and Control"; Ray Marshall, "The Negro and the AFL-CIO"

Suggestions for Further Reading

The Black Sociologists: The First Half Century

Introduction

1   Early Pioneers

W. E. B. Du Bois, "The Study of the Negro Problems"; W. E. B. Du Bois, "The Organized Life of Negroes"; George E. Haynes, "Conditions among Negroes in the Cities"

2   In the Robert E. Park Tradition

Charles S. Johnson, "Black Housing in Chicago"; E. Franklin Frazier, "The Pathology of Race Prejudice"; E. Franklin Frazier, "La Bourgeoisie Noire"; Charles S. Johnson, "The Plantation during the Depression"; Bertram W. Doyle, "The Etiquette of Race Relations—Past, Present, and Future"; E. Franklin Frazier, "The Black Matriarchate"; Charles S. Johnson, "Patterns of Negro Segregation"; E. Franklin Frazier, "The New Negro Middle Class"

3   Black Metropolis: Sociological Masterpiece

St. Clair Drake and Horace Cayton, "The Measure of the Man"

Conflict and Competition: Studies in the Recent Black Protest Movement

Introduction

1   Nonviolent Direct Action

Joseph S. Himes, "The Functions of Racial Conflict"; August Meier, "Negro Protest Movements and Organizations"; Lewis M. Killian and Charles U. Smith, "Negro Protest Leaders in a Southern Community"; Ralph H. Hines and James E. Pierce, "Negro Leadership after the Social Crisis: An Analysis of Leadership Changes in Montgomery, Alabama"; Jack L. Walker, "The Functions of Disunity: Negro Leadership in a Southern City"; Gerald A. McWorter and Robert L. Crain, "Subcommunity Gladiatorial Competition. Civil Rights Leadership as a Competitive Process"; August Meier, "On the Role of Martin Luther King"

2   By Any Means Necessary

Inge Powell Bell, "Status Discrepancy and the Radical Rejection of Nonviolence"; Donald von Eschen, Jerome Kirk, and Maurice Pinard, "The Disintegration of the Negro Non-Violent Movement"; Allen J. Matusow, "From Civil Rights to Black Power: The Case of SNCC, 1960–1966"; Joel D. Aberbach and Jack L. Walker, "The Meanings of Black Power: A Comparison of White and Black Interpretations of a Political Slogan"; David O. Sears and T. M. Tomlinson, "Riot Ideology in Los Angeles: A Study of Negro Attitudes"; Robert Blauner, "Internal Colonialism and Ghetto Revolt"; Charles V. Hamilton, "Conflict, Race, and System-Transformation in the United States"

Suggestions for Further Reading